ISSUES IN MISSIOLOGY

VOLUME V

How to Get to the Field
How to Stay on the Field
Second Edition

ROBERT D. PATTON, M.D., D.D.

Issues in Missiology, Volume V
Second Edition
October 2021

DISCLAIMER

The author of this work has quoted the writers of many articles and books. This does not mean that the author endorses or recommends the works of others. If the author quotes someone, it does not mean that he agrees with all of the author's tenets, statements, concepts, or words, whether in the work quoted or any other work of the author. There has been no attempt to alter the meaning of the quotes; and therefore, some of the quotes are long in order to give the entire sense of the passage.

Copyright © 2012 by Robert D. Patton, M.D., D.D.
Email: bobpattonmd@gmail.com
Website: www.teachingmissions.com

All Rights Reserved

Printed in the United States of America

ISBN 978-0-9860143-0-7

Dr. Robert D. Patton
The Crown College of the Bible
7311 Brickyard Road
Powell, TN 37849

All Scripture quotes are from the King James Bible except those verses compared and then the source is identified.

No part of this work may be reproduced without the expressed consent of the publisher, except for brief quotes, whether by electronic, photocopying, recording, or information storage and retrieval systems.

Publishing and Formatting by:
THE OLD PATHS PUBLICATIONS, Inc.
142 Gold Flume Way
Cleveland, Georgia, U.S.A. 30528
Web: www.theoldpathspublications.com
E-mail: TOP@theoldpathspublications.com

PREFACE TO VOLUME V

Dr. and Mrs. Bob Patton

My goal in this volume is very practical: how to get on the mission field, how to stay on the mission field, and how to have an effective ministry. I begin with my own personal journey, because I believe that we have seen the hand of the Lord in our lives and ministry, and that it may prove an encouragement to others. History does provide lessons when we learn from it. The book then progresses to follow the steps of the missionary prior to getting on the field, including a substantial section on deputation. I am including a brief monograph which my son wrote at the request of his mission under which they were serving at that time. His wife Charin added a section on the role of the wife during deputation which will prove very helpful.

There is also a fairly detailed section on practical cultural anthropology. My wife and I have lived in four continents, and the information provided will help the missionary avoid some of the traps which can snare the unwary. There is a section on culture shock, which often wipes out new missionaries, as well as a much longer section on how to adapt and work on the field. When you understand the cultural issues involved, it may not solve your problems, but it makes adjustment much easier!

I also asked my wife and daughter to contribute their thoughts on the role of the wife on the mission field. I could find little information on that subject. My wife cared for our four children for 5 years in Liberia, West Africa, when I was Professor of Medicine there, and has worked with me for 26 years in Suriname, with extensive experience in Bible club ministry, developing leadership in the women's ministry, working with teenage girls, and running our guest house, as well as serving as the bookkeeper for the church for years. My daughter has been on the mission field for 23 years. All of her children were born on the field. They moved to a remote jungle village reached only by boat when her first two sons were a toddler and a baby. Her two oldest daughters were born during those years of ministry in the remote village. They then moved to the mining town of Moengo where eventually five more children joined the family. She has homeschooled all of her children, and has had ministries with ladies, teen girls, and children. Both my wife and daughter are effective witnesses for the Lord, and well-qualified to share their thoughts.

In addition to the addendum on deputation, there are sections on the role of the Pastor and Church in missions, and a short section on worldview applied to evangelizing different people groups. Both subjects are important, and I believe that the addendums are worth reading.

It is my prayer that this volume will be a blessing to many, and will help many to get on the mission field, and stay there with a ministry which brings glory to our Savior.

Dr. Robert Patton
Paramaribo, Suriname
May, 2012

Additional Preface to the 2nd Edition

Nine years have passed since I wrote the first edition, which was published just prior to our leaving the mission field of Suriname, South America. We have been privileged to work teaching missions, Bible, and Human Anatomy and Physiology at The Crown College of the Bible during that time. This volume has served as the text for our capstone course Missionary Forum. I have attempted to summarize much of the materials which we teach in several missions courses as well as detailed information on deputation, and particularly deputation for missionaries from faith missions, in contrast to denominational missionaries. The denominational missionary, however, will find a great deal of practical information on preparation for the field and success on the field even though certain details will differ.

The situations when the book was written in 2012 have changed. My daughter and son-in-law have had nine children, all of whom have been home schooled. Five are back in the USA, and four in Suriname. Three children in Suriname are being home schooled. The oldest of the three is also taking dual credit courses from Crown College as she prepares to be a missionary to Brazil. Their son in Suriname is basically working as a missionary while he completes his college degree online. He currently runs the programming for a 24/7 radio station.

Our son and daughter-in-law are now empty nesters. All four children from Hungary graduated from the Hungarian school system, and the oldest three graduated from college. Two are married, and one is on the mission field.

My wife and I are in our 10th year teaching at The Crown College of the Bible. I have been teaching face-to-face courses at the undergraduate and graduate level, online classes on the undergraduate and graduate level, as well as a new adult learner online program. We have been blessed with 4 children, all married, 18 grandchildren, 16 great-grandchildren, and one expectant mother. We are grateful to the Lord to allow us to continue to serve the Lord.

Our prayer is that this book will be a practical guide and encouragement to many who are taking the gospel to the ends of the earth, whether at home or overseas.

DEDICATION

This volume on The Making of a Missionary is dedicated to my co-laborers on the field who contributed to the volume. First, my heart-felt gratitude is to my wife Liz, who for 62 years has been a superb helpmeet as we have lived in three continents. Second, I want to thank my daughter Kim, who for 32 years has labored with her husband Ethan Champlin in Suriname. Both contributed their advice concerning the role of the missionary wife. Third, I would like to dedicate this book also to my son, Marc Patton and his wife, Charin, who contributed a section on deputation, and have been serving the Lord in Hungary, East Europe for approximately 28 years. Thus, this volume has resulted from the input of six individuals with a total overseas experience of over 170 years on various mission fields.

TABLE OF CONTENTS

DISCLAIMER 2
PREFACE TO VOLUME V 3
Additional Preface to the 2nd Edition 4
DEDICATION 7
TABLE OF CONTENTS 9
INTRODUCTION 29
   A Personal Testimony 29
      A Concentration Camp Experience 29
      Repatriated 30
      Medical School 30
      Preparation For Missions 31
      My Spiritual Life 32
      Doing the Lord's Will 32
      Suriname 34
      God's Plan in Suriname 34
      Translating the Bible 36
      The Ministry Expands 36
CHAPTER 1 39
INITIAL THOUGHTS ABOUT MISSIONARY WORK 39
   Who Is a Missionary? 39
      False Ideas About Missionaries 40
      Missions Versus Colonialism 40
   The Challenge of Missions: Why Become 41
   A Missionary? 41
      All Life is For His Glory 41
      Be Passionate for God 41
      Facing Life and Death 42
      Trust God 43
      Some Dangers 43
      Acceptable Risks 43
      Foolish Risks 44
      Conquerors 44
   What About Money? 44
      Hudson Taylor's Experience 45
      Spiritual Warfare 45

Working, Not to Have, But to Give	46
Thought Questions:	47
CHAPTER 2	**49**
GOD'S CALLING	**49**
God's Calling Is More Than a Need	49
No Single Pattern	49
The Missionary Must Be Totally Consecrated	50
God's Will Must Be the Missionary's Will	50
God's Perfect Timing	51
The Missionary Call Versus Missionary Guidance	51
Recruitment Issues	52
Deputation Travel	53
Learning a Foreign Language	53
The Fear to Surrender to the Lord's Will	54
Some Problems and Issues for the Called Missionary	55
Commitment	55
Family Issues	55
Parental Opposition	56
Debt	56
Advanced Education	57
Adequate Bible Training	57
Vocational Qualifications	58
Love, Dating, and Marriage	58
Separation From Children	59
Single Missionaries	59
Unique Challenges	60
Housing Arrangements	61
A Lonely Single Missionary	61
Additional Requirements	61
Physical Requirements	61
Extra Training	62
The Missionary's Personality	62
Privation	62
Team Effort	63
Cultural Influences	63
Avoid Racial Prejudice and Impatience	63
Spiritual Qualifications	63
Mission Boards	64

TABLE OF CONTENTS

Personal Experience with the Scriptures 65
Facing Trials 65
Discipline in Body, Soul and Spirit 65
The Need for Christian Service Experience 65
Thought questions: 66

CHAPTER 3 67
THE MISSIONARY'S AUTHORITY 67
AND SUPPORT 67
God Deals with the Missionary: God Chooses the Man 67
God Chooses His Ministry 67
   God's Work Versus Man's Work 68
   God Works Through His Church 68
Why Missionaries Leave the Field 68
Missionary Effectiveness 70
   Know the Country and Culture 70
   Learn the Language 70
   A Strong Support Team 70
   Thought questions: 71

CHAPTER 4: CULTURAL ANTHROPOLOGY FOR THE MISSIONARY 73
Introduction 73
   Anthropology and Culture 73
   Theological Background 74
   Scriptural Authority 74
   The Organization and Operation of God's Realm 74
   Basic Concepts of Culture 75
   Worldview Summarized 75
   Additional Aspects of Culture 77
   Ethnocentrism 78
Dimensions of Culture 79
   The Bible Is Related to All Three Cultural Reactions to Sin .. 80
   Additional Features of Culture 81
Conclusion 82
   Thought questions 82

CHAPTER 5 83
DIFFERING ASPECTS OF CULTURE 83
Concepts of Time 83
   Time and Events 83
   Tension in Time — Time concepts 85

Time Considerations: Position of an Individual 85
Time Considerations: The Idea of Social Time 85
Time Considerations: An Event-oriented Society 87
  Assessment 87
  Concepts of space 88
    The Idea of Privacy 89
    The Concept of Territory 90
    Gods and Spirits Associated with Territory 91
  Assessment 91
    Stewards 92
    Thought questions: 92

CHAPTER 6 93
MISSIONARIES NEED TO UNDERSTAND CULTURAL SYSTEMS 93
  Differences in Kinship 93
    Tracing Kinship: Matriarchal or Patriarchal? 93
    Large Kinship Groups 94
  Assessment 96
  Achieved Status Versus Acquired Status 96
    The Caste System of India 97
    The Aristocracy of Europe 97
    Individual Roles Within the Family or Group 97
    Tensions About Self-worth 98
  Assessment 99
  People Orientation Versus Task Orientation 100
    People Orientation 100
    Task Orientation 101
    Task Orientation vs. People Orientation 101
  Assessment 102

CHAPTER 7 105
DIFFERING ASPECTS IN CULTURES 105
  Differences in Ways of Thinking 105
    Western Thought 105
    Holistic View 105
    Dual Brain Theory 105
    Differing Thought in the OT Versus the NT 106
  Differing Ways of Making Judgments 106
    The Dichotomists 106
    The Holistic Individual 106

TABLE OF CONTENTS

Differences in Educational Methods 107
    Practical Skills Versus Memorization Skills 107
Remembering Chart 108
Forms of Intelligence 108
    Attitude Toward Group Learning 109
Assessment 110
Shame and Guilt Cultures 110
Use Extreme Care in Shame Cultures 111
Assessment 112
    The Individual Concept of Sin as Breaking the law 112
    The Group Concept of Shame 113
    Sin Breaks Relationships 113
Openness and Vulnerability When the Individual Fails 113
    Differences in Terms of Handling Failures 113
Tensions Concerning Vulnerability 114
God Uses Our Weaknesses 115
Differences in Planning for the Unexpected 115
Ways to Handle Crisis: 116
Differences in the Roles of the Sexes 117
Differences in Economy 118
    Exchanges of Services or Money 118
    Group Labor 118
    "Stuff or Starve" Mentality 119
    Sharing 119
Assessment 120
The Concept of Limited Good 121
Differences in Life Cycle 122
    Birth 122
    Conception 122
    Childhood 123
    Adulthood 124
    Old Age 125
    Ancestors 126
Assessment 127
    Recreation and Humor 127
    Recreation 127
    Birthday Parties 128
    Health Concepts 128

Summary 130
CHAPTER 8 .... **131**
MISSIONARY ADJUSTMENT **131**
  Important Factors 131
  Childhood and Missionary Call 131
  Missionary Helps 132
    Overseas Experience 132
    Missionary Call 132
    Bible College 133
    Family 134
    A Strong Church 134
    Confident of Your Call 135
    Persistence 136
    Practical Experience 136
  Selection of Candidates 137
    Screening of Candidates 137
    Spiritual Evaluation 138
  Orientation 138
    An Effective Training Program 139
  Financial Support 140
    Denominational Board 140
    Non-denominational Board 141
    "Faith" and Deputation 141
    Getting to the Field 142
    Thought questions: 142
CHAPTER 9 .... **143**
THE MISSIONARY AND **143**
MISSION BOARDS **143**
  The Functions of a Mission Board 143
  Why Should We Work Through a Mission Board? 144
    Are Mission Boards Scriptural? 145
  Independent or Under a Board? 146
    Financial Guidance Needed 147
    Why Do People Go Independent? 148
  A Mission Board's Doctrinal Stance Is Vital 151
  Important Knowledge for the Missionary 152
  Important Questions for the Missionary 153
    How Does a Board Work With Missionaries In the Field? 155

TABLE OF CONTENTS

    What About Single Women and a Mission Board?........................155
    What Are the Priorities of a Mission Board?...............................155
    Mission Boards and Supervision 156
    Mission Boards and Financial Policies..156
    Conclusion: Mission Boards and Support 157
    Thought questions:..157
CHAPTER 10..159
DEPUTATION FOR THE MISSIONARY 159
  Introduction...159
    Deputation is a School for the Missionary 160
    Biblical Basis of Deputation 160
    The Missionary is the Servant of his Master...............................160
    A Missionary's Responsibility: Be Yielded to Him 161
    God's Three Specific Roles..162
    The Concept of Ambassador...162
    Deputation is a Call to Present Needs to the Church 163
  Lessons Learned from H. C. Loucks 164
    The Example of Noah 164
    The Example of Abraham 164
    The Example of Joseph 165
    The Prospect of Failure 165
  Our Responsibility is to the Lord 166
    Examples from the Book of Judges..166
    The Examples from the Kings of Israel.......................................166
  A Missionary's Trials and Temptations..168
    Examples During the Captivity 168
  Examples of Deputizing in the Three OT Roles 169
    The King 169
    The Prophet 169
    The Priesthood..169
  Examples of Deputizing From the NT 170
  The Called Missionary is Empowered 170
    Called to a Particular Ministry...171
    Deputation is a Call to Spiritual Maturity....................................172
    Deputation is Ministry..172
  World Missions is the Heartbeat of God..172
    Small or Big Church for Deputation...173
    Thought questions..173

CHAPTER 11 175
PREPARATION FOR DEPUTATION 175

- Scheduling meetings 175
  - Meet with Your Home Pastor 175
  - Your Home Church 176
  - Contacts 178
  - Setting up Appointments 180
  - Planning and Organization 181
- The Importance of Communicating 181
- The Importance of Scheduling 182
  - Organize Your Time 183
- Adequate Support 184
- Using the Telephone 185
- Talking with the Pastor's Secretary 186
- Specific Financial Planning 186
- How Many Meetings Are Necessary For Funding?......187
- The Need For Housing on Deputation 189
- Preparation for Your Presentations 189
  - A Field Brochure 190
  - Items Representing the Field 191
- Equipment Needs 192
  - DVD Projector 192
  - Direct Box Connection to PA Systems 192
  - Spare DVD's, Speakers, and Extension Cords 193
  - Cold Weather and Equipment 194
  - An Attractive Table-top Display 194
  - Literature Can Have an Impact 195
  - Prepare a Variety of Messages 195
  - Wife Should Prepare Also 195
  - Contact the Pastor Again Shortly Before Going 196
  - Allow Enough Time to Travel 196
  - Accept Accommodations Provided 197
  - Questions a Pastor Will Ask 198
  - Ask the Host Pastor What He Desires 198
  - Be Interested in the Pastor and Church 199
  - Proper Dress, Appearance, and Behavior 199
  - Express Appreciation 199
  - Furlough Meetings 200

TABLE OF CONTENTS

    The Two Biggest Problems on Furlough 201
    Writing Letters 201
    Expect a Certain Amount of Lost Support 202
    A Realistic Budget 203
    Thought questions: 203

CHAPTER 12 205
PREPARATION FOR OVERSEAS 205
    Legal Papers 205
    The Importance of a Will 206
    Medical Exams, Documents, and Medication 206
    Have Some Basic Medical Knowledge 207
        Consider Simple Medical Equipment 207
        Regional Diseases 208
    Packing and Preparing 208
        Electrical Equipment 209
        Baggage Requirements 210
    Foreign Currency Problems 210
    Vehicle Advice 211
    Specialized Training 211
    A Few Final Thoughts 212
        Thought questions: 213

CHAPTER 13 215
ARRIVING ON THE FIELD 215
    Culture shock 215
        Rules for Normal Living Change 215
        Stress from Culture Shock 215
        The Cycle of Culture Shock 216
        The Need for Positive Attitudes 217
    Reverse Culture Shock 217
    Other Problems Facing a First-term Missionary 218
        Lack of Security and Safety 218
        Lack of Conveniences 219
    Getting Over Culture Shock 219
    The Key to Getting Over Culture Shock 219
        Resolving Culture Shock 220
        Thought Questions: 220

CHAPTER 14 223
LANGUAGE ADJUSTMENTS 223

Accuracy in Pronunciation Is Important 223
Methods of Learning a Language Differ 224
    Patterns in Languages 225
    Total Immersion Versus Language School 225
    Formal Language School 226
    Learn One Place and Travel to Another 227
    Hire a Local National? 227
Conclusion 228
    Thought questions: 229

CHAPTER 15 ..... **231**
BONDING WITH "YOUR PEOPLE" **231**
Identification with a Missionary's People 231
    Work with Your People Rather Than as Boss 232
Developing Independent Churches 232
Negativism Hurts the Ministry 232
The Right to Privacy 233
Sharing 233
Situations Change 233
Dealing with Disappointments 234
    Expectations Are Often Not Met 234
Reasonable Goals 235
Reasonable Ways to Handle Disappointments 235
    Thought questions: 236

CHAPTER 16 ..... **237**
CONFLICT RESOLUTION **237**
Conflicts with the Mission Board 237
    Pastoral Care for the Missionary 238
    Financial Conflicts 238
    Conflicts in Philosophy 239
    Conflicts with Charismatics 239
Conflicts Between Missionaries 240
Personal Separation 241
Family Conflicts 241
Conflicts Between Parents and Children 242
    Home-school 242
    Local Schools 243
    Boarding School 244
The Missionary and His Own Parents 244

TABLE OF CONTENTS

Conflicts with National Workers 245
Conflicts in the Area of Finances.. 246
The Need for the Missionary to Work Himself Out of a Job 246
    Thought questions:... 247
CHAPTER 17 249
SPECIAL ADJUSTMENTS FOR MISSIONARY WIVES: THE ROLE OF THE MISSIONARY WIFE 249
by Liz Patton and Kim Patton Champlin 249
Introduction 249
What Should the Wife's Role Be in Terms of the Husband's Call to Missions? 249
    If My Husband is Called, so am I 249
    Liz: 249
    The Wife Determines Not to Be a Hindrance 250
    Surrender Our Rights to the Lord 250
    A Good Relationship Between Husband and Wife is Necessary ... 250
    Pray Together 251
    Kim: 251
What are the Challenges for the Wife During Deputation? 251
    Liz: 251
    Finances 251
    Do Not Spoil Your Kids 252
    Be Transparent 252
    Help with Displays 252
    Help with Communication 252
    Kim: 252
    The Missionary Wife and Deputation 252
    Timing and Finances 253
    Preparation of the Children 253
    Organization of Trips 253
    Attitude 253
    Ministry in the Churches 254
    Ladies groups 254
    Children's Classes 254
    Setting up the Display 254
    Availability to Answer Questions 254
    Helping with Administrative Tasks 254
Preparation for Overseas Life 255

ISSUES IN MISSIOLOGY, VOL. V, 2nd Ed.: MAKING A MISSIONARY

- Liz: 255
  - Suggestions 255
  - Your Relationship with the Lord and Heart Attitude 255
  - You Are Being Watched 255
  - Never Talk Badly About Your Husband 255
  - Being Versus Doing 256
  - The Wife Needs to Set the Tone in the Home 256
  - Language Considerations 256
  - Work as a Team 256
  - Household Help 257
  - Adapt Your Eating Habits 257
  - Learning from Nationals 257
- Ministry 258
  - Liz: 258
  - Your Children Are Vital to the Ministry 258
  - Work as a Team and Protect Your Husband 259
  - Family and Ministry Needs 259
  - Train Someone to Take Over 259
- Preparing for Overseas Life 259
  - Kim: 259
  - List What You Need 259
  - Packing 259
- The Missionary Wife and Overseas Life 260
  - Spiritual Growth and Prayer 260
  - Relationship with Her Husband 260
  - Adjustment to Climate 261
  - Adjustment to Food 261
  - Schooling for the Children 261
  - The Most Common Choice for Schooling 261
  - Purchasing Items for the Home, Food, Etc. 262
  - Household Help 262
  - Language Learning 262
  - Adapting to the Culture 263
  - Ministry in the Church 263
  - Support of Husband 263
  - Helping with Ladies Work 264
  - Helping with Children's Work 264
  - Training Nationals 264

TABLE OF CONTENTS

    Church visitation and outreach 264
    Ministry with Other Missionaries 264
    The Special Problems of Single Lady Missionaries 265
    Ministry with Other Nationals 265
    Furlough: The Missionary Wife and Furlough 265
        Schedule & Preparation 265
        Purchases While on Furlough 265
        Traveling 265
        Thought questions: 266

CHAPTER 18 269
RETURNING TO THE USA 269
    The Reasons for Returning 269
        Adjustments 269
        The Biggest Need: Finances 269
        The Second Big Problem 270
        Returning for Health Reasons 270
        Termination 271
        Thought questions: 272

CHAPTER 19 275
THE INCARNATIONAL MISSIONARY 275
    Incarnation and Enculturation 275
    Come as Learners, Not Know-it-alls 275
    The Problem with Ethnocentrism 276
    Cultural Relativity 278
    Compartmentalization 279
        Identifying with Certain Roles: Proper Attitude 280
    The Difficult Integration Problems 280
        Philosophy and Worldview 280
        Concept of Nature Versus Concepts of Animism 281
        Conquering Differences 281
    Learning from Anthropology as Missionaries 281
        Western Materialistic Values Versus Sharing 282
        Differing Views About Control and Planning 282
        Tasks Versus Relationships 283
        Quantitative Versus Balance and Beauty 283
        Independence Versus Dependence 284
        Rights of the Individual Versus Rights of the Group 284
        Equality Versus Hierarchy 285

- Informality Versus Respect 286
- Direct & Confrontational Versus Private Decisions 287
- Active & Productive Versus Elderly and Retirement 287
- The Western Approach 288
- The Biblical Approach 288
- One of the Missionary's Principal Tasks 289
  - Anticipation Versus Waiting 289
  - The Open-ended & Non-crisis Orientation 290
  - The Goal of Cross-cultural Missionaries 290
  - Guilt and Shame Cultures 290
  - How to Handle Situations 291
  - Thought questions: 293

CHAPTER 20 295
CULTURAL ORIENTATION AND GOSPEL PRESENTATION 295
- Introduction 295
- Presenting the Gospel 296
- How Are Our Messages Understood by the People We Are Trying to Reach? 296
  - Thoughts About Worldview 296
  - Assessing the Individual's Response to the Gospel 296
  - Individuals Hearing the Gospel Will Reformulate it 297
  - Protracted Decisions 298
- Worldview and Evangelism 299
- Worldview Structures 299
- Worldview System of Classification 300
  - Mono-cultural Worldviews: "My Way is the Right Way" 300
  - The Missionary Needs a Cross-cultural Perspective 300
  - Requirement for Evaluating a Culture 301
  - Differences in Endowment and Opportunities 301
- The Power of Language 302
  - Language Word Meanings Are Assigned by the Culture 302
  - Connotative Meaning: The Emotional Response to Words 302
  - The Use of Euphemisms 303
  - Language Can Shape Our Thinking 303
  - Behavior Also Communicates 303
  - A No De Mi Gwenti (It Is Not My Custom) 304
  - Be Careful to Be Not Offensive 304
  - Time Issues 305

TABLE OF CONTENTS

Social Structure and Evangelism 306
   Differing Emphasis in Western Society 306
   Status 306
   Different Types of Social Contacts 306
   Vertical Communication Between Classes 307
   Presenting the Gospel in Rural Societies 307
   Totalitarianism 308
Effective Communication 308
Media in Evangelism 309
   Books, Especially the Bible, Are Very Important 309
   Other Media Venues in Evangelism 310
   The Instruments, the Message, the Holy Spirit 312
   The Omnipotent Triune God 312
Psychology 313
   The Goal of Secular Psychology Versus the Goal of the Bible 313
   Guilt versus shame 313
   Repressive Versus Suppressive Societies 314
   Individual Decisions in a Family Oriented Society 314
What About Self-propagating, Self-governing, Self-supporting churches? 315
   Appeal to Both Shame and Guilt 315
   Stages of Decision Making and Discipleship 316
Contextualization 317
   Critical Contextualization 317
   Uncritical Contextualization 317
   Theological Support for Critical Contextualization 318
   Self-theologizing 318
   The Need For Clear Exegesis 319
   Culturally Specific Theology 319
   Realistic Contextualization 319
   Trans-cultural Theology 320
   Missionaries Must Refrain from Giving Answers 320
   Thought questions: 321
CHAPTER 21 323
A SUMMARY OF WORLDVIEW AND EVANGELIZATION 323
   A brief summary of common worldviews 323
      Naturalism 323
      Animism 324

Hindu-Buddhist Worldview 325
Buddhism 326
Warnings 326
Tao   327
Confucius 327
Chinese Traditional Religion 327
Communists 328
Muslims 328
Syncretic Religions 330
Presenting Christ 330
The Apostle Paul's Approach 330
Indians 331
Avoid Over-intellectualizing 332
Doctrine and Approach to Various Worldviews 332
Conclusion 334

ADDENDUM A 335
THE ROLE OF THE PASTOR AND CHURCH IN MISSIONS 335
Introduction 335
    The Responsibility of the Church 335
The Work of the Pastor in the Pulpit 335
    Missions Emphasis and Prayer 335
    Educate the People About the Missionary and His Ministry 336
    The Pastor as Recruiter for Missionaries 336
    Counseling for Missionary Service 337
    Facilitate the Specific Needs of a Missionary 337
    Direct the Young People 337
A Challenge to the Pastor 337
The Role of Parents 338
The Role of the Church 339
The Role of the Home Church 339
    Which Mission Board Should the Church Recommend 340
    What is the Stated Purpose? 340
    What are the Doctrinal Positions: Stated and Unstated 340
    What are the Financial Policies of the Board? 341
Ordination Services 341
Churches and Their Financial Support 341
Of Missionaries 341
    Faith Promise 342

TABLE OF CONTENTS

    Budgeting for Missions 342
The Vital Factor for Missions 344
Accountability 345
A Missions Committee 345
    Qualifications for Missionaries Set by the Board 347
    Financial Policies of the Church and Mission Board 347
    A Yearly Missionary Report 347
    Other Considerations for the Missions Committee 348
The Missions Conference 348
    The Assistance of the Mission Agencies 349
Responsibilities of the Sending Church 350

ADDENDUM B 353
DEPUTATION: A RUGGED BUT REWARDING ROAD 353
By Marc Patton 353
Forward 353
    The Process 353
    Success Belongs to the Lord 353
    There Is Not One Method of Deputation 354
Introduction 354
    Three Critical Areas to Avoid Deputation Problems 355

SECTION 1: GETTING STARTED 356
Start Early 356
Mission Board 357
Printed Materials 357
    1. Prayer Cards 357
    2. Letterhead 357
    3. Letters of Recommendation 358
    4. Resume 358
    Website 358
    Survey Trip 359

SECTION 2: SCHEDULING MEETINGS 359
Gathering Contacts 359
    1. Your sending church 360
    2. Your college 360
    3. Other missionaries 360
    4. Scheduled meetings 361
Planning Your Schedule 361
    Where Do I Start? 361

How Many Meetings Will I Need? 362
How Long Will It Take? 362
   1. Go to two different churches on Sunday 363
   2. Use mission conferences to fill in meetings between Sundays and
      Wednesdays. 363
   The Initial Contact 365
   Your Two-minute Opportunity 367
   The Final Question 368
   A Few More Thoughts 369

SECTION 3 - SO YOU HAVE A MEETING 370
Next Things 370
   1. Agree on a date and service 370
   2. Settle details 370
   3. Request accommodations as needed 371
   4. Send a confirmation letter immediately 371
   5. Send a second confirmation letter 371
   6. Call the pastor back 372
   7. If an emergency arises 372

SECTION 4: PREPARATION FOR THE MEETING 373
Projects That Must Be Completed 373
   DVD Presentation 373
   General Suggestions 373
      1. It should not be too long 374
      2. It should be sharp and professional 374
      3. (I eliminated point number three as irrelevant in this updated revision)..374
      4. Present your family as well as the field 374
      5. Emphasize the people more than places 375
      6. Tell the people what you plan to do 375
Display Board 375
Deputation Messages 375
   1. Stick to your purpose 375
   2. Stick to the given time frame 376
   3. Be prepared for anything 376

SECTION 5: AFTER THE MEETING 376
Follow-up 376
   1. Do not be too pushy 376
   2. Leave something with the pastor 377
   3. Send a thank you note 377

TABLE OF CONTENTS

    4. Leave the church on your prayer letter list 377
    5. Send an occasional personal note 378
    6. A follow-up phone call 378
    7. Your pastor or mission director could write a letter for you 378
  What Should Be Your Focus 379
Maintaining and Increasing Your Support After You Are on the Field 379
    1. Communicate well 379
    2. Invite key pastors and individuals to visit you on the field! 380
    3. Ask key supporters to help you gain new contacts and support 380
    4. When you are on furlough visit pastors and supporting individuals when you are driving through their area. 380
    5. Take advantage of modern technology. 380
THE MISSIONARY WIFE by Charin Patton 381
  The Unique Calling of a Missionary & Family 381
    The Helpmeet 381
    The Wife and Children's Responsibility 382
    Ways to Assist Your Husband 382
    1. Before Beginning Deputation 382
    2. Preparing for meetings 384
    3. Traveling 385
    4. The Meeting Itself 387
  Appendix A: Statistics 388
    A Few Thoughts 389
  Appendix B - Confirmation Letter Sample 389
  Appendix C - Second Confirmation Letter 390
  Appendix D - Call-back Letter 391
INDEX 393
ABOUT THE AUTHOR 397
BOOKS BY DR. PATTON 398
    ISSUES IN MISSIOLOGY, VOLUME I: 398
    ISSUES IN MISSIOLOGY, VOLUME II: 398
    ISSUES IN MISSIOLOGY, VOLUME III, THOUGHTS ABOUT TRANSLATION: 399
    ISSUES IN MISSIOLOGY, VOLUME IV, WORLDVIEW AND WORLD RELIGIONS 399
    ISSUES IN MISSIOLOGY, VOLUME V, Getting on the Field; Staying on the Field 400
    SRANANTONGO BIBLE 400

DVDS, MP3, ARTICLES 400
ENDNOTES 403

INTRODUCTION

As we begin an introduction to missions, I would like first to give a brief capsule of personal testimony. The rest of the chapter will outline some of the basic concerns for the person contemplating becoming a missionary. The remainder of the book will largely expand on many of these themes. You, the reader, may ask: "Why is there a large section of cultural anthropology in what is basically a practical book for missionary service?" It is because the concepts of cultural anthropology are vital for effective missionary service. I trust that the book will prove a blessing to you, dear reader. I would also strongly encourage you to look at the appendices at the back of the book, especially, if you are facing deputation, the section pertaining to this topic by my son, Marc Patton. I believe that it will be a great help.

A Personal Testimony

I want to start my personal journey speaking about my grandfather Patton. He was saved, as was his wife, and they were faithful members of the Presbyterian Church about the turn of the 20th century. He had a good tenor voice and sang in the choir. My grandmother played the organ for the church. Grandpa Patton worked selling suits at Wanamaker's Department Store in downtown Philadelphia. Grandma Patton supplemented their income by playing the organ for background music in the silent movies. She also had a boarding house, and her boarders were like family. I remember Uncle Walter and two Quaker ladies who influenced my father. My grandfather had a real burden for missions. At one time, the man who wrote the Korean national anthem stayed as a border in his home. My father's sister suffered brain damage at birth, and they had no other children. But my grandfather was delighted to see my father become a Presbyterian pastor and then decide to go on the mission field.

A Concentration Camp Experience

When I was three years old, my parents and I headed for China. The year was 1940. They enrolled in language school and had a Chinese nanny look after me. After a few months, the Japanese began to move from Korea into Manchuria, and Peking (now Beijing) was no longer safe. We were moved to the Philippine Islands and lived in Baguio in Northern Luzon. After the attack on Pearl Harbor, the Japanese invaded the Philippine Islands, which were then a United States' protectorate. They pushed up to Baguio, which was close to Clark Air Force Base. We were captured and imprisoned with about 500 people in Camp John Hay, which was turned into a concentration camp. That was a very intense time. Men and women were separated for two years, so I stayed with my mother. Food was very scarce. After a while, clothes wore out, and I had no shoes as my feet grew. When families were allowed to live together, our total space was perhaps 6 x 8 feet, separated by a sheet from our neighbors. We were finally released on February 3, 1945, and repatriated to the USA.[1]

Repatriated

It took some time to adjust to the USA. During my first year back in the USA, I caught most of the common childhood infectious diseases, including measles, mumps and chicken pox. My mother taught me to read during our first summer in the USA, and I was placed in third grade despite no previous schooling. However, I was a good student, and within a year I was one of the top students in the class. At age 11, I had a strong feeling that I should become a medical missionary to Africa. That feeling never left. I went through high school, graduated top in my class, and went to college on academic scholarships. In college, I majored in biology and chemistry, with minors in anthropology and philosophy and religion. During college, I met my wife. We dated three years and married just before my graduation from college. My wife was in nurses training, and I started medical school at the same school.

Medical School

My medical training went well. Again, I did well scholastically, and finished near the top of my class. I had not forgotten the idea of going overseas, and was able to create a special rotating internship program for two years, with six months in internal medicine, six months in pediatrics, nine months in surgery, and three months in obstetrics and gynecology. The head of Internal Medicine allowed me to count my

INTRODUCTION

second year as actually counting toward my Internal Medical residency, and then I stayed on for two additional years residency in Internal Medicine, and then spent two years in the Public Health Service to complete my military service. Our four children were born between my last year as a medical student and my first year in the Public Health Service.

Preparation For Missions

During this time, I was attending the Presbyterian Church, and decided to see about medical service. The board was very interested in my working in medicine but wanted me to work on an Indian reservation in the USA. I also mentioned to them that I had major questions about the deity of Christ and the inspiration of the scriptures. Remember, I was not saved at the time. These questions did not bother the board – and it bothered me that it did not bother them!

I returned to the University of Rochester for a two-year Cardiology fellowship. I wrote to 20 medical schools in Africa, explaining my background and my interest in Cardiology. I had correspondence with the medical school in Lagos, Nigeria, and almost went there. But in December 1970, in the middle of my second year of fellowship, I developed a spinal disc problem, and was on my back for 5 weeks. I thought that my career in Cardiology was going to be difficult because of my back problem. Then I received a telephone call from the Agency for International Development offering me a position as head of the Department of Internal Medicine in Monrovia, Liberia. My letter had arrived there concerning working overseas, and the head of the hospital sent a private courier to the airport to intercept a man from USAID who was just returning to the USA. He told him: "I want this man. Call him at once and recruit him." Thus, my back problem proved a great blessing, keeping me from going to Nigeria, but I went to Liberia instead.

We spent five years in Liberia, West Africa, under the Agency for International Development, which were very profitable professionally. I was Professor of Internal Medicine and head of the Department of Internal Medicine at the A. M. Dogliotti School of Medicine in

Monrovia, Liberia. I developed the program in Internal Medicine, taught medical students, and developed a training program including third-and-fourth-year students, internship, and two years of residency. Our cholera unit was used as a model for West Africa. We also developed an excellent tuberculosis control program during this time. When we left, I was decorated by the Liberian government.

My Spiritual Life

More important, however, was my spiritual life. My father had gone to Princeton Seminary just after the modernist split in the Presbyterian Church. All the strong Bible believers had left Princeton for Westminster Seminary, and although my father was saved, he became steeped in modernism. I was raised a liberal Presbyterian. At one time, just after marriage, I thought that I had made a personal commitment to Christ, but I had not really done so. However, in Liberia, I came under conviction and accepted the Lord as my personal savior. After doing so, our family left the liberal Lutheran church which we had attended in Monrovia, Liberia and ended up at ELWA, a church offshoot from the hospital and radio station begun by Sudan Interior Mission missionaries. Two of their missionaries had great influence on me. Dr. Bud Hurst challenged my faith to accept the Lord, and I made a decision after he had returned to the USA. Dr. Bob Schindler, the founder of ELWA Hospital, basically recruited me to join him at Southwestern Medical Clinic in the USA.

Doing the Lord's Will

At this point in my life, my goal was still to climb the academic ladder. I had co-authored a book on cardiac arryhmias and written or co-authored a number of professional articles. I had experience teaching and administrating a department of medicine. And I was still only 38 years old. I had an offer to go to the US Public Health Hospital in San Francisco, where I would be deputy chief of Internal Medicine until the chief retired in 6 months. I would have been able to retire at age 51 as I already had 7 years of service with the U.S. government. I had an offer to run the training program in a large hospital training their Internal Medical residents. But I knew that the Lord wanted me to go to Berrien

INTRODUCTION

Springs, Michigan to Southwestern Medical Clinic. Professionally this was a one-way street to oblivion. There was no academic teaching, and a smaller salary. But I decided that I had better do the Lord's will, and have been grateful for the decision.

We were in Berrien Springs for 10 years. I was in private practice, and was head of the Intensive Care Unit at a local hospital. For two years, we attended a strong Bible church, and then moved our membership to an independent Baptist Church where our children were attending school. We became totally involved as a family. We ran two bus routes. I sang in the choir, taught the adult Bible class, counseled, and ended up as deacon chairman. My practice was also going well, and we were basically content to remain where we were, until challenged by Dr. Darrell Champlin, who preached at our home church one Wednesday night in 1983. The following summer we visited Suriname, and came to stay in 1986, accompanied by our youngest daughter, who had just graduated from Bible college. She became engaged to Darrell Champlin's youngest son, Ethan, shortly after arrival, and was married the following year.

My original plan prior to coming to Suriname was to locate on the Tapanahony River in the interior and start a number of clinics along the river in a variety of villages, with the goal of starting a church in each place that we had a clinic. When we came to Suriname for an initial visit, we did travel to the interior. But we found a problem. Medizebs, the program providing medical care to the interior, insisted that if I were to work there, I would need to join them. But this was not a secular group, but a religious group from a liberal background, and I had major problems doing so. We did not know why at the time, but the Lord graciously created the problem.

Darrell Champlin noted that I had taught medicine before, and perhaps I could teach in the medical school, and keep a "foot in the door" for work in the interior. So we came to Paramaribo one day, and without any appointment ahead of time, the Lord orchestrated our meetings. We met with the head of the teaching hospital, the dean of the medical school, the head of medicine for the interior, and the minister of health all in one day! And they all said: "Come to the city. We need you." So, we changed our plans accordingly.

Suriname

On August 2, 1986, we arrived in Suriname, and went immediately to what was then the main mission station in Ricanau Mofo for two months of intensive language study. We returned to Paramaribo the last week of September, because the school year began October 1st. Two weeks later, a civil war broke out, and we were actually cut off from our mission station at Ricanau Mofo. And if we had followed my original plan, I would have been far behind enemy lines in the interior, cut off from our missionaries, and unable to communicate. The Lord was so good to protect us.

In retrospect, I was not really a good fit for the interior. I did not have the physical strength which is needed to wrestle barrels of fuel and oil, as well as other items from canoes to the shore. I was not a handyman and would not be prepared for the inevitable breakdowns that would occur. My instinct when something breaks is to reach for the telephone and call a repairman. But there are no close-by repairmen in the interior. And finally, the Lord wanted the development of certain ministries, which never would have developed had we been in the interior.

God's Plan in Suriname

At the time of writing this book, we have been in Suriname about 26 years. Initially I did continue teaching in medicine on a volunteer basis five hours daily from Monday through Friday, as well as church planting. We worked on learning Sranantongo and Dutch, went soul-winning, started a church, started training national pastors, and completed our first church building. But after five years in Suriname, I retired from teaching medicine and concentrated on the church planting and associated activities. The Lord made it very clear to me that I should leave my teaching medicine, although I loved the work and was good at it. Here is the story of what happened.

INTRODUCTION

My wife and I were discussing the ministry one night, and she pointed out that when I came to Suriname, the internal medical specialists were all too young to take over the department, as they had recently finished training. Now, five years later, they were fully capable to run the entire program without my help, and there was a real shortage of full-time fundamental preachers. I found it difficult to listen to these words from my wife. The following morning, I had a sharp pain shoot down my leg, and my toe went numb. I had had a spinal disc problem years before when in my fellowship training, and this was a recurrence, but without any precipitating injury.

I lay in bed in pain. A few days later, one of my soul-winning partners, whom I had taught to read, came to pray for me. Then he asked me: "Dominee (Pastor), do you know why you are sick?" My original reaction was to think: "Brother Andre, who are you to tell me why I am sick? I am the doctor, and you are the man I taught to read." But I didn't say that. He went on: "You are sick because you are one man, and you are trying to be two men." This was a typical "odo" or proverb saying, and I did not understand. He went on to explain. "You are trying to be both a doctor and a pastor, and you cannot do both." I did not care for his diagnosis!

A few hours later, Brother K. came to visit. I had not seen him in months, because he had been having some problems and was, at the time, out of church. He came to pray for me, and then asked me: "Dominee, do you know why you are sick?" He then repeated the same explanation, and I knew that the Lord had sent both men, because they had not met together before I received the message.

I struggled with the idea of leaving medicine for the next few days, but decided that I had better learn to trust the Lord. I recovered, and went to the hospital and resigned from my teaching schedule Monday through Friday. But I asked the Lord for a sign that I was in His will. Our men had asked me to preach on the radio about a year earlier, but when I tried to get on a local station, I had no success. However, what I really wanted to do was to preach on the national radio station from 6:15 to 6:30 pm, which was a fifteen-minute musical interlude between the Sranantongo news and the death announcements, to which every Bush Negro listens.

I would have a captive audience. I walked into the station, not knowing a soul. I walked out with a contract for Monday through Friday, five days a week at precisely the time I had asked for. That launched our radio broadcasts, which we have been doing 21 years.

Translating the Bible

Since I now had a block of time each morning, I began translating the Bible with a team of nationals whom I had trained. (I go into detail in *Issues in Missiology Volume III*.) Seven years later, the Bible was completely translated and printed, and is the most sold Bible in Suriname today. Our assistant pastor came to me, now ready to begin a second church, and we launched Winti Wai church. We also began our Bible Institute to train national pastors and leaders, which has now been in existence 21 years had has trained over 80 individuals.

The Ministry Expands

Over the years, we began training more national pastors, planting more churches, broadcasting on additional radio stations, and then inaugurated a TV ministry. In more recent years, we have started an Advanced Bible Institute, which is in its fourth year, broadcast on three radio stations, and broadcast two TV programs weekly. Eventually the Lord allowed us to see four churches planted, four church buildings completed, and 10 national pastors in our churches, with six pastors in other churches in Paramaribo. I have been able to write a number of discipleship guides as well as commentaries in Srananthongo.

Since we left Suriname in 2012, the national pastors have continued the work in all four churches. In 2018, it was possible for all the church properties to be transferred from the mission to the churches after they were officially recognized by the Suriname government. The radio ministry continued on three stations, and the two TV broadcasts per week have continued. Although the Bible Institute has fewer students than before, it has also continued. As more individuals now drive to church, the buses continue to run but in smaller numbers, paid for by the churches. It is amazing what the Lord can do if we simply yield to Him and allow His Holy Spirit freedom to work in our lives.

INTRODUCTION

Return to the USA

Our desire was to leave an intact church capable of supporting itself when we returned to the USA. I announced three years in advance that we would be leaving and started to drop some of our financial support for the churches, encouraging them to do their own maintenance and support their pastors and other staff. We also assisted in covering costs of buses which we rented but told the churches that our assistance would stop when we left. The churches rose to the challenges in covering their own expenses.

Two areas of finances I knew would be difficult – distribution of Sranantongo Bibles and our radio and TV programs. Both programs were designed not primarily for the local churches but for nation-wide evangelization. My son-in-law took over the Bible distribution and has continued to do so since our departure. Thus far we have had five reprintings of the Bible. We charge a low cost, which covers shipping and import duty (usually none on Bibles) and distribution. We make a small profit which is then returned to our printer to help cover the cost of the next reprint.

My son-in-law also arranges for both the radio and TV programs in Sranantongo. We have two TV fifteen-minute programs on a major TV station, and have been broadcasting several times a week on three radio stations, two in Paramaribo and one in the interior. More recently, my son-in-law has opened a 24/7 radio station in Moengo, Suriname, and we have additional programs broadcast as well.

My wife and I returned to Powell, Tennessee in August 2012. I have been teaching at The Crown College of the Bible. Although I primarily teach classes on various missions subjects, I also have taught Hebrews epistles, and teach Human Anatomy and Physiology. My wife attends all my classes and assists with administrative tasks as well as interacting with the students. I earned a Master in Missiology degree in 2013, a Masters of Biblical Studies n 2018, and was awarded a Doctor of Divinity degree in 2021.

CHAPTER 1
INITIAL THOUGHTS ABOUT MISSIONARY WORK

Who Is a Missionary?

So, you want to be a missionary — or at least know more about becoming one. First, we must ask: who is a missionary? Some say that he is an ambassador for Christ and a herald of the truth that Jesus is Lord. Of course, this is true. Paul, who I consider the greatest missionary of all time, and a model for us, says that we are all ambassadors for Christ. ***2 Cor. 5:20a: Now then we are ambassadors for Christ...*** It is our job to present Jesus Christ to the world as the true King of Kings and Lord of Lords. The missionary is an ambassador of love to the whole man — the body, soul and spirit. And he is an envoy of peace, ultimately bringing peace with God and with his fellow man. He is also a bearer of his culture. He cannot avoid bringing his culture with him. He must examine the culture which he brings, because he is not called to civilize the individuals on the field, but to present Christ by word and by a godly life.

Here is a more complete description of a missionary: he is a man or woman, called by God to a full-time ministry of the Word and prayer, who has crossed cultural barriers to preach the gospel in an area where Christ is largely unknown. This definition distinguishes between all believers (we are all witnesses and ambassadors) and those who have been specially called by God for a full-time ministry. Furthermore, it specifies a ministry of the Word and prayer. As a missionary, he has also crossed cultural barriers. These barriers can be categorized to give an idea of the distance of the cultural gap between the missionary and the group to which he ministers. There may be a bigger gap in an inner-city ministry in the USA than in many foreign fields.

False Ideas About Missionaries

We have many false ideas about missionaries. Some think that unless you cross the ocean you are not a real missionary. I would call this a baptism by salt water. Others think that you must live in a hut in the bush if you are a real missionary. When my wife and I were called to the city of Paramaribo in Suriname, she mentioned to a friend in the USA about buying some bedspreads. Her friend asked incredulously: You have beds? I guess she pictured us swinging in a hammock in a hut out in the jungle. Originally, I had planned to work in the bush, traveling by dugout canoe through rapids from village to village doing medical work and planting churches. When instead the Lord called me to a church planting ministry in the main city, some seemed disappointed that I was no longer a "real bush missionary."

Some have the idea that the heathen are waiting to flock to the missionary to hear the gospel. It is true that missionaries may eventually see many people saved. But it is far more common to labor for years before the first converts come. William Carey and Adoniram Judson both labored seven years before they saw a single convert. And in many cultures, they have had their own religious customs and holy books which antedate Christianity. Why should they reject their culture and beliefs to adopt a more recent western religion?

Missions Versus Colonialism

Further myths about missions: Missions ended like colonialism ended. The tie between missions and colonialism was unfortunate. Colonialism did make it easier for missionaries to get onto the foreign field in many cases. However, Christianity, which arose in the middle east, was often identified with the white man from Europe or the United States. Colonialism is basically over, but missions are far from over. Likewise, although short-term missions have become extremely popular, there is still a need for full-time missionaries. Some believe that we need only specialists on the field. But flexibility and adaptability are vital for successful mission work.

CHAPTER 1: INITIAL THOUGHTS ABOUT MISSIONARY WORK

The Challenge of Missions: Why Become A Missionary?

Why become a missionary? Because God created us to love Him, to enjoy Him forever, and to give Him glory. *Mt. 22:[35] Then one of them, which was a lawyer, asked him a question, tempting him, and saying,[36] Master, which is the great commandment in the law?[37] Jesus said unto him, Thou shalt love the Lord thy God with all thy heart, and with all thy soul, and with all thy mind.[38] This is the first and great commandment.[39] And the second is like unto it, Thou shalt love thy neighbor as thyself.* We are to show our love for God, among other things, by showing love to our neighbor. And what shows more love than showing him the way of salvation?

All Life is For His Glory

All life is to be lived for the glory of God. *Romans 11:36 For of Him and through Him and to Him are all things, to whom be glory forever. Amen.* We are to reflect what God is really like. We are to have a passion for what He is passionate about. God is passionate about His glory. We live in a universe which declares the greatness of God. *Psalm 19:1 The heavens declare the glory of God; and the firmament sheweth His handiwork.* When we show love to the dying soul without Christ, we declare to him the grace of God to the glory of God.

Be Passionate for God

God wants us to be passionate for Him. Paul was incredibly productive and effective. He focused on *one thing*. He did not dabble in a bunch of different directions, but on reaching the world for Christ. *Phil. 3:[9] And be found in him, not having mine own righteousness, which is of the law, but that which is through the faith of Christ, the righteousness which is of God by faith:[10] That I may know him, and the power of his resurrection, and the fellowship of his sufferings, being made conformable unto his death;[11] If by any means I might attain unto the resurrection of the dead.[12] Not as though I had already attained, either were already perfect: but I follow after, if that I may apprehend that for which also I am apprehended of Christ Jesus.[13] Brethren, I count not myself to have apprehended: but this one thing I do, forgetting those things which are behind, and reaching forth unto those things which are before,[14] I press toward the mark for the prize of the high calling of God in Christ Jesus.*

He boasted in one thing — the cross of Jesus Christ, where we find all the blessings for sinners. *Gal. 6:14 But God forbid that I should glory save in the cross of our Lord Jesus Christ, by whom the world is crucified to me, and I to the world.* And he lived out what he preached. We boast of the cross when we are on the cross. The old self dies, and the new self now lives by the faith of God in Jesus Christ. *Galatians 2:20 I am crucified with Christ; nevertheless I live, yet not I, but Christ liveth in me: and the life which I now live in the flesh, I live by the faith of the Son of God, who loved me, and gave himself for me.*

We boast of the cross when we bear the cross daily, as the Lord Jesus demands. *Mt. 16:24 Then said Jesus unto his disciples, If any man will come after me, let him deny himself, and take up his cross, and follow me.* Paul was determined to honor the Lord Jesus by his entire life, as well as his death. *Phil. 1:21 For me to live is Christ, and to die is gain.* Christ will be honored regardless of what happens.

Facing Life and Death

As we face both life and death, and place our lives in His hands, we make very apparent to all around us where our treasures truly are. This sort of missionary will have an impact, when the Lord Jesus is treasured above his health, wealth, and even life itself. *Mt. 10:[37] He that loveth father or mother more than me is not worthy of me: and he that loveth son or daughter more than me is not worthy of me.[38] And he that taketh not his cross, and followeth after me, is not worthy of me.[39] He that findeth his life shall lose it: and he that loseth his life for my sake shall find it.* The Lord Jesus taught: *Mt.6:19-21 Lay not up for yourselves treasures upon earth, where moth and rust doth corrupt, and where thieves break through and steal. But lay up for yourselves treasures in heaven, where neither moth nor rust doth corrupt, and where thieves do not break through nor steal. For where your treasure is, there will your heart be also.*

CHAPTER 1: INITIAL THOUGHTS ABOUT MISSIONARY WORK

Trust God

As we grow in faith, and also in effectiveness, we learn to trust the Lord Jesus for everything. We begin to realize that we have everything we need in Him. *2 Peter 1:3-4 According as his divine power hath given unto us all things that pertain unto life and godliness, through the knowledge of him that hath called us to glory and virtue. 4. Whereby are given unto us exceeding great and precious promises: that by these ye might be partakers of the divine nature, having escaped the corruption that is in the word through lust.* And as we die to self each day, and He lives through us, we find our faith growing, and Christ is magnified in our lives. The various trials and tribulations we encounter help perfect our faith and remove the rough edges that keep people from the Lord.

Some Dangers

What about the risks involved? When my wife and I went overseas, it was not like in the old days. When my parents went to China, we were evacuated to the Philippine Islands at the beginning of World War II, and still were captured and placed, for over 3 years, in a POW camp. My wife's parents escaped with, literally, the clothes on their backs from China as the Japanese troops advanced. My mother-in-law had each of the children wear three sets of clothing, because they could carry almost nothing with them when they escaped. Even when we were in Africa for 5 years under USAID, we had access to modern medicine and the possibility of evacuation to the USA. In Suriname, the situation is even better. The medical care is really quite good. When we arrived in 1986, they had at that time no full-time cardiologist, and I was the closest thing that they had. Now they have five well-trained cardiologists and a very modern catheterization laboratory. But although we missionaries are less likely to die of malaria or other diseases, or from cannibalism, there are the new dangers of war, terrorism, and abductions.

Acceptable Risks

So, what do we say about risks? Risks are acceptable if the cause is big enough. And no cause is bigger than reaching the world for Christ. In the eyes of God, of course, there is no risk, because He has all power, and knows the end from the beginning. **But God wants us to remain**

dependent on Him. When we insist on security and He is leading us in another direction, we may be clinging to a security which does not really exist except in our own minds. Jonathan Goforth and his wife were in disagreement about traveling into the interior of China. His wife was concerned about the children's health and basically refused to go. Ultimately before she went to the interior, one of their children had died. God did protect in their times traveling in the interior despite lack of cleanliness.

Foolish Risks

On the other hand, we are not to take foolish risks. We are not to be heroic for the sake of heroism, or for the desire for adventure. We see on television and read about extreme adventures. People who are bored with the usual, take ridiculous risks simply for excitement. We are not to simply show ourselves as self-reliant. But when we take risks (or forsake gain) for the sake of Jesus Christ, we show His value in our lives. God gives us everything we need for our spiritual growth. He gives us what we need to be happy for eternity, namely Himself.

Conquerors

We are more than conquerors in our trials and afflictions, and not by avoiding them when they must be faced. Shadrach, Meshak and Abednego were conquerors *in* the fiery furnace; not by compromising so that they would not be thrown into the furnace. They were also not alone. A fourth person "like the Son of God" was with them and protected them! We are also more than conquerors as long as we do not permit anything or anyone to separate us from the love of God.

What About Money?

In about 15% of his parables, Jesus talks about money. Jesus loves to show us those who have put Him above their love of money. He pointed out the widow who gave her last small coins into the offering, showing her trust of God and her love of Him. And so, we too must be willing to give our possessions over for the love of God. My wife and I had two excellent examples; our parents who were missionaries to China during World War II. My wife's parents were a missionary doctor and

CHAPTER 1: INITIAL THOUGHTS ABOUT MISSIONARY WORK

nurse. They could have lived comfortably in the USA, but they chose to serve 10 years in China and, later, another 11 years in India. During the invasion of the Japanese army, they fled leaving everything behind. My parents were students in language school. My father was a pastor. My mother married before completing her nurse's training. They were interned in a POW camp by the Japanese and lost all their earthly goods.

So, we must also be willing to put God before money. When we came to Suriname, my income dropped over 90%. We owned our own home free and clear. We sold it and gave the money to the Lord's work. The Lord has not only taken care of us financially, but abundantly blessed us. Truly, we found that you cannot out-give God. *Luke 6:38 Give, and it shall be given unto you, good measure, pressed down, and shaken into your bosom. For with the same measure that ye mete withal it shall be measured to you again. Mark 10:29-30 And Jesus answered and said: Verily, verily I say unto you, There is no man that hath left house, or brethren, or sisters, or father, or mother, or wife, or children, or lands for my sake, and the gospel's, 30. But that he shall receive an hundred-fold now in this time: houses, and brethren, and sisters, and mothers, and children, and lands, with persecutions, and in the world to come eternal life.*

Hudson Taylor's Experience

God used Hudson Taylor mightily. Hudson Taylor learned to give as a young man. God showed him that He was trustworthy. On one occasion, he gave away what was virtually his last money. God arranged for a gift to arrive the following morning worth four times what he had given. Taylor was able to trust the Lord for finances in beginning China Inland Mission, until there were over 1000 missionaries supported on faith. George Muller experienced the hand of the Lord on his own ministry to 2000 orphans, providing for them many times when they were virtually without food.

Spiritual Warfare

We must have a warfare mentality. When a nation is at war, we no longer have certain luxuries readily available. When the USA went to war in 1941, no cars were built from 1942-1945. We were at war. Tires were almost impossible to find. Certain foods were rationed. We are also at war, but not against human enemies. We are fighting not against flesh and blood, but against spiritual wickedness in high places. We must exercise ourselves positively carrying the gospel to the lost. We must take time in prayer. We must be willing to love others at cost to ourselves. Jesus said that to save our lives, we must be willing to lose them for His sake. He that loses his life for Jesus' sake truly finds it. And where is the first line of warfare being fought? In our own hearts. We must take the victory of the Lord and defeat the sinfulness of our own hearts. We must be in the world, but not of the world.

Working, Not to Have, But to Give

Most Christians in the USA will serve the Lord as they continue their secular jobs. They are thankful for His provision day for day and see His promises to them in their lives. They can live to His glory as they place Him first in their lives. Likewise, retired people will also want to live to the glory of God. We should allow Him to use us in our lives to spread the gospel. It is important to seek not only our own good, but to help others through our work, so that we work to serve others, and not just for our own profit. The quality of our work and our godly attitude can also open doors to the gospel and remove stumbling blocks. So, we work to be useful, and allow our work to develop redemptive relationships. We work, not to have, but to give. We give to His honor and glory, and to forward His work. We should have compassion for the lost, and be willing to give our lives for them, either at home or abroad.

When we truly love others, we will want them to receive what they need most; a personal relationship with Jesus Christ. As we give to send others abroad, this is a validation of the entire ministry of the sending church. We meet needs at home as a merciful church, and we send people out to plant merciful churches elsewhere. There is at this time a great need to plant churches where none exist, as well as develop national leadership to maintain churches which have been already started. We need to pray for workers, and that the Lord will use us with whatever skills He has given us.

CHAPTER 1: INITIAL THOUGHTS ABOUT MISSIONARY WORK

Thought Questions:
1. What do you believe are the main considerations for you for going to a mission field? Please make these personal to your own situation.
2. Are there some misconceptions which you had had about going on the mission field which this chapter exposed? If so, which?
3. What are your thoughts about finances and being a missionary?

CHAPTER 2
GOD'S CALLING

God's Calling Is More Than a Need

What about the call for the missionary?[2] Some individuals state that everyone is a missionary. There is no specific call necessary. Others state that everyone is called, which in many cases may amount to the same idea. If there is a need, all must go. But a call must be more than a need. I would agree that all are called to world-wide missions, but the question is where you are to serve. Some are to serve by staying, paying and praying. Others are to go. I believe that there is a definite call for the missionary which differs from saying that every member of the church is a missionary. Moreover, I believe that this sense of call is very important to the missionary when he is under testing. When tempted to quit, he can rest on the fact that he is there, not because of his own desires, but because of the call of God. And who God calls, God enables to do His will.

No Single Pattern

There is no single pattern in the Bible over the call of God to missions. There is no single verse or series of verses we can use. God uses several different methods to reach the missionary and varies His call. Some have a definite experience, while others have a gradual awareness that this is God's plan for their lives. Dr. Ida Scudder came from a missionary family. Her father was a physician but she really resisted becoming a missionary. After returning to the mission field from her schooling to help care for her mother, one night three different men came to her house asking her to help their wives. None of the three was able to deliver a child. Their culture would make it unthinkable for a man to treat a woman in labor. All three women died. Through that experience, Ida Scudder yielded to the missionary call, returned to the USA to train as a physician, and returned to eventually pioneer the medical center at Vellore, India, one of the premier training institutions in the country.

One of the first ways the Lord may work in our lives is to see the great spiritual need of the world, and to become aware of the great commission. We may begin to feel that this is something which we ought to do. That was basically my situation. Ever since I was 11 years old, I had an idea of becoming a medical missionary. The intensity of the idea fluctuated, but never left. We may also become aware that God has gifted us with certain gifts which should be used to His glory. In addition, our church may recognize and affirm that the Lord is calling and gifting us. God will also give us an increasing yearning to go to some field to do his will. As these various indications increase, we may become clearly aware of a call, although we have no specific experience of a call.

The Missionary Must Be Totally Consecrated

Furthermore, we can prepare ourselves for a call. The first point is to accept Jesus Christ as Lord of our lives. He must be Lord of all areas of our lives. He has the right to use, or reject, all aspects of our lives. To understand the will of God, we must be totally consecrated to Him. *Romans 12:1-2. I beseech you therefore, brethren, by the mercies of God, that ye present your bodies a living sacrifice, holy, acceptable unto God, which is your reasonable service. 2. And be not conformed to this world: by be ye transformed by the renewing of your mind, that ye may prove what is that good, and acceptable, and perfect will of God.* Note the main steps outlined. First, we must be totally consecrated, body, soul and spirit, to the Lord. We are to be holy; set apart for Him. Secondly, we must reject the thinking of the world system, which focuses on "me first," on the material blessings that are temporary at best, and on things we can see. We must focus on those eternal blessings which come from God. We must be open to the Holy Spirit, listening to His voice as He guides through the Word, and also recognize that God may guide us through providential circumstances.

God's Will Must Be the Missionary's Will

We cannot know God's specific will for our lives until our lives are in conformity to His general will. He promises to guide us, but begins with the basics first; our will. *Psalm 32:8-9 I will instruct thee and teach*

CHAPTER 2: GOD'S CALLING

thee in the way which thou shalt go; I will guide thee with mine eye. Be ye not as the horse, or as the mule, which have no understanding: whose mouth must be held in with bit and bridle, lest they come near to thee. God also will usually confirm our call through the local church. The task of world evangelism is given to the church. It is the church that is the pillar and ground of the truth. When we believe that the Lord is calling us to a task, is that task being confirmed by the church? Does our local church accept our call as from the Lord?

God's Perfect Timing

Timing is also important. Both my wife and I knew that we would eventually go back overseas after we returned to the USA following five years in Liberia, West Africa. We would feel a yearning when we saw missions presentations. At one point, after a missions conference, I went to our home pastor asking him about going to the mission field. At that point, we were very involved in the church. I was deacon chairman, sang in the choir, ran two bus routes with my wife and family, taught Sunday school, and was a counselor for the church. The pastor pointed out that my four children were all teenagers and doing very well at school. He felt that indeed we would go overseas, but that it would probably be better at a later date. He was correct. Four years later, our family situation was very different. Our two oldest daughters were about to marry, our son was a senior in high school, and one daughter a junior in college. We decided to wait a year to see the two daughters married and wanted to be home for our son's senior year of high school. We then started deputation and were on the field with our youngest daughter about 13 months later.

The Missionary Call Versus Missionary Guidance

Further, we need to distinguish between one's call and one's guidance. Paul was **called** as an apostle on the Damascus Road. He had been set aside from his mother's womb, but the specific call became clear to him then. However, he received on several occasions. In Acts 13, the Holy Spirit set Barnabas and Saul (Paul) apart for the work of missionaries. In Acts 16, he received the call to Macedonia after the Holy Spirit stopped him from traveling further north or east on his second missionary trip. I believe that I received a call as a missionary at age 11, or at least a strong impulse to do that sort of work. But in 1984 I was guided to go to Suriname, and later received guidance to leave medicine and devote time completely to the Lord's work in other areas.

What can we do to prepare ourselves for a call? First, we need an open mind. We need to totally surrender to the Lord and His will for our lives. We should avoid preconceptions or limitations placed on the Lord. How many people said that they would not yield to missions because they were afraid that God would send them to Africa. (Incidentally, our five years in Africa were life changing, a wonderful experience professionally, and the place where I received Christ as Savior.) We need an open ear to hear the voice of the Holy Spirit. And our heart needs to be pure; to know the Lord's will and to do it. We need busy hands working for the Lord. He is far more likely to use a busy person working for Him, than a lazy person waiting on the Lord, but doing nothing productive in the meantime. And we need to walk in faith. As we receive information, we need to get moving. As many have noted, a ship has to be in motion before you can steer it with the rudder. When it is anchored by the shore, turning the steering wheel changes nothing except the direction of the rudder; the ship remains unmoved.

Recruitment Issues

Recruitment is a major problem. The key in missions is the missionary, and not the money or things that accompany him. There is a 4-10% attrition per year.[3] There are a number of reasons people do not go to the mission field. In one study, 35% did not feel spiritually prepared to go on the mission field. This is to me a bit shocking. I have been concerned that some of our young people in college are depending on the college for their spiritual growth. They go to chapel daily and hear outstanding speakers. They go to church regularly. They have Bible conferences and revival meetings. They have nightly devotions. They live among Christians, often in a somewhat protected environment. But have they learned to feed themselves, or are they dependent on others for their spiritual food? On the mission field, all these props are usually gone. The missionary is often on his own. He needs a strong

CHAPTER 2: GOD'S CALLING

personal relationship with the Lord. Deputation can help in this area, as we learn to trust the Lord and see His will manifested in our lives.

Deputation Travel

Over 30% stated that they did not want to have to raise support. This, of course, depends on the type of mission you join. My parents and my wife's parents were in denominational mission boards and they did not raise support. My wife and I joined a faith mission where it was necessary to raise personal support. I personally found deputation a challenge, an eye-opener, and an opportunity to set a foundation of prayer support for our ministry. There is a separate section on deputation below, as well as an excellent exposition of "how to do it" in the appendix by my son, Marc Patton.

As we travel on deputation, several points are helpful to remember. It is important to recognize that most missionaries are no more or less spiritual than others. They have their problems like everyone else. They should not be put on a pedestal; it can be painful falling off. Also asking for support is not begging. It is giving churches an opportunity to work together in missions. They need the missionary to go; the missionary needs their support to be able to go. It is a team effort. The section on deputation goes into detail about this topic.

Learning a Foreign Language

Another area of challenge is learning a foreign language. Language was never my strength in school, and I knew that it became more difficult to learn languages, especially after age 35-40. But when the Lord called us to Suriname, we had to become at least functional in two languages: Dutch and Sranantongo. The Lord does help and enable you to do what He has called you to do. Remember that it is His power that does the work, and not your wisdom or ability. Language learning is a challenge. However, learning it as a missionary on the field is quite different from learning it as a student.

I have a doctor friend who lived as a missionary child in China until his parents were chased out when he was age 12. He spent many years as a missionary physician in Africa, learning Swahili. Finally, when

China opened up to foreigners, near retirement age, he had a chance to return with a group. He said nothing on arrival there, but listened carefully until he remembered the Chinese that he had not used in over 50 years. After a week in the country, he started talking fluent Chinese to those around him. Everyone was amazed. How can you speak Chinese? He said: Well, I have been here a week. But they said: Chinese is a difficult language! He replied: It can't be too difficult. All the little children here are speaking it without any trouble! Then he told them the truth.

But in truth, if the Lord calls you, then He must enable you as well. My wife also spoke Chinese as a child, but forgot it. When we went to language school at age 48, initially she had lots of problems with language. But she clung to the fact that if the Lord had truly called her, then the Lord would help her, and indeed He has done just that. At first, my youngest daughter lived with us as a missionary in Suriname. She worked with my wife, and she ran our first Bible club. My wife was her assistant, and she depended heavily on Kim, who learned the language quickly. However, when Kim returned to the USA to get married, now my wife was in charge. She wondered what she would do but found that she started to say things she had no idea that she could say. She became fluent in Sranantongo and functional in Dutch. Over the ensuing years, she has taught women, teenage girls, and children in Suriname.

The Fear to Surrender to the Lord's Will

Many are afraid of a full-time commitment. In fact, they are afraid of total surrender to the Lord's will. When we do this, we doubt either the Lord's goodness or His power. If we think that He will require us to do things to make us miserable, or to fail in what He has called us to do, then we doubt His goodness. And if we are afraid to go, but we believe in His goodness, then we doubt His power to enable us to do what He has called us to do. At the cross, we see both the goodness and love of God displayed; His goodness in dying for our sins on the cross, and His power in raising Jesus from the dead. This is the same power that Paul craved, and we can have it too. *Phil. 3:[10] That I may know him, and the power of his resurrection, and the fellowship of his sufferings, being made conformable unto his death;[11] If by any means I might attain unto the resurrection of the dead.* The Holy Spirit lives in us and longs to control us and empower us.

Some Problems and Issues for the Called Missionary

Commitment

There are a number of obstacles to getting on the field. One of the biggest problems is that of lack of commitment. In my generation 60 years ago, most of us knew what we were going to do by the time we were out of college. Often, shortly thereafter we were married, had a career, and were starting a family. Things are different now. Many delay commitments for years, including the commitment to the mission field.

Family Issues

There are several problems possible in the family of the missionary candidate. His spouse may be unsympathetic to the call. I believe that if the Lord calls the husband, then he has called the wife as well. If the wife is in opposition, this raises a red flag, and presents a major challenge. I have been grateful that my wife has always been totally supportive of our ministry. She has never balked at a location where we have gone, or the financial limitations which we have experienced.

A number of effective missionaries had major problems in the family. William Carey's wife did not want to go to India, and later after going there, became mentally ill and even tried to kill her husband. She died after a number of years of mental illness. Mary Moffat, who married David Livingstone, had major adjustments, especially as David Livingstone became more of an explorer and constantly traveling. She was left back in England when he was exploring but later returned to travel with her husband. She eventually died while on a trip in the interior of Africa. I have faced a challenging situation where it appears that the wife was called to the mission field before marriage, but not the husband, who simply agreed to go. The stress of the mission field created many difficulties, and eventually they left the field during their first tour.

They later served the Lord very effectively as a family in the United States.

Parental Opposition

Many missionaries have experienced parental opposition to their going. I believe that you must respect your parents and listen carefully to the reasons for their opposition. However, ultimately you must obey God rather than man. Having a large family can also present problems, especially the costs involved in transportation, schooling, and even deputation. We were very fortunate. Both sets of parents were totally supportive of our plans. I remember pulling out of the driveway after seeing my parents before going overseas. Tears were streaming down the faces of my wife and daughter. My dad was 80 at the time, and we wondered if we would ever see him again. The Lord was gracious, and he lived to be 94. We were able to see him several times before his death.

Debt

Another area of concern is debt. Most mission societies will not permit candidates to leave the country until their debt load is paid. For that reason, we must be careful when taking student loans or other major expenses during our training time. This has presented a huge problem in some types of work like medicine, where the average doctor is facing a debt of well over $100,000 when he finishes training.[4] (In recent years, that cost has continued to rise, and for some, it may be doubled.) He may be able to pay off that debt over several years working as a doctor in the USA but working on a missionary salary is a different story. Most mission boards will not allow the applicant to leave the USA without clearing his debt first.

Raising support is a challenge but a growing experience in prayer, faith and determination. For a young couple or a single individual, the challenge is very real, but it is even greater when one has a family with a number of children. On the other hand, God can block the wrong candidate if no support is forthcoming. If God calls, God does provide, but it is important to take enough time to get adequate support before leaving for the field.

CHAPTER 2: GOD'S CALLING

Bruce Olson is a well-known missionary author of "Bruchko," where he relates his adventures and ministry among the Motilone Indians. He went to Venezuela with virtually no support and God did provide, often in miraculous ways. I would not state that this is the usual way God works, but we have seen many students getting support even for short-term missions trips. Crown College has had a semester overseas in England as one of our ways to help students get a missionary experience. On one occasion, one member of a group just could not get support enough to go, but because the team had bonded, he decided to ride to the airport with them. He felt an urge to take one last look at his mail before going and found enough money for the entire trip. He quickly packed and left with them. He is currently in England as the director of that work along with his wife and six children.

Advanced Education

It may seem strange, but advanced education can also be a hindrance to going to the field. The more education you receive, the more tempted you will be to remain in a teaching position, or in an attractive offer from a large church. Furthermore, it may seem like a waste of talent and training to go somewhere where you will not be able to use all your training. However, recent studies have shown very positive reports from those who have gone on to receive advanced degrees. They have actually done better than those with less formal training in many situations. Most missions do prefer a college graduate, but it is more important to keep learning and growing in your faith. I have always considered my college training as primarily a preparation for lifetime learning.

Adequate Bible Training

Adequate Bible training is important. I was extremely well-trained in medicine, as a specialist and sub-specialist. However, my Bible knowledge was very limited. I spent several years while in practice in the USA doing correspondence courses to enhance my Bible knowledge prior to going on the mission field. I also participated in personal soul-winning, counseling, and ran a bus route for practical experience in soul-winning. My wife was a very effective soul-winner, prayer warrior, and bus captain. She was totally supportive of our ministry before going to the field and all our time on the field.

Remember, crossing the sea does not convert you to an effective soul-winner. If you cannot win souls in your own country without cultural and language barriers, what makes you think that you will suddenly become a soul-winner when you have these additional hurdles to overcome between you and the lost person?

Vocational Qualifications

Of course, vocational qualifications depend on the sort of work you will do as a missionary. For someone translating the Bible, special training in linguistics and translation are invaluable. For the pilot flying in the bush, not only knowledge of flying, but also of maintenance as a mechanic is usually advisable. The training in medicine varies tremendously. I spent most of my time teaching Internal Medicine, and I needed specialty training and board specialization to be effective. That degree of medical training would not be required for someone working in a bush clinic. Training for nurses varies greatly as well. Those working in a hospital setting would need very different training from those working alone in the bush where they function more as a doctor.

Love, Dating, and Marriage

What about dating and marriage for the potential candidate? It is important to make some basic decisions early in a relationship. After my son was called to missions while he was in college, he decided that he would let any young lady know that he was called to the mission field before pursuing a relationship. He did not want to start a relationship and find later that the other individual was not interested. As a senior in college, he wondered what would happen if he did not find the right wife. Then she showed up; she was a freshman in college who had surrendered to missions in seventh grade. They have been in Hungary as missionaries about 30 years. My youngest daughter was on the verge of becoming engaged when she went with us on our survey trip to Suriname. During the three-week trip, she surrendered to the Lord's call to the mission field. Because she knew that the young man did not feel called to missions, she broke off the relationship. She met her future

CHAPTER 2: GOD'S CALLING

husband when we arrived on the field, and they were married the following year.

Separation From Children

Additional family considerations include separation from children and single missionaries. We will address both areas in more detail below. The question of education of children is a major challenge to the parents. Should the children go back to the USA, or attend a boarding school in the area where you are working? Should you home-school them? Or should they attend local schools in the local language? These are important decisions, and no single answer is correct for all concerned. Our daughter in Suriname has been homeschooling her nine children with excellent results. The four oldest all did well in college. Our son in Hungary opted for all his children to attend Hungarian schools. Our son-in-law was sent to boarding school in both Suriname and Brazil. He especially loved his time in Brazil. He also lived with a family in the USA for a while and had some of the adjustment problems of a third culture kid. With internet access, DVD's and other technology such as Skype and Zoom, it has become easier to homeschool in recent years. This direction was accelerated when the COVID-19 epidemic forced most schools to adapt to distance learning.

Single Missionaries

The situation with single missionaries is also a concern. Most of the single missionaries are ladies rather than unmarried men. Each situation has its challenges. One young lady worked with us very successfully for five years. In her previous situation in Africa, she worked with a young couple, and many of the Africans assumed that the missionary had two wives, a natural assumption in their culture. The situation of a single woman in a remote area with a couple can create major problems. The young lady has her need of socialization; the couple has their need of teamwork together in their marriage. Stresses can come. In some cultures, there is no cultural equivalent to an unmarried woman. The nationals may wonder what is wrong with her that her parents could not arrange an appropriate marriage. The single woman is freer to devote her time to ministry directly with the nationals; often the wife has more of a supportive role with the husband and children. In some locations it is not safe for a single woman to travel or live alone. This may create major problems when the unmarried woman missionary must be accompanied by the male missionary to go to her ministry in some remote areas, and at the same time, the missionary's wife is at home, caring for the children. We had two single nurses living together in the bush and running a clinic. A few times a year they would close the clinic for a few days and take a break in the capitol city. The nationals were convinced that they were going to the city to meet their boyfriends.

Unique Challenges

A number of single missionaries have served the Lord in remarkable ways. This is true for both men and women. The single missionary is not held back by family responsibilities and is freer to move as he or she feels the Lord indicates. However, there are a number of unique challenges facing the single missionary. I would recommend any single missionary reading the section on this subject in *Honorably Wounded*, by Marjory F. Foyle, a single missionary psychiatrist who speaks both from personal experience as well as from the care of many single missionaries on the field.[5]

Sexual Feelings

One of Dr. Foyle's recommendations is that the missionary candidate decide what he or she believes about his singleness before going to the field. Furthermore, it is advisable to discuss this situation with some representative of the board, and also make plans concerning how to handle any attraction to missionaries or nationals of the opposite sex, or even, in some situations, the same sex. She points out that sexual feelings are part of one's nature, and do not automatically disappear when the decision is made to be celibate and head to the mission field. But it is possible to have many creative alternatives to normal sexual activity which allow the missionary to have fulfillment in a God-honoring way.

Sexual Problems

We have seen problems both for men and women in Suriname. Women may be propositioned, or a national may seek a longer relationship, hoping for marriage as an entrance into the USA. Men are constantly approached by women. When my son-in-law was setting up a station in the interior, he would never go alone but always went accompanied by his brother. He was approached by women even when his wife was physically present!

Housing Arrangements

Housing arrangements are sometimes a headache, especially for single women. It is often not safe for them to live alone. Living with a couple is usually not a good idea on a long-term basis. We were able to arrange in Suriname to have a single lady missionary live in her own apartment which was attached to the house of a couple. Both had privacy, but there was security for the lady. Sometimes it is best to have a pair of single ladies living together. This may or may not work out well, depending on the individuals. Some are able to provide fellowship and long-term support for each other; at other times, the relationship between the two missionaries does not work well.

A Lonely Single Missionary

The situation with a single woman missionary living near a couple may work out well in a developed situation but may prove extremely difficult in a remote area. The single missionary will need some companionship and will naturally seek it from the couple. This can create problems in the marriage, especially if the man becomes attracted to the single lady.

Additional Requirements

Physical Requirements

Physical requirements are not as restrictive as formerly. Many locations have good medical care, so that persons with chronic diseases like hypertension, diabetes, etc. can be treated effectively. Even third world countries are advancing. When I went to the USA with a heart attack, I had triple vessel disease. I was asked if I wanted to have stents or open-heart surgery. The cardiologist was concerned that if I opted for stents and got into difficulties, no one could change a stent. However, although we had no open-heart program, over the last year that I was in

Suriname, there were five cardiologists capable of invasive cardiology including insertion of stents and pacemakers. While this is exceptional, the medical situation in many "developing countries" is improving.

Certain basic health considerations are important. You should work at keeping your weight under control. This can be a real challenge during deputation and furlough. In Suriname, there are blooming trees and flowers year around. It is not a good place to live for people with severe allergies. We had a missionary who left after two years on the field. Recurrent asthma attacks became a major problem for her.

Extra Training

Some extra training can be helpful to bridge certain gaps in the missionary's preparation. Special courses in grammar and linguistics as well as language learning can help bridge the language gap. Courses in cultural anthropology can help bridge the cultural gap. And learning about the worldview, thought patterns and religious beliefs of those where you will be serving will help bridge the religious gap. We will briefly outline many of these issues in more detail below.

The Missionary's Personality

What is the personality most desired for a missionary? Missionaries come in all sizes, shapes and personality types but there are some characteristics which are helpful. It is important to be emotionally stable and to be driven by character rather than emotions. We can expect culture shock on arrival on the field, and if we are driven by emotions, we are in for a roller-coaster ride. We are far better off making decisions based on solid character. It is also important to be flexible and adaptable. This extends beyond the actual work which we do, but also includes our work ethic and what we expect of others, our concept of time, and the importance we give to interpersonal relationships. One big help is a good sense of humor; especially being able to laugh at yourself.

Privation

As missionaries, we need to be prepared to endure what we may consider privation and hardness. Some of the things we normally would have in an American culture may not be available. Not only is it possible

CHAPTER 2: GOD'S CALLING

that you may not have a dishwasher, but you also may not have a washing machine, stove or refrigerator. In some places, there is no electricity or running water as well.

Team Effort

We need to be willing to work as a team. We are in this together, and need to survive as a team. We need to be willing to take orders as servants of Christ. We need to serve those to whom we minister. We are not on the mission field to play big boss. And we need to be willing to work under nationals as well as fellow-missionaries.

Cultural Influences

We must be very careful not to allow our western culture to unduly influence us and our relationships to nationals. In the last century, many tied Christianity to western culture, and many missionaries felt that they must change the culture of the person to have a real Christian. There was a strong feeling of superiority of Western cultural values, including many western values which conflicted with Biblical truth. We must not try to impose our culture. Our goal is to see persons conformed to the image of Christ, and not to make them westernized.

Avoid Racial Prejudice and Impatience

We must be very careful in our thoughts and attitudes as well as our actions to avoid racial prejudice. We must be prepared to wait. Most of the third world is event-oriented rather than time-oriented. We will go into much greater detail concerning these issues in later chapters.

Spiritual Qualifications

Spiritual qualifications begin with a genuine conversion experience. Although this should go without saying, I have met a number of unsaved missionaries on the field. My wife saw one lady accept the Lord who was unsaved, and later was divorced by her unsaved MD missionary husband. Another good friend of ours, a white American Lutheran, was saved in a black Baptist church while on furlough in the USA. I believe that this is much more common among missionaries sent out by old-line denominations, where often the majority of members, including the staff, may be unsaved.

Although I will expand on this concept elsewhere, it is appropriate to mention that salvation from the penalty of sin is just the beginning of our spiritual qualifications. The truly born-again believer has Christ actually indwelling him in the person of the Holy Spirit. The missionary needs to die to his old nature, our self-life, and allow the new nature, the life of the Spirit of Christ, to rule in his life. Not only is he saved from the penalty of sin, which is separation from God eternally in hell, when he receives Christ, but he is potentially freed from the power of sin through the indwelling power of the Holy Spirit. He must learn to yield to the leading of the Holy Spirit on a moment-by-moment basis to experience His supernatural power.

Our tendency as missionaries is to depend on our own strength and wisdom. But as missionaries, we must rely on Jesus Christ. The apostle Paul explains in *2 Corinthians 12:7-10 And lest I should be exalted above measure through the abundance of the revelations, there was given to me a thorn in the flesh, a messenger of Satan to buffet me, lest I be exalted above measure. For this thing I besought the Lord thrice, that it might depart from me. And He said to me, My grace is sufficient for thee: for My strength is made perfect in weakness. Most gladly therefore, will I rather glory in mine infirmities, that the power of Christ may rest on me. Therefore, I take pleasure in infirmities, in reproaches, in necessities, in persecution, in distresses for Christ's sake, for when I am weak, then am I strong.* Here Paul shows us that sometimes our trials are present in our lives to drive us to dependence on Christ.

Mission Boards

As I mentioned in my personal history, I applied to a liberal board early in my medical career, and even went for interviews. I was in the midst of my medical training. First, I noted that although I made it clear that I wanted to work overseas as a physician, I ended up talking to a recruiter for home missions who was determined to send me to a needed post on an Indian reservation in the western USA. I had great difficulty getting any information from the same board about overseas posts. The director of national missions seemed to be primarily interested in recruiting to meet his own needs. Second, at that time I was unsaved, and clearly stated that I had real questions about the deity of Christ and

CHAPTER 2: GOD'S CALLING

the inspiration of the Bible. They assured me that this would be no problem! Even in my unsaved state, I knew that something was wrong!

Personal Experience with the Scriptures

Further, we must know the scriptures, not only theoretically, but by personal experience. In Dutch, there is a difference between *weten* and *kennen*. Both would be translated by the word know. But the first is really to know about something or someone without personal experience. The second speaks of personal experience. Science is *wetenschap;* to know about things. There is a dating service advertised as *kennismaking*. When we speak about knowing Christ, obviously the second word would be used if we were to use Dutch. We must know Christ and the truths of the Bible, not just theoretically but personally.

Facing Trials

When trials come, it is a great blessing to be confident of divine guidance. Then we know we are where the Lord wants us and doing what He would have us to do. We can rest assured that trials will come, and then that certainty is invaluable. In my time in Suriname, I know, and most of our people know, that God sent us here to do His work.

Discipline in Body, Soul and Spirit

In addition, we need discipline of our body, soul and spirit. Paul kept his body under discipline. We need a strong personal devotional life. As mentioned above, we can no longer coast on the spirituality of our school, our church, our chapel attendance, etc. When we allow the Holy Spirit to guide us and fill us, we can have a heart of love which is true agape love for our people. I knew that I was called not only to Suriname, but also to the Bush Negro people. We had contact with other groups, and saw some saved as well, but we knew that our primary ministry was with this group of people.

The Need for Christian Service Experience

Finally, we should have had some success in Christian service before going to the field. My wife and I spent eight years working on a church bus route with our family. We saw a number of people saved and discipled. This experience was invaluable when we started our ministry in Suriname. And even today some of our churches are running buses.

Thought questions:

1. Describe your own call to missions. Are you convinced that God has actually called you to be a missionary?
2. What are your main concerns and challenges concerning going on the mission field, especially as outlined in this chapter?
3. Under the section Recruitment Issues, at least 8 different issues are mentioned. Are any of these issues raised a personal problem to you? If so, which? And how will you resolve the problems?
4. Do you expect to go overseas as a single missionary? If so, what are your thoughts about singleness and the challenges listed?
5. More requirements are listed under Additional Requirements. Which of these requirements presents a personal challenge to you? How will you meet the challenge?

CHAPTER 3
THE MISSIONARY'S AUTHORITY AND SUPPORT

God Deals with the Missionary: God Chooses the Man

First, God chooses the man. Jesus said: *Ye have not chosen me, but I have chosen you, and ordained you, that ye should go and bring forth fruit.* God not only chooses the man, but He calls the man to His service. He called Moses. He called Jeremiah. Jesus personally chose and called His disciples. Paul was an apostle, not by the will of man, or his own will, but by the call of God. When God calls a man, he is not just a volunteer.

God Chooses His Ministry

Second, it is God that chooses his ministry. It is the Holy Spirit who decides what gifts He receives. It is God who chooses the location and the sphere of the ministry. It is God who determines the length of the ministry. And it is God who determines the success of the ministry. Is it good in His sight? The very times and seasons are under His control.

God commands evangelism in good times and bad times. But it is God that opens and closes doors. He told the church in Philadelphia: *Rev. 3:7-8 And to the angel of the church at Philadelphia write, These things saith he that is holy, he that is true, he that hath the key of David, he that openeth, and no man shutteth, and shutteth, and no man openeth, 8. I know thy works: behold, I have set before thee an open door, and no man can shut it: for thou hast a little strength, and has kept my word, and hast not denied my name.* Open doors are our responsibility; closed doors are His to open.

God's Work Versus Man's Work

We need to remind ourselves that there is God's work and man's work. God abundantly dispenses His grace, but He manifests His power only when needed, and not just for show. If a man can do the job, God expects him to do so. When Jesus went to the grave, He expected the men to open the grave by moving the stone. He expected the men to remove the grave clothes that were hindering Lazarus. These things they could do. But He was the one who raised Lazarus from the dead. In the feeding of the five thousand, the disciples found a young boy and brought his lunch. The disciples made the people sit down and distributed the bread and fish. The disciples gathered the baskets of pieces left over. But Jesus multiplied the fish and loaves, which man could not do. Jesus provided redemption, but we must preach it. God uses human agents in proclaiming salvation.

God Works Through His Church

Likewise, God works through His church. He has given us the ministry of reconciliation. When the church stops its outreach and ceases to be a missionary church, it has denied its faith and betrayed its trust. God expects the church to reach out to the lost, and ultimately to see other churches planted. Many independent Baptist mission agencies concentrate on church planting.

Why Missionaries Leave the Field

Of course, we all must leave our work on this earth sometime. But it is very sad when a missionary leaves the field before his effective ministry is (or should be) finished.

(1) He may have personal problems that prevent him from continuing.

(2) Perhaps he simply lacks spirituality or commitment.

(3) Some missionaries sadly are involved with drugs and/or alcohol.

(4) Sickness may lead to departure.

(5) Missionaries are not immune to immorality on the field.

CHAPTER 3: THE MISSIONARY'S AUTHORITY AND SUPPORT

(6) Family problems are aggravated by the stresses of the field. I have seen couples who had the mistaken idea that their problems would be easier to solve overseas. They seemed to forget about the additional stresses of culture shock and the loss of many of the support structures they had had before. Furthermore, the wife often has more adjustment problems than the husband. This may be particularly true if the husband has a rather specialized task. For example, I first went overseas as an internist to teach medicine in Liberia. I had the opportunity to work in a hospital with students and staff. We did lack many of the facilities which we had in the USA, but basically most of the work remained the same. My wife had to adjust to many differences: weather, heat, lack of many labor-saving devices, having household help, the question of school for the children, and adjustment to language and culture.

(7) Children may do very well in adapting to a new culture. They have a broader view by living in a different culture, speaking another language, and being used to traveling. However, especially in the teenage years, it may be difficult to adjust overseas. Children have various options for schooling, including home schooling, attending a school in English or the language of the country, or a boarding school. Most do well; some don't.

(8) Problems may occur with other missionaries. Usually, you do not get to choose your fellow workers directly. Your choice of a mission board may help in terms of theology, standards, and approach to ministry. But there may well be personality clashes. You may be thrown into close proximity with those with whom you would not choose to associate with normally. In remote areas, the interaction may become very intense, as there are few other choices of friendships or partners.

(9) Nationalism is strong in many nations. I had little problem with that situation in Liberia, even though I was chief of Medicine. Even though I worked hard to avoid that image in Suriname, I had one young preacher who resented me any time I assumed a position of authority as the senior pastor. He was attending the university and then went to work for Amnesty International. A number of years later, he realized that he had misjudged my motives, and we are good friends now. Our goal as

missionaries is to see national churches which are truly independent. We must take the role of a servant or a partner with the national leaders.

Missionary Effectiveness
Know the Country and Culture

A few things that can make the missionary more effective, include studying the country and the language where he will be ministering. Any information gleaned in advance is a help. When I went to Liberia for the US government as a physician, I spent many hours studying information about the country and the culture. The US government often prints some information in book form which is very helpful, and usually up-to-date and reasonably accurate. I also studied the Dutch language some before arriving in Suriname. This also helped me. There are some language courses available in many of the more common languages, but those languages limited to a smaller area, like Sranantongo, are unlikely to have formal courses available. Rosetta Stone courses are relatively inexpensive and available for many languages.[6]

Learn the Language

Some languages prove very difficult for English speakers. Tonal languages like Chinese are very different and give many English-speaking missionaries great difficulties. The Slavic languages are also difficult. Many missionaries decide that the language is too difficult, and work through an interpreter. Do not make that decision. You will be permanently limited. You will be separated from the people. Furthermore, language is often a clue to the national's thinking processes. In fact, language may structure your thinking. Take enough time to learn the basics of the language, and then make it a lifelong project to keep learning. I continued to learn Sranantongo for the entire 26 years that I was in Suriname. For me, it was especially important as I was working on translating the Bible as well as commentaries and study materials. A textbook called LAMP — *Language Acquisition Made Practical* can be very helpful in getting started in learning a language.[7]

A Strong Support Team

To avoid burnout, and to continue successfully on the field, it is important to have a strong support team. **First**, you must set reasonable goals for yourself. **Second**, your family must be in agreement. **Third**, it

CHAPTER 3: THE MISSIONARY'S AUTHORITY AND SUPPORT

is important to have a team of prayer warriors, especially in the USA. As you develop your ministry, you can have further support members on the field as well. Deputation is an ideal time to develop prayer support as well as financial support.

Summary thoughts

These first three chapters serve as a brief introduction to many considerations of missionary life and work. We will go into much greater detail in the following chapters, beginning with the subject of cultural anthropology. We trust that this information has been a blessing as well as a challenge, and I wish you success in your future ministry.

Thought questions:

1. What is the relationship between the work of God in and for the missionary and the missionary's work?
2. Who has the ultimate authority for you as a missionary? To whom are you responsible. How does this work out between your relationship to God and his call, your church, to whom the work of world-wide evangelization is given, and your mission board and mission field?
3. A list of 9 common reasons why missionaries leave the field are listed. Which of any are potential traps for you personally? How will you handle them?
4. The chapter lists important factors which help you to be more effective as a missionary. How are you appropriating them in your life?

CHAPTER 4: CULTURAL ANTHROPOLOGY FOR THE MISSIONARY

Introduction

Anthropology and Culture

It is vital for the missionary to understand culture. Culture is the patterns and way of life by which people order their lives.[8]

For the first six years of life, we have intensive training from parents and others, but the training never stops; we have life-long enculturation. During the teen years, peer groups become very important as well. We tend to congregate with those of similar values, which thereby reinforce our own cultural values. We over-learn these values and ways of thinking until they are automatic, and we assume that they are correct. Each individual is different in accepting or rejecting certain portions of his culture as he develops his lifestyle. However, living with cultural expressions which differ from ours can bring stress into our lives.[9]

The study of culture falls under the general heading of anthropology. Anthropology is the study of man, and it attempts to deal with what people actually do and think.[10] It describes their total of behavior and deals with their worldview.[11] When I studied anthropology 50 years ago, the concept of anthropology focused on non-western people, and usually "primitive" tribes. However, it deals with all types of people. The culture of a people shows how people meet their needs within the restrictions imposed by their environment. No single culture is intrinsically superior to all others, and cultures demonstrate the ingenuity of people in meeting their basic needs in a wide variety of situations.

When we study anthropology, we take a holistic integrative approach to people. We use a cross-cultural perspective. This not only helps us to appreciate others and their culture, but it helps us understand ourselves and our own culture, which we often take for granted. Furthermore, it helps us to understand the Bible and the culture of biblical times. Finally, anthropology can help us understand how best to communicate the message of the gospel, how to make the gospel relevant to the people whom we seek to reach, and how to build bridges between their culture and that of the Bible.[12]

Theological Background

We need to remember that the subject of missions begins with God, and not man. Many think that man is seeking God, whereas in truth, God is seeking man. Adam hid after he sinned, but God sought and found him, confronted him, chastised him, and restored him. The mission is God's, but He calls us to be a part of that mission. We, of course, need His input, guidance, and power.

Scriptural Authority

God has given us an authoritative revelation, which is our message to a lost world. This message of the gospel has been given within a specific historical and cultural context. Our task is to communicate that message. Jesus Christ is God's perfect representative and His perfect communicator through His incarnation. The good news is that salvation is available to all who accept Jesus Christ, and He calls each of us to a life of discipleship. God the Holy Spirit was sent to draw mankind to Christ, and to empower us as Christians to minister to the lost and broken of this world.

The Organization and Operation of God's Realm

First, the kingdom of God is where God is king. Second, His community here on earth is the church, and it is the church's responsibility to reach out to the world. Third, each member is a priest of God. Fourth, a member of the church has the responsibility and right to interpret scripture. We must be careful to understand and explain His Word clearly, and this task is especially relevant to the missionary.

God has allowed man to adapt here on earth through culture. Man has certain physiological, psychological, and social needs which can be met through cultural adaptation. We need to recognize that man is a

CHAPTER 4: CULTURAL ANTHROPOLOGY FOR THE MISSIONARY

sinner, and that his culture, therefore, is affected by sin. The gospel, which is without sin, needs to be expressed within a cultural framework. The gospel is above culture, but expressed via the culture, although not determined by it.

Basic Concepts of Culture

Culture is a broad and difficult concept to define. It is the comprehensive way that people meet their needs and desires. Culture includes not only the knowledge possessed by the people, but their emotions and values as well. Culture includes communication, and the quality of relationships between people. It includes the worldview of the group, which are the deep underlying assumptions of reality that we usually accept without question. Culture includes far more than worldview, but the worldview of a given people influences virtually all aspects of the culture.

Worldview Summarized

As an introduction, I will briefly summarize several different worldviews which differ from both western missionaries and a biblical world view.[13] This subject is discussed in detail in *Issues in Missiology Volume IV*, which covers the topics of Worldview and World Religion.

We missionaries believe that we live in a real world which really exists outside us. It is a rational world, orderly, and works under natural laws. We believe that science is important. There is a biblical basis for our beliefs. God created the universe, which is outside of Him, and also depends on Him. On the other hand, in eastern religion, the outside world is considered imaginary. People may be just projections of the mind of God. Time is cyclical. Truth comes from meditation, when we become one with the universal spirit. It is difficult to appeal to history and science with this worldview.

As we look at the history of western thought, there was a real shift from biblical dualism to neo-Platonic concepts. In the Bible, the fundamental division was between God as Creator, and all of His creation. The creation included spirits, humans, animals, plants, and inanimate matter. In neo-Platonism, dualism exists not between the

Creator and His creation, but between spirit and matter.[14] Thus the division became between the invisible universe of God and the spirits, including both angels and demons, and the visible created universe. This led to a split between the natural observable world and the supernatural world.

Originally, science was a servant to religion, but then later became totally separated from religion. Science concentrated on the material created universe, and basically ignored the supernatural. Missionaries from the west, where science dominates, likewise tended to separate their spiritual ministries from the social gospel, which was manifested in the visible world. In this way, missionaries actually spread secularism, because the culture in which they ministered often accepted western science, which the missionaries brought as part of their western culture, but rejected Christianity, which they viewed as a foreign religion that they did not need to accept.

We also find a difference between the concept of nature in western civilization and the concept of animism. The division of the animate and inanimate universe corresponds to a western perspective. But many cultures, particularly animistic cultures, look at all nature as alive. Animals, and even inanimate objects such as stones and trees, have spirits. This may even be reflected in the language. For example, Sranantongo is without a passive tense. You cannot say: "I was cut by the knife.." You have to say: "the knife cut me" (*Da nefi koti mi*). You cannot say that you were caught in the rain. You have to say that the rain beat you. (*Alen ben fon mi.*) All nature is alive.

There are still further shifts of worldview in the west with the development of post-modernism. This philosophy denies the possibility of objective truth. All truth is relative to the observer and his desires. Therefore, what is true for you may not necessarily be true for me. This rejection of both absolutism and the authority of the Scriptures undermines the attempts to present salvation as absolute truth.

In some ways, post-modernism has been a corrective. We as missionaries are often ethnocentric. We believe that our way is not only the best way, but perhaps the only sensible way to think and approach

CHAPTER 4: CULTURAL ANTHROPOLOGY FOR THE MISSIONARY

reality. We fail to recognize that the underlying assumptions of our worldview are indeed assumptions. We tend to accept our cultural patterns as the normal way that everyone should think or do things. We need to be open to other cultures, and it is important to see that the western worldview is based on assumptions, and not on infallible truth.

Our own culture often blinds us to certain truths of the bible, because these truths clash with what we view as undeniable truth. We tend to equate western civilization with Christianity. This assumption was openly stated in the 19th century. The policy was to civilize the native population first, so that you could Christianize them. We now recognize that many of our western worldview beliefs are actually anti-biblical, and that other cultures may be closer in some ways to the biblical ideal.

We need to realize that we see incompletely now. Only God sees perfectly. All our perceptions are affected by our own culture, personality, and experience. Also, our sins affect the way we perceive. Thus, we always filter reality. We learn incompletely. Our experiences in life modify our mental maps. We may change when we are confronted with another model or paradigm of reality. We may actually experience a paradigm shift to a new perspective. However, often people place their worldview in compartments, and shift back and forth from an old view to a new view rather than integrating them into a new way of looking at things. After I was saved, I still operated largely on my worldview which was rooted in my education and liberal theological background. It took about a year for me to re-integrate my thinking with a Biblical worldview.

Additional Aspects of Culture

Culture consists of learned patterns of concepts and behavior. It consists also of underlying perspectives. The important fact to remember is that culture is agreed upon patterns, and culture is learned. Different cultures represent the creativity of mankind. The power of culture is that we have the propensity to live by habit. Then we do not have to consciously think about the multitude of activities we do each day.

Culture is learned beginning in earliest childhood and continuing throughout life. It is not inherited, nor primarily racial in character. For example, I recently read about a black young man on the volleyball team for China. The Chinese coach said that he was chosen, not because he was black, but because he was a very good volleyball player. Furthermore, culturally he is Chinese. He does not look Chinese, but he thinks Chinese and speaks Chinese. A few years ago, a young lady visited us who had grown up in Japan. Her parents were American missionaries, and she was white. However, she showed many characteristics of a proper Japanese young lady in how she spoke, walked, and ate. A third example is a professor of missions who had spent years as a missionary to Koreans. I spoke with a Korean student in an American college, who said that the missionary was more Korean than American in how he thinks and behaves.

We need to honor cultures, and we need to remember that we need culture to survive. Cultures can be used for good or for evil, because all cultures are infected by our sin nature. It is the choices that people make which determine if that culture shall be used as instruments for God, or instruments for Satan. Culture is complex; it is tightly integrated around our worldview; it is a total design for living; and it is adapted to our circumstances.

Ethnocentrism

Normally, we learned culture as if our culture was perfect. We call this ethnocentrism. We have a tendency to want to impose our culture on others. Remember that culture makes sense to those who are in the system. If something doesn't make sense to you, then you are missing something in understanding the culture. We need to remember also that the Bible stands above culture. As we will show later, portions of the culture may be anti-biblical. For example, in the Bush Negro culture of Suriname, the society is matriarchal. This means that the woman is boss in a number of areas, and that the inheritance passes through the mother's line. Furthermore, the male relationship that is most important is not the father, but it is the brother of the mother.[15] This arrangement does not correspond to the biblical pattern.

CHAPTER 4: CULTURAL ANTHROPOLOGY FOR THE MISSIONARY

Culture is based on group agreement. Culture contains a historical legacy, linking us to the past. Culture is also a way to regulate your life. Furthermore, there is an explicit, conscious culture, and an implicit, unconscious culture. There is also an ideal culture, and then the actual culture which you find present around you. It is important to be aware that "all culture is not the same culture." No one within the culture meets the requirements of the cultural ideal.

Dimensions of Culture

Three main aspects of culture should be mentioned at this point. **First**, there are cognitive aspects of culture. This speaks of the knowledge, logic, and wisdom that is manifested within the culture. Knowledge includes the assumptions about reality which we have already mentioned, as well as the nature of the universe around us, how to cope with our environment, and how to change things. Wisdom speaks about how to apply our knowledge in effective ways. Knowledge and wisdom may be stored in literature, but also in songs, drama, or poetry. In the Bush Negro culture, some wisdom is stored in what are called "anansi" stories, which are animal tales about a spider. Some is stored in "odos," which are short pithy statements with a point which they wish to illustrate.

A **second** aspect of culture is the affective realm, which looks toward beauty and feelings. This may involve taste in food, as well as the form of housing, furnishings, planting flowers, and dress, which gives insight into the aesthetic values of the culture.

A **third** area is in the values which are established within the culture. This includes what is considered moral and what is considered immoral. Also included is what is believed as truth. Values vary tremendously from one culture to another. For example, which is more important – to tell the absolute truth or to bend the truth a bit to avoid hurting someone's feelings? In my culture, you should tell the truth. But in Suriname, that is not the case. I have had many people promise that they will be coming to church next Sunday, but after I had been here for a while, I realize that they are just being polite and not wanting to appear rude. They are not deliberately trying to deceive me and would expect that any Surinamer would pick up the clues.

Here is another question: Which is worse, to commit sexual immorality or lose your temper? For us in the west, the answer is easy – sexual immorality! But in India and much of the East, losing your temper is worse. Imagine the impact that this should have on a hot-tempered missionary in such a country. I know that Baptist World Mission makes clear that sexual immorality will result in the missionary immediately leaving the field. But a hot-tempered missionary creating tension with nationals in the East can also be a disaster.

The Bible Is Related to All Three Cultural Reactions to Sin

Cultures can be characterized by three different reactions to sin. Some cultures are dominated by guilt. This is especially true in western cultures. You are guilty and need to be forgiven. The focus is on the individual and his personal sense of guilt. Many cultures are shame oriented. These cultures are usually group oriented, and the individual who sins brings great shame on the entire group. We need restoration and erasing our shame. The cultures of the Middle East and Far East are usually shame cultures. A third reaction is fear, which is primarily found in oral societies of animistic cultures. Of course, no society is strictly bound to one of these reactions, and there is a mixture of all three, but usually one reaction dominates.

We can find all three reactions in the very first sin, which can serve as a prototype. When Adam and Eve ate the fruit in violation of God's specific command, they immediately experienced guilt. They hid out of fear. And they were ashamed to appear before God because they were naked.

God's salvation through Jesus Christ meets our need. Jesus took the guilt of our sin on Himself. Our sins, as it were, were nailed to His cross, and His robe of righteousness now clothes us. Our sins are washed away by the blood of Christ. Our shame in appearing naked before God in our sins has been met when we are clothed with the righteousness of Christ.

CHAPTER 4: CULTURAL ANTHROPOLOGY FOR THE MISSIONARY

And when Jesus Christ died in our place, He freed us from the fear of death, especially eternal separation from God.

We missionaries need to recognize that the Bible relates to all three aspects of culture. Of course, the Bible is filled with factual knowledge, and the Bible is totally reliable in the facts that it relates. But the Bible also instills awe and the fear of the Lord as we allow it to work in our lives. We realize that we need to submit to such an awesome God. And the Bible shows us that we need to evaluate our lives and culture according to Biblical principles. We need to give God and His word the ultimate allegiance in our lives.

Additional Features of Culture

In addition to the worldview mentioned briefly above, we expect to find myths, symbols, forms and rituals in every culture. The term "myth" in anthropological literature has a different connotation than the usual use of the word, which is for a story without any factual basis. In anthropology, the term myth speaks of an overarching narrative which expresses or explains the basic worldview and philosophy of the culture. It is called alternatively a "metanarrative." This myth often explains creation and why there is a separation between mankind and the God or gods who created the universe.

Certain symbols come loaded with meaning from the culture. For the Christian, the cross talks about more than just the method to execute criminals under the Roman Empire. It speaks of the sacrifice of Christ to redeem mankind, and the separation of the Christian from the world system. Likewise, for the Jew at the time of Christ, a lamb would speak of an innocent sacrifice for sin.

Forms and rituals also have special meaning. In general, those raised in western civilization tend to separate out the form and the meaning, so that they are two discrete entities. This separation is often not true in other cultures, who then take the form much more seriously than those of the west.

Conclusion

Anthropology focuses on communication, especially on the quality of relations, perceptions, felt needs, acceptance, and appreciation. Anthropology also looks behind the form to the meanings of the form. What does the form that we see here trying to communicate? Anthropology also looks at the worldview: those assumptions, values, associations, and allegiances that we have in our culture. Anthropology works with people in the field where they live, and not in isolation. Anthropology also studies how culture changes.

We all have culture, customs, rituals, and worldview. We need customs, but not someone else's customs. We need rituals, but not someone else's rituals. And we need to remember that culture is like a river. We see the top, which is superficial. Most is deep beneath. And beneath the river of cultural language, rituals, myths and customs, lies the worldview of the individual.

Culture is structural. People work within the structure, either to strengthen it or to change it. Culture is a strategy for survival which belongs to a society and is operated by it. God's Word is above culture and is absolutely true. We must learn to adapt the truth of God's Word to the culture in such a way that we maintain its truth and yet communicate it to others so that they may understand the gospel.

Thought questions

1. What concepts about culture do you find most helpful in your understanding? What is the difference between a nation and a people group?
2. How does your worldview differ from the rest of our western culture, and from the Bible?
3. What are the basics of the worldview of your chosen people group?
4. How does the worldview of your people group line up with that of the Bible? If the Bible is supra-cultural, then does it have priority over our own worldview, and also the worldview of the people-group to whom we minister?
5. How can you adapt your message of salvation to the felt needs of the culture, especially in terms of guilt, shame and/or fear?

CHAPTER 5
DIFFERING ASPECTS OF CULTURE
Concepts of Time

There are huge differences in values of time.[16] In the West, time is highly valued and organized and linear. "Scientific time," is linear, and is divided into equal units of seconds, minutes, hours, days, weeks, months, and years. Time can be accurately quantitated and projected to the future. We Americans are basically future-oriented. Time moves ahead and can never be made up. We can "lose time." Clocks abound. I feel lost if I do not have my watch. Of course, with the new generation, the cell phone has replaced the watch.

In many agrarian cultures and simple oral cultures, time is viewed as cyclical. There is a planting time, a cultivating time, a harvesting time, and perhaps, in colder climates, a time of rest during winter. Many of our older Bush Negroes have no idea of exactly how old they are, especially if they were born in the interior. The year was simply not that important. Now that the Suriname government gives retirement income, or "old people money," it is important to have some idea of the age of the individual, and so it is calculated from well-known events. For example, during World War II, a German vessel was sunk in the Suriname River. So the interviewer might ask if the individual was born then, and if so, to estimate how old he might have been as a child. Perhaps he had just started school. Then a date would be estimated, written down, and that was the person's age from then on. In other parts of the country, people have been more conscious of birthdates, which then are accurate.

Time and Events

Other cultures focus on events as the main focus, or might even consider time as pendular. While Americans are usually future-oriented, traditional African thought focuses on the past. They may describe a mythical past, or the recent past, remembering the recent ancestors. They may talk about what they did at that time. The present and near future are also considered, but not as important as the past.

The Chinese tend to think especially about the present and try to integrate all the current happenings into the current situation. Americans focus on time, which disappears. Other cultures may focus on space where things happened, rather than time. They may say something like this: "we cannot go back, but this is where such as such happened."

What is considered late in one culture is very different in another. There has been a huge problem initially in the companies working in the interior because of the Bush Negro sense of time. Americans are very time conscious. Time is money. Bush Negroes are not. The mining company Suralco had to let a number of workers go because they could not be depended on to show up on time. Likewise, when we have meetings at our church, I was still usually the first person there for a 7 pm meeting. Some members were chronically late.

This attitude actually effected a political election. The Bush-Negroes had had little influence in elections for many years but banded together and found that they had considerable political clout. In a recent national election, which occurs only every five years, the Bush Negro parties had a number of candidates for office. They were required to submit the names to be placed on the candidate voter lists on a certain day at a certain time. However, they were casual, and submitted several lists after the deadline. This raised a big ruckus when they were denied the right to register their candidates, and the decision finally went to the judiciary. The question was whether "Suriname time" would be accepted (Suriname time is up to a few hours after official time), or whether the judge would rule for official time. To the surprise of many, the judge ruled: three o'clock is three o'clock and late is late. The candidates were not able to be registered.

Of course, we see the same thing in the USA, where there is a difference in attitude of "being on time" at work or school, and being on time at church or for a social occasion. I remember when I was a college student, I had to catch a ride with others for my summer job. The job had a time clock to punch in. The driver loved to come just at the last minute. I can remember racing to punch in before the 8:00 on my timecard. Fortunately, I had won a number of half-mile races that year and was able to run fast! Otherwise, I would have been late. No one in

CHAPTER 5: DIFFERING ASPECTS OF CULTURE

Suriname would do such a thing. We rarely have time clocks. They would think that I was crazy to race to work like that.

Here is a small chart showing the difference in concept of time in various societies:

Tension in Time — Time concepts

	Lateness excused	Tension	Hostility
Yapese	2 hours	3 hours	4 hours
Latin America	? 30 minutes	1 hour	2 hours
North America	5 minutes	15 minutes	2 hours

Time Considerations: Position of an Individual

Another consideration is the position of the individual. When I was in college, the students were basically allowed to leave if the professor was late to class, assuming that he would not come. However, how "late" was late depended on his status. For an instructor, after 5 minutes you could leave; for an assistant professor, it was 10 minutes, and for a full professor, it was 15 minutes. Likewise, I read about two other situations which played a role. In some Arab countries, if you agree on a time to meet, and two are of equal status, you really meet an hour after the agreed time. However, if you are a servant, you are expected at the "correct" time. So, if an American meets his Arab colleague at the agreed time, then the Arab will wonder why his colleague is acting like a servant, and the American is annoyed that he is shown no respect if his colleague arrives an hour after the scheduled time. The same situation may occur with friends in some countries.

Time Considerations: The Idea of Social Time

When I was in Liberia, the idea of social time was also different. Once I wanted to do something with our children in the evening, and would not be done until nearly 11 p.m. However, I felt an obligation to go to a birthday party given by the head of the surgery department which was scheduled the same night at 9 p.m. My good friend and co-worker, Dr. S., was an Indian medical specialist, but had spent years in England. Therefore, like a proper Englishman, he and his wife arrived at 9:05. They were right on time. The wife came down in a robe with curlers in her hair. "O my goodness," she said. "I didn't expect anyone so early!" I arrived with my wife at about 11:30. As a good American, I started to apologize profusely that I was late. "Come on in!" Dr. B. greeted me. "The party's just starting!" And indeed it was. On another occasion, my wife and I had a dinner party which included some Liberian government officials and friends to begin at 6 p.m. Most arrived by 6:15. One Liberian doctor and his wife did not arrive, and we finally started eating about 7:00 p.m. They arrived around 7:30, which was fine in their culture.

For years, we had wanted to start our church services "on time." Two of our churches were particularly notorious for beginning at least 30 minutes after the stated time. One finally changed the hour from 9 AM to 10 AM, and now the service begins approximately on schedule. We have succeeded in having a regular scheduled service beginning at the stated time, although some individuals chronically arrive well after the scheduled time. It is interesting that the same individuals do so week after week and arrive almost invariably at the same time each week, perhaps 15-30 minutes after the service begins. Yet two individuals hold very responsible positions with the government, and I suspect are "on time" when required at work.

Our concepts of time are surprisingly deeply ingrained within us. Even when I know that I will be the first individual at a meeting, I have difficulty deliberately arriving after the scheduled hour. However, the ingrained pattern is also true of the individuals to whom we are to minister, and we are not likely to change them. I have read of an epitaph on the grave of an individual, perhaps in India, which described the individual as a man who tried to hurry the East. So, it is best to understand, and to recognize what we should and should not try to change. When I wrote this section a number of years ago, we had already spent six years trying to get paperwork done through the Suriname government. The government must recognize our churches as independent entities. I resigned myself to the fact that I would leave

CHAPTER 5: DIFFERING ASPECTS OF CULTURE

Suriname with those papers not yet completed. Actually, the paperwork was completed and the churches turned over to the nationals about 10 years after we started the process.

Time Considerations: An Event-oriented Society

Also tied into the concept of time is the question of an event-oriented society versus a program-oriented society. Americans tend to want to have programs, with a proper beginning and ending time as a primary focus. Most of the world is much more event oriented. It is not so important when the event begins or when it is completed, as long as it is done well. And Jesus moved through His life much more event-oriented than worrying about a time schedule.

Assessment

It is important to recognize that the Bible teaches that time does move on and is not strictly cyclical. There is no reincarnation. There is a judgment, and we will be judged on what we do during our stay on earth. History is moving ahead and is under the control of God. *Hebrews 9: [27] And as it is appointed unto men once to die, but after this the judgment:[28]* So Christ was once offered to bear the sins of many; and unto them that look for him shall he appear the second time without sin unto salvation.

We are also to make use of our time, as we will be judged for what we have done on earth. *Ephesians 5:[15] See then that ye walk circumspectly, not as fools, but as wise,[16] Redeeming the time, because the days are evil.[17] Wherefore be ye not unwise, but understanding what the will of the Lord is.* But we must have the proper priorities and have time for people. One of the complaints made against missionaries is that they are always too busy to have time for others. Jesus was aware of His task and His ultimate goal. However, He moved ahead steadily, and never was hasty; He made time for people. On several occasions, people tried to kill Him, but "His time had not yet come." We need to realize that our time is in the Lord's hands, and to allow Him to work through us to minister to others.

Concepts of space

Another area of difference is space. We have a "space" around us that is like a bubble, and we don't feel comfortable with others invading "our space." Americans stay at a certain distance when talking. Latin Americans talk closer. I had doctor friend who acted like a Latin American. He would come to about 18 inches away when talking. I would back up, and he would move forward.

When a lady is sitting at a public restaurant with stools in front of a table, if the stool next to her is empty, she will probably put her purse there, keeping her "space." The same thing is true in sitting with a number of empty seats. I notice the same situation when sitting in an airport awaiting a flight. We would not think of sitting directly next to a person when empty spaces are available. That is not necessarily true in other cultures. When my wife sat in church with some of her children from the Bible club, they would sit right against her even though there was plenty of space on the bench. If she would move away, they would move closer. She learned to stay put. They wanted the physical contact with their teacher.

In Suriname, when you go to a doctor's office you greet the others in the waiting room, acknowledging their presence. A similar situation was present in Liberia. Dr. Cooper was the president's personal physician as well as the director of the J.F.K. medical center. We had a special request requiring his approval. When we arrived to see him, there was a large room with chairs around the edges of the room. We went from person to person, individually greeting every person in the room.

There are also variations in what is public space that you greet or not depending on the country. Most times you will ignore persons beyond about 15 feet or so in the USA, but it may differ in other lands. My wife was looking for a child to walk to church. Usually the properties had a nicer home in the front and some "shanty-like" houses behind. A man was on the porch, and she asked if the child was in the house behind. He said: "*Mi na wan libisoema toe.*" (I am a living human too.) She had failed to greet him personally. She understood and immediately apologized.

CHAPTER 5: DIFFERING ASPECTS OF CULTURE

The Idea of Privacy

Likewise, the idea of privacy is radically different. The nationals often are very curious as to the life of the missionary, who may have limited privacy. They often love to have lots of company. A family we knew well helped us learn the language when we first came to Suriname. They stayed in a very small wooden house. When visitors came from the interior, there were people sleeping everywhere! You could hardly walk. The day after the visitors left, my wife visited, and asked how things were going. She expected the lady to say with relief that she finally got her house back. Instead, the lady bemoaned their leaving: "I am so lonely..."

The same situation is true in the hospital. We like privacy and are willing to pay extra at times for a private room. But some individuals do not want to sleep alone in a hospital room. They want other people sleeping near theme. This was certainly the case when my wife was hospitalized. They also are reluctant to leave children alone at night. Often the smaller children will sleep in the same room as their parents.

My son found the Hungarians prize privacy more than even the Americans. When they were building their church, I was amazed to see windows in the roof rather than the walls. When I asked Marc, he said that if the windows were lower in the walls, they could see into the neighborhood but not if the windows were higher. When they wanted to pass out salvation tracts, they found that you do not go house to house and deliver them personally. You could place them in mailboxes. Later, they found a unique method. They ordered an insert in a local paper with colored pictures, information on the pastor and the church. The cost for 20,000 copies in the local paper was comparable to printing individual tracts, and the newspapers were delivered to the homes for them.

Hungarians are great readers. Marc went to the local open market to request a booth for selling books. He would have free salvation tracts also available. The market refused, saying that they already had two booths selling books. He returned, asking for permission to sell American popcorn. American popcorn? No problem! And next to the popcorn were free tracts. He learned to stay away from the tracts and allow the Hungarians to browse at their leisure.

When Marc's family came to Suriname to visit, he and his son Ben went soulwinning with me. When I approached a home, I met the man and turned to introduce them. They had stayed perhaps 50 feet away. In Hungary, they were not accustomed to go together right up to a house like we do in Suriname. So, privacy concerns are different. Americans really prize their privacy, but Hungarians seem to prize theirs even more.

The Concept of Territory

The concept of territory also varies. The Bush Negroes with whom we work often live in what we would consider dangerous parts of the city. In fact, even in our church area, where I had worked for over 25 years and done a lot of soulwinning, I had been advised not to venture on foot at night. Our young ladies sometimes must walk from a bus to their homes in areas where I would not want to venture as an outsider even though I am an adult man. But if they are in their own area, they sense no fear or problems. However, walking in another area would be a totally different story. My wife used to drop off young ladies after her girls' club. One girl asked her to walk back to the house where she was staying. She was in a different neighborhood than her home and did not feel safe.

Most people have a clear sense of territory as well, but different ideas about who "owns" the land. In many cultures, it is not possible to sell or buy the land, but simply purchase the right to use it. The land may belong to the clan or tribe, who may believe that they have a right to the land but they may feel that the gods own or protect the land. Among the Bush Negroes, the people in a certain clan or village have rights to cultivate the ground, go hunting and fishing, and perhaps to cut lumber from the land, but that does not mean that they own the land outright. Some of our church members are doing strip-mining for gold, again in the areas which belong to their clan. However, the local leaders will decide who can use the land.

When the whites came to America, they bought land from the Indians – or at least they thought they did. The American Indians, on the other hand, like many tribal people, believed that land could not be bought or sold, or even exchanged, especially when some of the land was sacred. They believed that they were giving the whites the right to use the land for a time. Thus, when the Indians needed the land again or ran into problems with many settlers coming into the land, there were major problems when they wanted their land back. Apparently, the term "Indian giver" was coined because of this problem.

Gods and Spirits Associated with Territory

Furthermore, many cultures have gods or spirits associated with their territory. For example, in the Bible, we read about the Israelites defeating the Syrians in the hills of their territory. The Syrians decided that their gods were the gods of the plains, but those of the Israelites, the god of the hills. So, they fought again, this time on the plain. But God had promised the king of Israel that He would defeat the Syrians to demonstrate that He is not limited to the hills but that He is also the God of the plains.[17] Of course, the God of the Bible is the God of the entire earth.

When the Syrian general Naaman came to Israel to be cured of his leprosy, the prophet Elisha sent a messenger telling him to wash in the Jordan River seven times. When he did so, he was cured. He decided that the God of Israel would be his god. But he did something very interesting. He brought two mule loads of earth back to Syria with him.[18] I believe that he felt that the God of Israel was effective in the territory of Israel, and so he brought back a bit of Israel's territory with him! I picture him carefully spreading out the dirt on a special location, and then praying on that dirt. He thought that he was literally on "praying ground!"

Assessment

Ultimately God owns everything. *Psalm 24:[1] The earth is the LORD's, and the fulness thereof; the world, and they that dwell therein.[2] For he hath founded it upon the seas, and established it upon the floods.* He decided where the various people of the world would go. *Acts 17: [24] God that made the world and all things therein, seeing that he is Lord of heaven and earth, dwelleth not in temples made with hands;[25] Neither is worshipped with men's hands, as though he needed any thing, seeing he giveth to all life, and breath, and all things;[26] And hath made of one blood all nations of men for to dwell on all the face of the earth, and hath determined the times before appointed, and the bounds of their habitation;[27] That they should seek the Lord, if haply they might feel after him, and find him, though he be not far from every one of us.*

Stewards

In reality, we are stewards of the earth by God's grace. We need to recognize that different folk have different ways of handling space and territory and be sensitive to their system. In the Old Testament, land was owned by the tribes, and Moses even prayed especially to God about a situation with a man who had five daughters and no sons. The daughters ultimately were given the right to "own" the land but had to marry within their own tribe so that the land would not pass over to another tribe. Land could be purchased, but in most cases, it reverted back to the original owner at the time of jubilee.[19] Other land was purchased permanently, as, for example, the cave where Abraham buried his wife.[20] Understanding these concepts helps us realize why Naboth did not want to sell his property to King Ahab for money or a better location. We need to understand the basic differences in space, privacy concerns, and territory between our own culture and the culture for the people group to whom we minister so that we can be more effective ministers of the Lord.

Thought questions:

1. Why is it important to understand another culture's attitude toward time? Why is it important Biblically that time is not cyclical but linear? And what about "being on time?"
2. Why is it important to understand the differences in our "personal space" between various cultures?
3. Why is it important to grasp differences in the desire for privacy and the concept of territory in our people group?

CHAPTER 6
MISSIONARIES NEED TO UNDERSTAND CULTURAL SYSTEMS

As missionaries, we need to understand the system of the culture in which we are living, and make appropriate choices. For example, my son-in-law lives in the mining town of Moengo, where much of the land is "purchased" for essentially a century but it is not a permanent possession. Our church land in the city of Paramaribo is permanently ours.

Differences in Kinship

The kinship in America is rather simple, focusing on the nuclear family. In the immediate nuclear family, there is the husband and father, the wife and mother, and the children of both sexes. The relations are considered bilaterally, with the father's mother and father and the mother's father and mother both considered grandparents. The brothers and sisters of both the father and mother are considered uncles and aunts, and their children are considered cousins. There is no distinction as to which family comes from the father or the mother in terms of names or relationships.

Tracing Kinship: Matriarchal or Patriarchal?

Many kinship groups, however, are traced on one side of the family, but not the other. For example, the Hebrews were primarily patrilineal, and traced the family through the father's line. The mother came into the family by marriage, but the primary kinship pattern was patrilineal, and this can be easily seen in the lists of the families found in the Old Testament. They are traced from father to son. In contrast, the Bush Negroes of Suriname are matriarchal. The line goes through the mother. At least one individual explained to me that at least you can know who the mother is! The father can choose to accept the child as his, but that is a separate decision which he must make unless the couple is legally married. Then it is assumed that the infant is his own child.

Unfortunately, immorality and short-term relationships are common in the Bush Negro culture. Therefore, a woman may have several different husbands over a period of time. The man may have relationships with multiple women. In this situation, it is a little easier to understand why the focus is on the mother's brother. His position remains stable. However, this means that the family is tied to the mother, and not to the father. The father often has little say in what goes on in his own family and tends to focus on his sister's family more than his own. This matriarchal pattern is anti-Biblical and undermines the role of the father in the family. As you can imagine, it also can present a distorted view of God if we look at God the Father in such a context. Biblical marriage creates stress in this situation because the old cultural patterns are anti-Biblical. A truly biblical marriage may bring many readjustments to the relationship with other members of the family.

One of our preachers lost a son during a severe asthma attack several years before he became a preacher. I noticed that he had virtually nothing to say as far as the funeral was concerned. The attitude of the wife's brothers was that he had no say, because he "only made" the child, but the child came from their "bere" — the womb of their family. It is difficult for a man to take his position as head of the home under these circumstances.

Large Kinship Groups

It is difficult for us as American missionaries to fully appreciate the importance of the family to the individual in a large kinship group. The family is always there and will protect the individual against virtually any attack. I remember hearing about a fight in a Bush Negro village between two families. The future wife of one young man was being strangled by a member of the young man's family, and he pulled the other man off his future wife. Later, he was beaten by two of his uncles. They told him that you never go against your own family, even for your future wife. Family is family.

I saw a similar situation once after our church had just begun, when two young ladies from different families began to argue and fight. In a matter of a few seconds, there was a tremendous uproar, much to the

CHAPTER 6: MISSIONARIES NEED TO UNDERSTAND CULTURE

interest of the entire neighborhood! Fortunately, it did not escalate and was eventually cooled down. I am most grateful that I have never seen a repeat at church. However, family is family.

Stepping out against family is extremely difficult, especially in areas such as the interior of Suriname. My son-in-law and daughter worked for five years in a village in the interior. No one was saved when they arrived. They did see a few individuals, mostly children or young adults, come to receive Christ personally. But not a single one was willing to be baptized, although they held regular church services during their entire five years. They found that children who became serious and on the verge of accepting the Lord suddenly stopped attending Bible club or services. The family withdrew them. To come out boldly for Christ would mean standing against the entire family and having no one to help in time of need. My son-in-law Ethan Champlin had a good Suriname friend in Bakoe. He told Ethan that if he were to become a Christian that no one would give him a daughter to be his wife, no one would help him to build a house or to assist him in any way. Sadly, a tree fell on him while the Champlins were on furlough, and he died before he could be taken to the city for medical help.

Some of the nationals told Ethan that they could not be saved because the spirits had known them and controlled them since childhood. They could conceive that perhaps a young child would be able to get saved early in life. In some locations, the adults would state that although they could not leave their old ways, their children were free to make their own decision, but in reality, when children did pray to receive Christ, the family withdrew them from the church. Ethan prayed to the Lord about whether or not they should remain at Bakoe in the interior. He told the Lord that they would announce their plans to relocate back in the mining town of Moengo. But if one single individual asked them not to go because who would show them the way of salvation, they would stay. Many asked them to stay. They said: Who will repair our outboard engines? Who will bring us medicines, etc. However, not a single individual spoke to them about concern for their souls, although they had heard the gospel many times. They relocated in Moengo, where they have been for more than two decades. Some individuals from the same villages who have come to Paramaribo have received Christ in the city. The family is not totally dominating in the city as it does in the interior.

Assessment

Our family and culture are not earned. They are a gift of God, and we should respect and appreciate them. *Exodus 20: [12] Honour thy father and thy mother: that thy days may be long upon the land which the LORD thy God giveth thee.* There were severe penalties outlined in the Old Testament for those who failed to honor their parents.[21] And Jesus honored His parents as well. *Luke 2: [51] And he went down with them, and came to Nazareth, and was subject unto them: but his mother kept all these sayings in her heart.[52] And Jesus increased in wisdom and stature, and in favour with God and man.* Jesus cared for His mother while dying on the cross, placing her in the care of John the apostle.

However, there is a higher call than our physical family, whom we must respect. *Luke 11: [27] And it came to pass, as he spake these things, a certain woman of the company lifted up her voice, and said unto him, Blessed is the womb that bare thee, and the paps which thou hast sucked.[28] But he said, Yea rather, blessed are they that hear the word of God, and keep it. Mark 3: [32] And the multitude sat about him, and they said unto him, Behold, thy mother and thy brethren without seek for thee.[33] And he answered them, saying, Who is my mother, or my brethren?[34] And he looked round about on them which sat about him, and said, Behold my mother and my brethren![35] For whosoever shall do the will of God, the same is my brother, and my sister, and mother.*

Thus, the Christian has an even larger and more permanent family, the family of faith. He is bound with other believers in the body of Christ. Our loyalty to our physical family is extremely important, but to our family in faith is even more important.

Achieved Status Versus Acquired Status

In America, we state proudly that anyone can be president. Although that is not totally true, as there are a number of criteria to be met, such as age and citizenship, still the statement shows that America is an achievement-oriented society, with considerable social mobility.

CHAPTER 6: MISSIONARIES NEED TO UNDERSTAND CULTURE

This is radically different from a number of other societies, where status is ascribed, not achieved.

The Caste System of India

Perhaps the most well-known situation of ascribed status is the caste system of India. The Indian society has four main caste categories, and then a fifth and lower category, the untouchables, or Dalits. Although the caste system is now illegal formally, it is still very much functional in many aspects of Indian society, especially in marriage. You are expected to marry within your caste. And, in fact, there are many sub-categories of castes, and the individual is expected to remain within that framework. Even if a Dalit, or untouchable, is able, through his ability, to become wealthy, he is still socially inferior to a Brahman, who might be simply a schoolboy.

The Aristocracy of Europe

Another well-known area of ascribed society is the aristocracy within Europe, especially prominent a few centuries ago. It was virtually unthinkable that royalty would marry a commoner. In fact, one man slated to be king of England gave up the throne to marry his love, a commoner. There was so much inbreeding that in some situations, there were problems with congenital diseases.[22] In a number of societies, the king and queen married within a group which was quite inbred. In such a society, the upward mobility is much more limited.

Individual Roles Within the Family or Group

The role of the individual may be settled, even at birth, by such criteria as the family into whom the individual is born, whether he is male or female, and whether the individual is older or younger than his siblings, especially if he is the oldest son. These responsibilities are automatically assigned. For example, the oldest son in a Chinese family has special responsibilities. In the Bible, we find that the oldest son received a double portion of the family inheritance as part of his birthright, as well as the spiritual leadership in the family. The oldest son was expected to care for his mother and any unmarried sisters. Thus Esau, although he was born just a few minutes before his brother Jacob, had this position, but despised his birthright, which he sold to Jacob for a meal of stew.[23]

We have had two brothers who were separated by birth by only one year. Both were living with their grandmother. The younger was kidding his older brother and said in jest: "Joe lei!" (You are lying). Suddenly his grandmother slapped him across his face and said: "Don't you ever talk to your older brother like that." The older brother had additional responsibility for his younger brothers and sisters. The older sisters often cared for the younger ones like a surrogate mother.

Some of the differences between ascribed and attained status are outlined in the following chart:

Tensions About Self-worth

Status focus – ascribed	Achievement focus - attained
Personal identity is obtained by position, birth, and rank	Personal identity is obtained by one's achievements
Amount of respect is permanently fixed; those with high status honored despite personal failings	Amount of respect determined by one's achievements or failures
Play your role; be willing to sacrifice to achieve higher rank	Self-critical, and sacrifices to achieve even greater goals
People associate with social equals	Associate with people of equal accomplishments regardless of background

In each situation, we are expected by society to play out our role according to the status which we have obtained, either by inheritance or by achievement. The differences are quite clearly outlined by this chart from Lingenfelter.[24]

CHAPTER 6: MISSIONARIES NEED TO UNDERSTAND CULTURE

Assessment

Jesus was not impressed with status, much to the chagrin of the Pharisees. *Luke 15:[1] Then drew near unto him all the publicans and sinners for to hear him.[2] And the Pharisees and scribes murmured, saying, This man receiveth sinners, and eateth with them.* Jesus responded with the parables of the lost sheep, the lost coin, and the prodigal son. On another occasion, He pointed out that it is not the healthy, but the sick who need a physician.[25]

In Luke 14, Jesus points to the need of humility. *Luke 14: [7] And he put forth a parable to those which were bidden, when he marked how they chose out the chief rooms; saying unto them,[8] When thou art bidden of any man to a wedding, sit not down in the highest room; lest a more honourable man than thou be bidden of him;[9] And he that bade thee and him come and say to thee, Give this man place; and thou begin with shame to take the lowest room.[10] But when thou art bidden, go and sit down in the lowest room; that when he that bade thee cometh, he may say unto thee, Friend, go up higher: then shalt thou have worship in the presence of them that sit at meat with thee.[11] For whosoever exalteth himself shall be abased; and he that humbleth himself shall be exalted.[12] Then said he also to him that bade him, When thou makest a dinner or a supper, call not thy friends, nor thy brethren, neither thy kinsmen, nor thy rich neighbours; lest they also bid thee again, and a recompence be made thee.[13] But when thou makest a feast, call the poor, the maimed, the lame, the blind:[14] And thou shalt be blessed; for they cannot recompense thee: for thou shalt be recompensed at the resurrection of the just.*

The disciples struggled with the question of their position in the Kingdom. But Jesus showed them a different way. *Matthew 20:[25] But Jesus called them unto him, and said, Ye know that the princes of the Gentiles exercise dominion over them, and they that are great exercise authority upon them.[26] But it shall not be so among you: but whosoever will be great among you, let him be your minister;[27] And whosoever will be chief among you, let him be your servant:[28] Even as the Son of man came not to be ministered unto, but to minister, and to give his life a ransom for many.*

These were important lessons for me to learn. The last three years that I was in Suriname, I turned over the ministry to the national leaders. I learned to give them the major responsibility for making decisions and was their servant. When a pastor from one of our churches asked me to come and preach, I would ask them if they had checked with "my pastor" (the pastor of the church which I was attending).

It is also key to recognize that our worth comes primarily from our relationship with Jesus Christ. We are forgiven sinners, and we do not have the right to subjugate others to do our will. *Romans 3: [21] But now the righteousness of God without the law is manifested, being witnessed by the law and the prophets;[22] Even the righteousness of God which is by faith of Jesus Christ unto all and upon all them that believe: for there is no difference:[23] For all have sinned, and come short of the glory of God;[24] Being justified freely by his grace through the redemption that is in Christ Jesus:* We have not earned our righteousness. It is a gift of God.

People Orientation Versus Task Orientation
People Orientation

I am a typical American, highly organized, task-oriented person. I like to have my plans for the day worked out and scheduled. I get frustrated if my plans are delayed unexpectedly. I had major adjustments to Suriname, which is very much a person-oriented culture. The problem, of course, is not simply the frustration, but the danger of seeking one goal after another, some of which may not always be in the will of the Lord. The task-oriented individual often prefers to work alone, and social relationships can sometimes simply be an extension of his work.

The typical people-oriented individual uses all occasions to build extensive networks of relationships. He thrives in the stimulation of the group, and often expends much energy extending and maintaining those relationships. He is willing to sacrifice some personal achievements for the sake of the group, and believes that the quality of relationships is more important than achieving his own independent objectives.

Task Orientation

The task-oriented individual may succeed well as a teacher, preacher, someone in Bible translation, or in administration. He does well if given a chance to schedule his own activities independently, and often is frustrated with fellow workers who spend large amounts of time on "frivolous conversations."

For six years, I had a male secretary who did not work efficiently. He was frustrated by being in an office where he often worked alone. When cell phones became popular, I finally had to purchase a special telephone which could not be used to contact cell phones because my telephone bill had skyrocketed. Some individuals can work and converse at the same time. Not this man. When our bus driver from the church would come, he would visit with my secretary, sometimes talking as long as an hour. The work stagnated. I tried to help my secretary, who was struggling to finish high school, which he finally did. But it seemed that the more I reduced his workload to help him study, the less work and the less studying occurred. We eventually parted ways — and we were probably both relieved. Our cultural orientations clashed, and even though I knew this intellectually, I had difficulties handling the situation emotionally. I mention this to help others who may struggle with similar situations.

Lingenfelter gives us another very helpful chart.[26]

Task Orientation vs. People Orientation

Task Orientation	People Orientation
Focus - task and principles	Focus - people and relationships
Satisfaction in achievement of goals	Satisfaction in interaction

Seeks friends with similar goals	Seeks friends who are group oriented
Accepts loneliness and social deprivation to achieve personal goals	Despises loneliness. Gives up personal achievement to have group interaction

Furthermore, western missionaries generally separate work from play. There is a time for work, and a time for recreation. Much of the world has a different attitude and combines both aspects together. Of course, it is possible to abuse this situation, and simply to have pleasure without work. But it is also quite possible to combine the two, and in some situations, the individual may actually be more productive.

Assessment

Jesus was people oriented. He knew that His Father had sent Him into the world to redeem the world, and never deviated from that goal, even at the cost of the cross and temporary separation from His Father. Although He met his goals, it was never at the expense of people. Jesus had time for people and shared His life with them. One problem for task-oriented people is the temptation to use others to reach their goals. This is the antithesis of the life of Christ, which we are to manifest in our lives.

Philippians 2: [3] Let nothing be done through strife or vainglory; but in lowliness of mind let each esteem other better than themselves.[4] Look not every man on his own things, but every man also on the things of others.[5] Let this mind be in you, which was also in Christ Jesus:[6] Who, being in the form of God, thought it not robbery to be equal with God:[7] But made himself of no reputation, and took upon him the form of a servant, and was made in the likeness of men:[8] And being found in fashion as a man, he humbled himself, and became obedient unto death, even the death of the cross.[9] Wherefore God also hath highly exalted him, and given him a name which is above every name:[10] That at the name of Jesus every knee should bow, of things in heaven, and things in earth, and things under the earth;[11] And that every tongue should confess that Jesus Christ is Lord, to the glory of God the Father.[12]

CHAPTER 6: MISSIONARIES NEED TO UNDERSTAND CULTURE

Wherefore, my beloved, as ye have always obeyed, not as in my presence only, but now much more in my absence, work out your own salvation with fear and trembling.[13] For it is God which worketh in you both to will and to do of his good pleasure.

The apostle Paul also shared his life with others. *I Thessalonians 2: [6] Nor of men sought we glory, neither of you, nor yet of others, when we might have been burdensome, as the apostles of Christ.[7] But we were gentle among you, even as a nurse cherisheth her children:[8] So being affectionately desirous of you, we were willing to have imparted unto you, not the gospel of God only, but also our own souls, because ye were dear unto us.[9] For ye remember, brethren, our labour and travail: for labouring night and day, because we would not be chargeable unto any of you, we preached unto you the gospel of God.*

Paul urged others to do the same. *Ephesians 5:[1] Be ye therefore followers of God, as dear children;[2] And walk in love, as Christ also hath loved us, and hath given himself for us an offering and a sacrifice to God for a sweetsmelling savour. Colossians 3: [12] Put on therefore, as the elect of God, holy and beloved, bowels of mercies, kindness, humbleness of mind, meekness, longsuffering;[13] Forbearing one another, and forgiving one another, if any man have a quarrel against any: even as Christ forgave you, so also do ye.* As missionaries, we need to be humble servants of others.

Thought questions:
1. What do you know about the kinship arrangements of the people group to whom you plan to minister? Why is it important to understand this question?
2. Notice the importance of family relationships. Does this have a significant impact on how you will present the gospel within a group of individuals from a family?
3. Does the Bible support special responsibilities for certain individuals in the family such as the father, the mother, and the older brother?
4. Are you a highly driven task oriented individual? How are you going to adjust if you find yourself (as is highly probable) in a relationship-oriented culture?

CHAPTER 7
DIFFERING ASPECTS IN CULTURES
Differences in Ways of Thinking
Western Thought

Our western background has influenced even the way that we think. Westerners like to categorize things into black and white, or true and false, even when there appear to be shades of gray. We like to sort things out into clear patterns, and of course, this fits with our use of such things as the computer, which has binary codes of positive and negative. We want specific criteria to sort things out into clear categories, and file them like you file something, placing them in the right box or folder. We feel secure knowing that we are right and fit into a specific role in society.

Holistic View

On the other hand, much of the world takes a much more holistic view, believing that the whole is greater than its parts. Judgments are then open-ended and take the entire person into consideration. Security comes from knowing that there are multiple interactions within society, and the individual may feel insecure if he is confined to making judgments by himself alone.

Dual Brain Theory

Some of the differences have been attributed to the "dual brain theory." There does appear to be a difference in the function of each hemisphere of the brain, and the dominant hemisphere seems to vary from individual to individual, as well as from culture to culture. The left hemisphere is primarily verbal, rational, analytical, and digital (separating into separate categories.) In contrast, the right hemisphere is more signal-pictorial, emotional, holistic, and analogical (multiple categories.) There is a tendency to think that individuals from a western culture are more oriented to using the left brain, and those of oral cultures more the right brain. Of course, there are individual differences and orientations among all groups, and everyone uses both sides of the brain, although one may dominate.

It is true that different individuals vary. I am, for example, a left-brain type individual. I am probably typical of the individual who is favored at present by the western educational system. On the other hand, many in the developing world seem to be much more right brain in orientation. However, the truly healthy individual will use both hemispheres. I also doubt that one can categorize a culture across the board as either right brain or left brain, especially after my experience teaching in developing countries for 30 years, when I have had students working primarily in either way.

Differing Thought in the OT Versus the NT

In terms of the Bible, we find a difference between Greek and Hebrew thought. Paul is perhaps a classic example of one who thinks in the logical framework of Greek thought. The book of Romans is a classic book with very tight reasoning. On the other hand, Jesus used the pictorial language of the Hebrew culture, often speaking in analogies or parables. He often focused on the issues of the day, such as healing on the Sabbath. He used vivid illustrations, such as straining a drink to remove a gnat but then swallowing a camel, or washing the outside of the plate, but leaving the inside filthy.[27]

Differing Ways of Making Judgments
The Dichotomists

We need to be tolerant and understanding of other ways of making judgments. The dichotomist, who tends to see things in black and white, may feel that the holistic individual lacks character and principle, and is inconsistent in his judgments.

The Holistic Individual

On the other hand, the holistic individual may consider the dichotomist as legalistic and unfeeling. The Bible urges us to avoid making incorrect judgments, especially about the motives of others. *Mt. 7: [1] Judge not, that ye be not judged.[2] For with what judgment ye judge, ye shall be judged: and with what measure ye mete, it shall be*

CHAPTER 7: DIFFERING ASPECTS IN CULTURES

measured to you again.[3] And why beholdest thou the mote that is in thy brother's eye, but considerest not the beam that is in thine own eye?[4] Or how wilt thou say to thy brother, Let me pull out the mote out of thine eye; and, behold, a beam is in thine own eye?[5] Thou hypocrite, first cast out the beam out of thine own eye; and then shalt thou see clearly to cast out the mote out of thy brother's eye. I Corinthians 4:[3] But with me it is a very small thing that I should be judged of you, or of man's judgment: yea, I judge not mine own self.[4] For I know nothing by myself; yet am I not hereby justified: but he that judgeth me is the Lord.[5] Therefore judge nothing before the time, until the Lord come, who both will bring to light the hidden things of darkness, and will make manifest the counsels of the hearts: and then shall every man have praise of God.

Differences in Educational Methods
Practical Skills Versus Memorization Skills

When I began teaching in Liberia, West Africa, I noticed immediately that there were differences in the ways that my students learned compared to my training in the USA. This has been confirmed not only with the 5 years teaching medicine in Africa, but also with an additional 10 years teaching medicine in Suriname, as well as teaching in a Bible Institute in Suriname for over 20 years.

I was an excellent student in the USA, capitalizing on my scientific and mathematic skills. These two skills allowed me to graduate valedictorian from my high school and salutatorian in my college class. However, my weaknesses were in language and art, and although I enjoyed sports, I was not an exceptional athlete. Memorization was always a challenge to me. I remember struggling to remember 1000 words in Latin which I memorized for my Regents final in third year Latin, and promptly forgot the vocabulary as soon as I passed the test.

However, much of the third world education is very different. Of course, in many areas, until recently there was no formal education possible. Most persons were oral learners and illiterate. I was surprised to learn that literacy actually may diminish one's ability to remember oral facts, because now things are written down, and it is possible to return to them. Previously, most learning was done by observation and imitation. Today, even in western culture, combining both visual as well as oral methods seems to aid in retention.[28]

Remembering Chart

What we remember:	After 3 hours	After 3 days
What we hear	70%	10%
What we see	72%	20%
What we see & hear	86%	72%

I might add: what we see and hear and do is even better remembered.

Forms of Intelligence

We now recognize that there are many forms of intelligence, including spatial, kinesthetic and musical intelligence as well as the linguistic and mathematic intelligence mentioned above. My medical students were all intelligent individuals; otherwise, they would have never been able to get into medical school. Nevertheless, there was an emphasis on memorization of facts rather than logical application of facts, and it was necessary to work on their getting a better grasp of medical topics with a broader base of skills. Since I was teaching Internal Medicine, much of the training was much more "hands on" practical training, which made teaching easier. Training in surgery is even more practical, with years of supervised "hands on" training. Because I was more skilled intellectually than in hands on work, although I had nine months of surgical residency, I decided to return to Internal Medicine.

Judith Lingenfelter related her broad experiences in teaching in a developing world context.[29] She also noted the emphasis on memorization, and that many of her students were able to memorize far more than her USA students. For example, one student had just

CHAPTER 7: DIFFERING ASPECTS IN CULTURES

completed memorizing the book of Hebrews and was starting to memorize Luke. Practical skills are also very helpful, although some students resisted, stating that this is "not school."

I am currently teaching several courses in college including Human Anatomy and Physiology. There are many facts to know and remember. I try to help the students in a number of ways. In addition to repetition, I demonstrate how various parts of the body function together and cause common experiences. For example, today I was discussing the structure of the face including the nose and eye. I mentioned that when we cry, the tear gland releases tears on the eye. The eyelids was the tears down, and the lower lid has a small hole where the tears flow into the tear sac next to the nose and dump into the nose. I mentioned that when we cry, we often blow our nose because of the tears flowing there, and if too many tears form, they overflow the drainage system and flow down our cheeks. These simple facts help them to learn. I often have them feel parts of their body, such as bones and muscles, to understand what they do.

Our music teacher was teaching a young lady to play the violin. She had real difficulty producing the proper tone for the notes. He then guided her hand and elbows in the proper position after she did not understand what people had told her. She learned kinesthetically, and she left as the best violinist from the college.

Attitude Toward Group Learning

Another important difference is the attitude toward group learning. This is also emphasized in Suriname. I found the whole concept difficult, as I had been very competitive, and had always striven to be the best or close to the best in my class. Classmates were classmates, but also competitors. However, the interest in group learning is becoming much more widespread.

One of our young preachers is excellent working with his hands and with practical knowledge. He always seems to be able to figure things out. He had troubles in school, partially because of a civil war during his childhood that interrupted his training. He never quite finished high school. Finally, he obtained a job as a chauffeur for the Maritime Authority.

One day they had a technical problem that no one of their technical men could solve. He solved it, was moved to the technical service, and rose quickly to head up the technical service. He was recently sent to the USA to learn about some jet propulsion marine engines. The final exam for their course was to assemble an engine correctly as a team. He is now a captain of a ship, having advanced beyond his technical skills.

Team learning and more practical experience is also being emphasized in online learning programs. So, we in the west are moving toward more practical experience even using high tech teaching. And of course, apprenticeship has been used successfully throughout the world for centuries, not only training for trades, but also in a variety of professions. Teaching in groups also avoids a major problem with many developing countries, which is the problem of shame at being unable to answer questions correctly. When the entire group yells out the correct answer, those who are afraid of answering incorrectly hope that their answer will be swallowed up in the group answer. We will describe the difference between shame cultures and guilt cultures below.

Assessment

It is important to realize that there are many different types of intelligence and provide opportunities for individuals to learn within the framework of their talents. We should not squeeze them into a western mode which may be awkward for them and may not apply to their own situation. Practical experience is also important. Our goal should be life transfer, helping mold the life of the student to resemble his teacher. *Matthew 10:24-25a [24] The disciple is not above his master, nor the servant above his lord. [25] It is enough for the disciple that he be as his master, and the servant as his lord.* Jesus, of course, was successful in transforming the lives of his disciples. *Acts 4:[13] Now when they saw the boldness of Peter and John, and perceived that they were unlearned and ignorant men, they marveled; and they took knowledge of them, that they had been with Jesus.*

Shame and Guilt Cultures

When Adam and Eve sinned in the garden of Eden, they felt both guilty before God, and ashamed of their nakedness. Some cultures

CHAPTER 7: DIFFERING ASPECTS IN CULTURES

emphasize shame more, while others put the emphasis more on guilt. They also experienced fear and hid from God.

Those cultures that emphasize shame are usually tight-knit societies. The emphasis then, is on the fact that you have let down the group and brought shame to the entire group. There is usually strong social pressure on the individual to conform. In some situations, the individual may try to escape the shame by suicide. Countries such as Japan or small oral societies often emphasize shame.

Middle East cultures also have a strong shame emphasis. The tendency is to first try to hide the shame by denying or covering it up. If that is unsuccessful, the group or individual may react violently. They may attack the individual bringing shame (for example, a woman who is pregnant out of wedlock with so-called honor killing) or even the individual who exposed the shame so that others could see it. One problem in shame culture is that hiding shame is often given priority over dealing with sin by confession and repentance.

Guilt is more commonly seen in cultures with more emphasis on individual responsibility. The concept is that you have broken the law and are thereby guilty. The emphasis is more on the conscience of the individual than on the sense of letting down the group. Guilt is seen in such countries as the USA or Germany. However, in a guilt society, the individual may fail to grasp the fact that he has sinned and rebelled against God Himself and that his sin has social ramifications.

Use Extreme Care in Shame Cultures

American missionaries must be very careful when working in a shame culture. Direct reprimand may lead to severe consequences. Usually it is possible to deal with a situation without compromising your values, but usually direct confrontation, as we do in the USA, will not be taken well. The individual does not want to "lose face," and bring shame to his family. I have learned to allow much more latitude in judgment in Suriname, and to depend much on the nationals. They understand the nuances of the culture and what can have an impact on others. They know the right way to deal with their people.

For example, we had a young woman who was a baptized member of the church, and she became pregnant out of wedlock. My idea was to talk privately first with the girl, but the nationals called first on the mother. The mother thanked us for *"poeroe da sjem gi hem"* — taking away the shame from the family. She agreed with us, called the girl, who came forward at church and confessed what she had done (a very difficult step in a shame culture like the Bush Negroes), and was restored to the church, and continues to attend. I have made a number of errors bypassing the right chain of authority by using my western ideas. The nationals, on the other hand, have been very helpful.

I remember reading about a similar situation of another missionary. Someone needed to be reprimanded. The missionary called the individual and spoke to him privately, which is what I would have done according to my western training. The individual was furious, and the missionary was deeply troubled. When a similar situation arose, and he asked advice from the nationals, they said to go through an intermediate. Although he doubted, he did so, and the individual took the reprimand well, and corrected his behavior. In that culture, direct confrontation is used only for correcting children. He had shown respect by going through an intermediary.

Assessment
The Individual Concept of Sin as Breaking the law

We in the west concentrate on the concept of sin as breaking the law or overstepping the mark which God Himself has set. This is indeed true. Our picture of justice is lady justice, with her eyes blindfolded, holding a scale in her hand. The idea is that if our sins are heavy, the scale will demonstrate our guilt. It is true that God has set His laws, such as the Ten Commandments, and that we are all guilty of breaking the law. I think that it is also significant that lady justice is blindfolded. Our idea is that lady justice is impartial, and that despite your position, you will not escape justice. On the other hand, lady justice may also be blind to many extenuating circumstances that would better be handled by mercy than simply applying "the letter of the law."

CHAPTER 7: DIFFERING ASPECTS IN CULTURES

The Group Concept of Shame

It is also true that we are bound together in groups, and when one rejoices, we all rejoice, and when one sorrows, we all sorrow together. And if one member brings shame on the group by failing to fulfill his duty, he brings shame on the total group. When Christ died on the cross, He died a most shameful death. I believe that He was probably totally naked. His punishment was reserved for the worst of criminals, and the Jews believed that the individual was actually cursed by God. He died to take the curse and shame of our sin, which warranted death, on Himself, as well as its guilt and payment.

Sin Breaks Relationships

However, there is another aspect of sin which we must never forget. Sin is not merely breaking some impersonal law, as one would do driving too fast around a curve and spinning off the road. The laws of God are not impersonal, but they are His personal commands. Thus we need to have our relationship with the Lord restored, and this requires a sacrifice. Because God is an infinite God, only a perfect sacrifice of infinite worth is appropriate, and God Himself provided that sacrifice on the cross. Jesus Christ removes both the shame and guilt of our sin when we cast ourselves upon Him. He is the ultimate answer whether our culture emphasizes shame or guilt.

Openness and Vulnerability When the Individual Fails

Differences in Terms of Handling Failures

Another way of looking at this tension between shame and guilt is what Lingenfelter called vulnerability.[30] Using this broad term, he was speaking not only of sin, but also failure to perform. There is a difference between cultures in terms of handling such failures as he outlines in the following chart.

Tensions Concerning Vulnerability

Conceal vulnerability	Expose vulnerability
Protection of self-image at all cost; avoidance of error and failure	Relative unconcern over error and failure
Emphasis on quality of performance	Emphasis on completion of the event
Reluctance to go beyond recognized performance or enter the unknown	Willing to push the limits and go into the unknown
Denial of culpability; withdrawal from activity to hide weakness or shortcoming	Ready admission of culpability, weakness and shortcomings
Refusal to see alternate views or accept criticism	Openness to alternative views and criticism
Vagueness as regards personal life	Willing to talk freely about personal life

As I study the tensions shown in this chart, I come back to the differences often seen between a shame culture and a guilt culture. The shame culture would correspond more to the group which wants to conceal vulnerability, and the guilt culture is more willing to expose vulnerability.

The Bible teaches that we should be humble, and also assess the areas of our weakness so that we do not make foolish decisions because of pride. *Luke 14:[28] For which of you, intending to build a tower, sitteth not down first, and counteth the cost, whether he have sufficient to finish it? [29] Lest haply, after he hath laid the foundation, and is not*

CHAPTER 7: DIFFERING ASPECTS IN CULTURES

able to finish it, all that behold it begin to mock him,[30] Saying, This man began to build, and was not able to finish.[31] Or what king, going to make war against another king, sitteth not down first, and consulteth whether he be able with ten thousand to meet him that cometh against him with twenty thousand?[32] Or else, while the other is yet a great way off, he sendeth an ambassage, and desireth conditions of peace.[33] So likewise, whosoever he be of you that forsaketh not all that he hath, he cannot be my disciple. Wisdom indicates that we should recognize our weakness to avoid making foolish decisions.

God Uses Our Weaknesses

Another consideration is that God uses our weaknesses to exalt His strength to His glory. *2 Corinthians 12:[7] And lest I should be exalted above measure through the abundance of the revelations, there was given to me a thorn in the flesh, the messenger of Satan to buffet me, lest I should be exalted above measure.[8] For this thing I besought the Lord thrice, that it might depart from me.[9] And he said unto me, My grace is sufficient for thee: for my strength is made perfect in weakness. Most gladly therefore will I rather glory in my infirmities, that the power of Christ may rest upon me.[10] Therefore I take pleasure in infirmities, in reproaches, in necessities, in persecutions, in distresses for Christ's sake: for when I am weak, then am I strong.* God showed this principle, not only in the life of Paul, but on many other occasions in the Bible.

Moses, 80 years old, with his 83-year-old brother Aaron confronted the most powerful ruler in the world armed only with a walking stick. Gideon, a young man in a small tribe, defeated 135,000 Midianites with 300 men armed with torches, clay pots and trumpets. Jehoshaphat defeated three kings with an army led by the choir; three opposing armies destroyed themselves before the Israelites even arrived. Thus, we need a balance between humility and trust in the Lord.

Differences in Planning for the Unexpected

Sherwood Lingenfelter gave a very clear explanation of the difference between planning for a crisis and not making plans for the crisis.[31] He contrasted the Yapese, who ignored a warning for a typhoon, and the American military, who had already planned for the typhoon and sat comfortably in their building to wait it out. Some attempt to plan for all potential crises, while others are in a more flexible mode. Here is his chart:

Ways to Handle Crisis:

Crisis Orientation	Non-crisis Orientation
1. Anticipates crisis	1. Downplays possibility of crisis
2. Emphasizes planning	2. Focuses on actual experience
3. Quick solution to avoid ambiguity	3. Avoid taking action; delay decisions
4. Repeatedly follows preplanned authoritative decisions	4. Makes ad hoc decision on spur of the moment from multiple options
5. Seeks expert advice	5. Shuns expert advice
6. Pessimistic	6. Optimistic

Lingenfelter mentioned that the natives received frequent warnings about a potential natural disaster. Most of the time the disaster never really came so that any special preparation was unnecessary. They would rather scramble in the event of a real emergency than respond to many false alarms. Furthermore, sometimes they did not have the necessary resources to prepare adequately ahead of time.

Once again, balance is important. One consideration is that in many countries, there are many variables which cannot be controlled, so that it is impossible to plan effectively long-term. However, it is very helpful to look ahead and have a "back-up" plan. Flexibility is an important characteristic of the missionary. Paul demonstrates this flexibility in *I*

CHAPTER 7: DIFFERING ASPECTS IN CULTURES

Corinthians 9:[19] For though I be free from all men, yet have I made myself servant unto all, that I might gain the more.[20] And unto the Jews I became as a Jew, that I might gain the Jews; to them that are under the law, as under the law, that I might gain them that are under the law;[21] To them that are without law, as without law, (being not without law to God, but under the law to Christ,) that I might gain them that are without law.[22] To the weak became I as weak, that I might gain the weak: I am made all things to all men, that I might by all means save some.[23] And this I do for the gospel's sake, that I might be partaker thereof with you.

Differences in the Roles of the Sexes

In oral small societies and peasant societies, the roles of the man and woman are usually sharply defined. Their work, their education, their clothing, and their interaction with the opposite sex are clearly understood. In many of these societies, from a young child, the girl will associate with women and the boy with men. Each sex has clearly defined responsibilities.

However, in western civilization, we find that the roles of men and women have been less and less clearly differentiated. Unisex clothing and haircuts have become common. In terms of sports, we find that women are demanding and receiving very similar sports programs as those for men. In recent years, with a surge of transgender protests and programs, the differences are even more blurred.

Since World War II, the roles have changed dramatically. During the war, women began to take the jobs and wear the clothes of men. "Rosie the Riveter" was a model to help in the war effort. When I was a medical student in 1960, we had five women in our class of 70 students. Now the ratio is more women than men. Surgery used to be pretty much a male medical subspecialty. One recent year, in the medical school which I attended fifty years ago, for the first time, all eight new surgical residents were women.

Dresses were standard clothing for girls and women when I was in school. Now they are the exception, and not the rule. About a decade ago, I was unable to find a dress for my mother in the standard department stores. The demand was not there, and they did not carry them any longer.

Differences in Economy

The most basic economic system is where the individual or family unit is completely self-sufficient. The members raise their own crops, or depend on their own hunting and fishing prowess. They make their own clothes, their own instruments, and build their own houses. It would be extremely rare for a small family unit to be self-sufficient in most of today's societies, but a number of small oral societies have very little contact with those outside their own group.

Exchanges of Services or Money

A second, more developed, method of economy is to have reciprocal exchange. If I am better than my neighbor in some activities, and he is better than I am in others, it makes sense to allow each of us to work in the area where we are more competent and help each other in that area. Sometimes, instead of direct exchange of goods or services, it is possible to have mutual exchange of gifts.

However, as the society becomes more complex, it is very useful to have some sort of independent medium of exchange, such as money. Then it is much easier to purchase items with money rather than to find someone willing to make the necessary exchange. Although some simply buy and sell, in many cultures, especially traditional cultures, shopping becomes a social activity with bargaining. No one is expected to pay the first price asked, but one bargains back and forth until the price is agreed upon. The social interchange is enjoyed, and they also may expect the wealthier person to pay more because he has more resources. For that reason, a number of western missionaries would send their housekeeper to the market to purchase items, because she could get them at a lower price.

Group Labor

The ways of paying individuals also varies. In some of the villages in the interior of Suriname, they find it to their advantage to work as a big group to clear area for planting their gardens. So a group may work

CHAPTER 7: DIFFERING ASPECTS IN CULTURES

together, rotating from one of the individual's garden to another. The person whose property is being cleared will provide drinks and food for the day. However, more and more, the individuals are working for pay, with a certain wage for a day's work.

I read about a missionary, who was operating on a very tight budget, trying to get some students to his school. They needed to go by rickshaw, and the men who would run carrying the students were demanding an exorbitant price, probably because they expected that the missionary could and would pay far too much for the service. But the missionary, who had been in China many years, said something to this effect: "Honorable sirs, you do not understand me. I am not asking to buy your rickshaw, but simply to rent it." The men laughed, and then agreed to a reasonable price.

Of course, we often do the same thing in the USA with certain items, as for example, a car. One usually does not pay the asking price and can reduce the price substantially by bargaining. This is also possible in other purchases as well.

"Stuff or Starve" Mentality

Many oral societies have a "stuff or starve" mentality. When food is available, they will eat generous portions, but when it is not, they go hungry. Some have little concept of "budgeting" food. When we arrived in Suriname, cooking oil was difficult to find, and my wife used it very conservatively. She gave a liter bottle to a family which we knew, but in two days, they had used it completely. They were accustomed to using a lot of oil and were not about to change their pattern because of a shortage.

Sharing

Possessions are often shared within the group, especially in small villages, or within the clan. If someone kills a large animal, the meat is divided among the entire clan. If there is a successful fishing expedition, everyone gets some fish. We were touched when my wife made a cake for a Bible club and passed the pieces out. The children carefully saved some of the cake to share with their siblings at home. This also makes economic sense. In these cultures, it is often difficult to preserve food for long periods of time. If the group shares, then all benefit from the benefits of whomever had a successful hunt.

Possessions are also to be seen in some cultures. "Show" is a big thing in the lives of some of our Bush Negroes. When one of our missionaries in the interior put some new linoleum on the floor of his bedroom, they asked him: "What did you do that for? How is anyone going to be able to see it?"

Many persons in a third world country live just above subsistence level. They do not have resources to be able to save enough to care for themselves in their older years. The emphasis is on the well-being and the survival of the group. Thus the good person shares what he has with others, is generous, and not boastful. The person who refuses to share is greedy. The group is to take care of the elderly. This is in sharp contrast to the USA, where the good person is able to take care of himself.

Good as that is in theory, in practice, we have seen cases where the elderly were neglected by their family. They did not receive adequate food or care, especially when they were unable to care for themselves. Some have also exploited them, taking their "old people money" (like our social security.) Of course, sometimes the same things occur in the USA. On a number of occasions, some of our missionaries in Suriname have ministered to the elderly.

Assessment

The area of finances is a very difficult problem for many missionaries. I deal with this situation in considerable detail in *Issues in Missiology Volume I*.[32] There is a tremendous discrepancy between the salary of the average missionary and the salary of the individuals where he has come to work. The entire economic system is also radically different, as is the question of how much one can share in a situation where sharing is done within the family or clan.

Some missionaries simply isolate themselves from the situation by simply associating with their own expatriate companions, or with nationals of equal financial resources. Some try to pare down, and some even live at the level of the poor. One suggestion which has merit is living as the "righteous rich," a term that might be used of persons like Abraham and Job. They were generous and helped others, but did not live in poverty.

I would like to suggest several thoughts in this area:

1. A man's life does not consist of his possessions.
2. Our resource is the Lord, and not a person or institution.
3. We are responsible for what we do with the talents and goods which the Lord has given us.
4. God expects us to share with the poor, and blesses us when we do so.
5. God wants us to have humility, and certainly not to be proud over our possessions.
6. We should live relatively frugally, though not as a pauper.
7. We should not be greedy.
8. The effectiveness of our ministry is not necessarily enhanced by having financial resources.

The Concept of Limited Good

In many parts of the developing world, the nationals hold the concept of limited good. By this, they mean that there is a limited supply of goods, which not only include food, clothing, and material goods, but also relationships and positions. If this is true, then if I get more of something, then someone else is going to get less. Therefore, there is a strong impulse not to allow others to progress too much, believing that this will diminish the resources available to others.

However, this concept is generally limited to insiders within the system, and not to outsiders. Outsiders can bring in additional goods, materials, etc., without reducing the amount that others may receive. I might give a simple example even from medical practice. There has been a tendency to limit the number of medical practitioners in the city of Paramaribo, especially in the medical specialties, because there were a limited number of patients who could afford to pay for private practice. However, when I came as a specialist to simply work in the hospital, and had no private practice, I was no threat to the income of anyone. I was involved in training specialists in Internal Medicine. The internists already working had a tendency to control how many in training would be able to go abroad for specialty training, and in which area to limit the amount of competition in some areas, and better provide specialty care in multiple areas of medicine.

Differences in Life Cycle

Different cultures have very different approaches to the various stages in life. We will outline a few of these differences below:

Birth

Some cultures look at birth strictly from a biological perspective. Others, who believe in reincarnation, believe that the individual has been alive before, but he is reborn at this particular moment. Cultures may vary greatly over when they believe that life actually begins. Those believing the Bible have generally considered life to begin at conception when the sperm and egg unite. However, in the USA, those who are pro-abortion often tell the mother that the baby is not a baby, but just a piece of tissue, or a fetus. Anti-abortion advocates want the mother to see that there is actually a child in her womb under ECHO, and not simply a blob of tissue.

Conception

Other cultures may believe that supernatural help is required at conception, and that a spirit must enter the woman before she can conceive and give birth. If a Bush Negro woman cannot conceive, she will normally consult a bonoeman or bonoe-oema (witchdoctor) to see what is preventing conception. She may be given a variety of things to do to help her become pregnant. She may have many things which she must avoid doing as well.

Likewise, there are differences in views of the role of the man in conception. Some believe that the man plants his seed, and the woman bears the child like the ground bears plants. Others believe that the man has little to do with the process. Among some Bush Negroes, it is felt that the man must continue to have intercourse with the woman for a substantial period of her pregnancy, which will assist her to deliver the baby.

Pregnancy may have many taboos and limitations on work. When the actual delivery occurs, usually older women will assist with the delivery. In some cultures, it is unthinkable for a man to examine a pregnant woman or assist in a delivery. You may remember that the reason Dr. Ida Scudder became a physician was that in India it was not appropriate for a male, even a physician, would be involved in a pregnancy and delivery. It was because of these cultural taboos that she returned to the USA to learn medicine, and then came back to India to set up training for women, first as nurses, and then as physicians.[33]

There are often a number of regulations about intercourse following a delivery. In some societies, there is a considerable delay, perhaps as long as the mother is lactating and breast feeding, or until the child begins to walk. In other societies, the delay is perhaps 6-12 weeks or so. Among the Bush Negroes, the woman must wash herself with hot water in which certain leaves are placed. She must wash twice a day, usually at the same time, and is often assisted by her mother or aunt in washing in the right manner. It is felt that this is necessary for her to regain her figure and be attractive to her husband. After three months, she can have sexual relations again.

Childhood

Childhood is usually a time of intensive learning and protection. The mother is extremely important for the child in many cultures, although that is changing, especially in the west. In cultures with a larger kinship group, such as a clan, other women may also be involved in raising the child, especially sisters and the sisters of the mother. Usually in these less developed cultures, the children associate with those of the same sex – the children learn the roles that they will play as adults.

This period is much prolonged in those countries with extensive education. The child is removed from the immediate family situation for much of the day and is placed in a formal school situation. The child therefore has a stronger relationship with the teacher, and this may somewhat weaken the relationships at home. With more advanced education, the adolescence of the child may be greatly prolonged. This is increasingly a feature of western civilization.

When I was a child about 60 years ago, in the USA, everyone was expected to finish high school unless there was an unusual problem. Then many graduates began work immediately, and soon began to seek a mate and begin a family. Some would go on to college, and again, at the completion of college, the majority of students would immediately begin work, and many would marry. A few would go on to post-graduate education.

However, the situation is radically changed today in the west. There is a very long period of prolonged childhood and adolescence. Many go on to further education, and even after completing their education, they have no desire to "settle down," work and marry. They may even continue to live with their parents during this period into their late 20's or even into their 30's. The individual may well be sexually active but not want the responsibility of marriage and family. Further, the individuals are often encouraged to choose a life-partner on the basis of emotions when they are not experienced in their lives, and without advice from their family, and they often reap problems in their lives. There is often a severe generation gap, with lack of understanding between the young and the older adults.

Adulthood

Many stresses may occur to the adult. There may be competition for limited resources, and stresses of warfare. The individual may need to rein in his impulses and appetites and is usually under pressure to conform to the expectations of society. Some individuals are bored with monotony and dissatisfied with human relationships. Health issues and finances can also bring additional stress.

No society is totally free from these problems. Certainly, western culture has not solved all the problems for her people, and those of the developing world can often see the limitations of western culture. They often reject the family arrangements of western society. They may conclude that the cost of the technological advances is too high in terms of human relationships and happiness.

Old Age

Cultures differ radically in the treatment of the elderly. In modern western civilization, there seems to be a great emphasis on youth. The elderly person is often marginalized. The family may not feel a great responsibility for him. Modern medicine has also created a crisis of sorts. Life expectancy has increased dramatically, and the population of the elderly has exploded. This change in demography has placed great financial strains of the economy, especially on the social welfare costs. In the kinship type of organization, the kinship group takes care of the elderly, but that same sense of responsibility is not always seen in the nuclear family. The elderly person is often expected to provide enough for an adequate retirement, which at one time might have been 10 years or so, but now may stretch for 20 or more years.

Furthermore, the cost of caring for the elderly has skyrocketed with the advent of modern medical technology. The west seems to place a high priority on keeping the individual's biological body going on as long as possible. The incidence of Alzheimer's disease may be approaching 50% in those over 85, and the cost of care is prohibitive. Many families now have elderly parents who must be cared for at home, and others have them in a nursing home.

I mentioned above that sometimes the kinship group does take care of its elderly, but in other instances, it does not do so, and leaves the individuals to care for themselves or die. In certain societies, it is expected that individuals will basically remove themselves from society when they become a handicap. The elderly Eskimos, for example, may deliberately wander off into a blizzard or bitter cold to die when they are no longer able to keep pace with the society.

On the other hand, some countries, such as China, greatly admire the elderly, and give them great respect. In a number of societies, the older woman really comes into her own at a more advanced age, where she is greatly respected. The family may seek advice from the older men as well and give them great respect.

Ancestors

It seems strange to consider ancestors in the phases of life, because we in the west basically stop considering individuals to have an impact directly on our lives after death. We may greatly respect the work that they have accomplished, and build monuments to their honor, but do not expect them to directly affect us.

However, this is not true in many societies. They view life as a continuous stream from the unborn through life and to the ancestors, especially those ancestors which you can remember. In many cases, the clan believes that the ancestors are the most powerful members of the clan, as they live where the spirits are, and can give advice and protection in time of need. On the other hand, if the ancestors are not respected properly, they are in a position to do great harm.

Among the Bush Negroes of Suriname, they believe that family evil spirits, which are displeased ancestors, can do great harm to the living, and even result in death. Therefore they are appeased in many ways. At the burial, they are prayed to, and given gifts to go inside the casket. They are given food (*trowe njanjan*) during the burial ceremonies prior to burying the body. An individual is assigned to carry mourning for the departed and must place food and drink beside him for the dead. He may wear some of the clothes of the departed and be mournful for about 6-9 months until they have a ceremony terminating the mourning period. When a new baby is born, the ancestors are also "informed" in a ceremony *"poeroe da pikin na doro."*

Many in the Far East also revere their ancestors. It is sometimes difficult to distinguish between respect and worship. The oldest son has a special responsibility in Chinese families, and this is one reason that with a "one child" policy in China, some would abort a female fetus. Chinese have burned paper money, and even computers and cars to make them available in the life beyond. Likewise, there are special ceremonies in Cambodia for the departed.[34]

Assessment

There are tremendous variables between cultures as we study how they deal with life cycles. We missionaries need to look carefully at our own western civilization and notice a number of serious problems in our own culture, before we make harsh judgments about other cultures. We have struggled in the USA with the incredible number of abortions, which has divided the country. Our prolonged adolescence has created a number of problems as well. Our focus on "success" in terms of material goods and emphasis on youth have also added to our problems. In addition to placing high value on youth and productivity rather than old age and wisdom, we have had an exploding shift in population toward the elderly and skyrocketing cost of medical care, especially in the last years of life. These situations create tensions in the USA, and also in many ways reflect an anti-biblical stance of western civilization.

Recreation and Humor

In terms of humor, I still struggle to understand what the Surinamers find incredibly funny. This has been especially true with *"toneels,"* or plays. Our Suriname people are very adept at acting, and love to have plays, which they often write themselves. The actors also often improvise, and are very free to do so, even in their teenage years. Many times the audience is convulsing in laughter, and my wife and I look at ourselves and ask: what is so funny? Of course, the same is true in reverse. Our American humor often escapes them. These subtleties of the language are very difficult to pick up. One of the skills of some Bush Negroes is to insult someone in such a way that they do not realize that they have been insulted until later. Of course, if even the national does not pick up the clues initially, then such things go right over our heads as expatriates.

Recreation

Recreation is also different. This is true even in the area of sports. In much of the world, soccer (called football in almost all countries except the USA and a few others) is the biggest sport, and soccer stars are heroes and well-known over the entire world. Our missionary children often play soccer by preference, and should they go back to the

USA for schooling, they often excel, in contrast to their USA counterparts. I was surprised to find that such things as chess, checkers, and even cricket were big sports in some parts of Suriname.

Birthday Parties

Birthday parties are important in Suriname. They especially emphasize the first birthday, and then birthdays that are divisible by five — especially such birthdays as 40, 45, 50, 55, 60, 65, 70, etc. These are called *"bigi yari"* (big years). Typically, the individual will hold a birthday party at his own expense, and if he can afford it, may provide food and drinks for all in attendance. Many birthday parties may have a church service at the beginning. Later, the usual party, especially for the unsaved, will involve dancing, preferably with a live band. As is typical in the tropics, often the actual party begins about 10 pm, and finishes in the wee hours of the morning. Of course, the party is held outdoors with loudspeakers making it possible for the entire neighborhood to participate, whether they want to or not.

Health Concepts

Every culture has different methods of dealing with sickness. We in the west primarily use scientific explanations of illness and use medications or surgical interventions for cure. In terms of physical illness, modern medicine has been remarkably effective, especially for such sicknesses as infectious diseases caused by bacteria or parasites. We have also been effective in treating basic heart disease, hypertension, and other common organic diseases. We ask the basic question: "how did this sickness occur, and what can stop it?" Then we treat with medicine, surgery, radiation, etc.

But much of the world, especially those areas where animism predominates, asks a different question. Why did this sickness occur, and why at this particular time? In cultures where the spirits seem to dominate everything, it is natural to believe that for some reason, the spirits caused the illness at a particular time. Perhaps the individual angered an ancestor. Perhaps someone performed witchcraft to cause him to become sick. He may have broken a *trefoe* (a law of his clan, such as not eating a particular thing). Thus, the individual will seek out a

CHAPTER 7: DIFFERING ASPECTS IN CULTURES

shaman or witch doctor (*bonoeman* in Suriname) to discover the cause and find a cure.

Therefore, we find a number of interesting differences in treating patients from an animistic background. For example, when we were in Liberia, many patients felt that if I wrote a prescription for a medication, because I was the head doctor of Internal Medicine, that the prescription had more power than if one of my students or residents wrote the same prescription. Once, a radiologist friend really helped my reputation. He was known for his expertise reading x-rays and diagnosing illness. He said: "You know that I can see your sickness with this machine (the x-ray). You see that white man? He doesn't need a machine." I can only imagine their ideas — that perhaps that I had x-ray vision.

It is also understandable why many individuals will consult a doctor, get a prescription, and then go to the shaman or witch doctor. They go to the doctor to handle the physical aspect of the illness, but then to the shaman to see what the spiritual cause is, and how to correct that cause now or avoid it in the future. They view this as two different aspects of the disease, and it is common to "cover all the bases."

I should also mention that any Internist knows that in about 30% of the patients who come to us, we can find no physical organic illness. It appears to be some psychological or spiritual problem. The individual often will respond to virtually any medicine, as long as he believes that the medicine will help. We call this "placebo effect," and it may give a positive result in perhaps 20 or 30% of cases. You need to control for this effect when testing an unknown medicine. Therefore, the usual technique to control for this problem is to use a double-blind method of assessing results. In the double-blind controlled method, medicine is given, but neither the patient nor the doctor knows which medicine is real and which is placebo. Therefore, it is called double (both patient and physician) blind.

I mention the above to make it more understandable why people do go to the shaman, and at least partially explain his success in treatment. But I should also mention that real demonic power is often present, and demonic illness is possible. Therefore, the spiritual aspects of disease should not be neglected. It is also possible to have cures of organic diseases on a demonic basis. The question about treatment is not just empirical, of whether something works or not, but also what source provided the cure. I have seen a number of manifestations of demonic attacks, and at least in one case, a patient who was demonically blind for a few years who later totally recovered.[35]

Summary

We as missionaries should look carefully at the practices of the culture to which we are ministering and support those aspects which are biblical. We should look at the possibilities of substituting biblical alternatives also in the areas of the culture which need to be directed to a more biblical stance.

Thought questions:

1. What kind of learner are you? Visual, "hands on" or some other type? How can you adapt your teaching methods (including presenting the gospel) to methods for your people?
2. What sort of adaptations must you make when dealing with a shame culture? Mention some potential dangers if you do not adapt.
3. How will you approach a situation where nationals are repeatedly approaching you for a loan of money?
4. How will you work with the concept of limited good to best utilize your talents?
5. What cultural adaptations of your people will impact your ministry, and how can you adjust to accommodate them?
6. If you are involved in the physical care of the health of your people, what concepts do you need to understand?

CHAPTER 8
MISSIONARY ADJUSTMENT

Important Factors

We will trace a series of themes concerning adjustment of the missionary, including (1) his early life and call, (2) deputation, (3) arrival on the field, (4) his time in service, and (5) the end of the missionary service. We will attempt to see some of the factors which can assist the missionary to have a successful ministry, and some of the pitfalls which need to be avoided.

Childhood and Missionary Call

There is no single pattern of successful early childhood training which can predict the success of a missionary, but certainly poverty is no handicap. A number of very successful missionaries, such as Hudson Taylor, Mary Slessor, and Gladys Aylward grew up in poverty. On the other hand, God worked in remarkable ways with such wealthy individuals as William Borden and C. H. Studd, who were also greatly used in His missionary service.

Strong family background is certainly a help. In my own case, my grandfather Patton's home was open to missionaries, although financially they struggled to make ends meet. His life influenced my father, who left his position as a Presbyterian minister to go to China as a missionary. His missionary career was cut short by World War II, where he, my mother and I spent 38 months in a Japanese POW camp in the Philippine Islands. My mother's health and my father's age prevented their return to China, which rapidly closed when the communists took over following the war. My father continued to work as a Presbyterian minister until his retirement, but my exposure to missions planted the seed of mission work in my heart.

My wife's father was one of six boys working on a dairy farm. They were of reformed background, but not strongly church oriented. He felt the call to overseas service, and went to China after receiving training as a physician, accompanied by his wife, who was trained as a nurse. All four children were born in China. They were chased out of China by the advancing Japanese troops in World War II, returned to the USA, where my father-in-law specialized in Psychiatry, and later returned for 10 years of service heading a psychiatric hospital in India.

The number of missionary children returning to overseas service is higher percentagewise than other groups, and often reflects the family life of the missionary on the field. We have been blessed; we spent five years overseas in medicine with our four children. God called two children to the mission field, one to Hungary, and one to Suriname. Two grandchildren are also involved in missions officially. We currently have one grandchild in Zanzibar, East Africa with his wife and child. A second is now in the process of going to South Africa with her husband and three children. A third is functioning basically as a missionary in Suriname while he completes his college degree within the next year.

Missionary Helps

Overseas Experience

Overseas experience in itself is helpful for future missionary adjustment. Of course, if the individual returns to the same field where he grew up as a child, he usually has adjusted to the culture and often speaks the language, usually with better pronunciation and idiomatic expression than his parents. But even in the case that the child ends up on a different field, the previous experience in a different culture helps the individual to be more flexible and less subject to culture shock. It appears also to be helpful to speak more than one language when one is working on learning a new language (or languages) in the field where he will be serving.

Missionary Call

The future missionary often feels "special," with a call from the Lord. The actual type of call varies greatly from individual to individual. In my own case, it was just a sense that the Lord wanted me to go overseas as a medical missionary to Africa. I first sensed this call when I was 11 years old, and although there were times that I thought of doing

CHAPTER 8: MISSIONARY ADJUSTMENT

other things, the call never really left, and at age 33, I ended up moving my family to Liberia, West Africa, where I headed up the Internal Medical department in a new teaching hospital for five years. During that time I realized that I was not saved and received Christ as my savior. After returning to the USA, I spent 10 years in a mission-oriented Christian medical group practice, and then went to Suriname, South America under Independent Faith Mission, and later under Baptist World Mission.

Bible College

In many cases, the individual will go to Bible College and receive special training in missions courses, which may assist the individual in his preparation for overseas service. It is also possible to get specialized training in the area of service before heading overseas. I thought that I might be practicing medicine alone in a remote area. I deliberately took additional training in Pediatrics, Obstetrics, and Surgery to have a broader base of training than just Internal Medicine. Then I took additional specialist training before going to Liberia. When I returned to the USA, I realized that I needed Bible training. Since I had major family responsibilities with a wife and children in Christian day school and college, leaving medicine to go to Bible College was not a very attractive option financially. Therefore, I took two correspondence courses, one from Moody Bible Institute and then the Liberty Home Bible Institute prior to going overseas.

I might mention that there are many more opportunities for training now than when we went overseas. Online training has become commonplace, especially since the COVID-19 epidemic beginning in 2020. I have been working for the last nine years as a professor of Missions and Health Care at The Crown College of the Bible. We have been expanding a variety of two-year programs in several trades (diesel mechanic, HVAC, welding, construction, cosmetology; and others are planned), in applied science, in business, and teaching. It is also possible to receive certification in different skills such as TESOL (teaching English as a second language.)

There are many advantages to having a trade or skill in addition to formal missions training. These skills may be the best way to get into a restricted country – for example, as a businessperson, a teacher, or a health care expert. English is often a key skill desired in other countries, and native speakers, especially those who speak American English, have many opportunities available. If you are trained and certified in Teaching English as a Foreign Language, many doors are open for work.

Family

Your family in the USA can be very encouraging, or they can be a problem when considering overseas service. In our situation, both sets of parents were strongly supportive of our going overseas. Other parents may be reluctant to allow their child to go overseas, not only because they do not want to lose contact with their child, but also contact with their grandchildren. They may think: Who will take care of me in my old age? Or perhaps a businessman has developed his business with the thought that his son will take over the business when he retires.

If there are major problems within the family relationships before a missionary goes overseas, this should be a warning of potential future problems. Running overseas to avoid family problems is a futile choice. The missionary will bring the problems with him. We have seen both individuals with problems with parents and problems between husband and wife creating major problems overseas. The emotional support which was previously available and enabled you to cope was now gone, coupled with the additional stresses of overseas living. Ideally these problems should be dealt with prior to going overseas.

A Strong Church

A strong church can also be a great help to the missionary, both in confirming his call and also in opening the individual to the needs of overseas service. Some churches have very active programs in missions, featuring missionary speakers, promoting missions conferences, and sending groups overseas for short term mission experience. These various opportunities to serve in your church are also great ways to assess and develop your talents and spiritual ministries while in the USA.

CHAPTER 8: MISSIONARY ADJUSTMENT

Confident of Your Call

I can speak from personal experience that it is very helpful to be confident of your call. This was true in my own life even before I was truly saved at age 36. I went overseas to Liberia at age 33 and was unsaved but religious. After I had been working a few months, I realized that several of the doctors who were under me did not really want me there. However, I did have confidence that God had called me, and that I needed to stay. (I am still amazed that I believed that God brought me to Liberia even though I was unsaved.) After more time with them, I became personal friends with many of the doctors, and had a wonderful five years in Liberia.

In the same way, I had a number of problems meet me in Suriname. But I was absolutely convinced that I was in the will of the Lord. What was of additional help was the fact that most Surinamers were also convinced that God had called me to Suriname to work with them. Therefore, when the trials came, I was confident that one way or another, the Lord would bring me through.

Although the missionary has confidence in the Lord's call, and that he has been specially chosen for a specific task, he needs to avoid pride, or the attitude that "I gave up so much to come here." Many persons in the USA had spoken to me about "giving up" material goods to come to Suriname, because I was leaving my well-paying job as an Internist. My wife and I have spoken a number of times that we feel that we gave up nothing significant. We gained much more and consider it a rare privilege to serve the Lord in this ministry. A number of times we have asked: "Lord, why were you so good to us, to save us, and to allow us to serve You here, when so many of my doctor friends are lost and heading toward a Christless eternity?"

It is important to separate out the call for specific service from the need of salvation. The apostle Paul recognized his need of salvation when he was confronted by the risen Christ on the Damascus Road. A number of years later, while the leaders of the church in Antioch were praying, the Holy Spirit made a specific call to both Paul and Barnabas as missionaries. Still later, the Holy Spirit directed them to specific locations. We see a striking example in Acts 16, where Paul and Silas were stopped from going in several directions (Ephesus & Bithynia) and ended up in Troas, where Paul saw a vision of a man from Macedonia calling for his help.

Persistence

One of the characteristics which the missionary candidate needs to develop during his training period is that of persistence. He will need persistence in deputation, in adapting to a new culture, in learning a new language, in training nationals, and especially if engaged in such things as translation work. Most of us have had challenges in our lives before going to the mission field and an opportunity to develop persistence to succeed in difficult endeavors. In my case, probably the biggest challenge was to complete my medical training although we had few financial resources. When I went overseas, I had finished 16 years training after high school, with 8 years after receiving my MD degree. Another much less demanding even in my life was in sports. I was a fairly good distance runner, but plenty of better runners were around. It took persistence to finish a cross country race and not give up. Even such simple things as sports, music, or other activities can serve to help us not to quit.

Practical Experience

Another factor which will help the candidate is some practical experience in ministry prior to arriving on the field. It is hard to visualize someone effectively winning the lost in a strange culture and language who has never done so in his own language and culture. These ministry experiences will add creditability to the candidate, and also give him more confidence that he is actually capable of doing the work.

During the eight years prior to our leaving for Suriname, my wife, my family and I were very active in our local church. We ran two bus routes as a family, an experience which was very helpful background. We all were effective soulwinners. I was active in the choir, taught an adult class in Sunday school, counseled, took correspondence courses in Bible as well as counseling, and was eventually deacon chairman.

CHAPTER 8: MISSIONARY ADJUSTMENT

All these experiences helped when we arrived on the field. It should be no surprise that when we were in Paramaribo, Suriname, we started a transportation ministry. We carried many persons in our own vehicles, and eventually hired buses to bring children and adults to church.

Selection of Candidates

In fact, there are two selection processes. (1) The candidate selects the mission board to apply to, and (2) the mission board selects the candidates whom they will approve as candidates. The selection process can be a time of stress for the candidates, especially when they come before the board.

Mission boards, of course, are interested in finding candidates who will stick it out, especially since many boards experience attrition as high as 50% during the first term. There are a few criteria that seem helpful. The best predictor was the individual's previous behavior, followed by a clear sense of God's call and motivation. The individuals should also show flexibility, adaptability and good interpersonal relationships.

One result was the fact that the more aggressive candidates did better than those who would be passively accepting the supervision of others. I might add here that it takes a fairly aggressive and well-organized individual to be able to actually raise sufficient support to go overseas.

Screening of Candidates

In terms of screening of candidates, I would like to make a personal plea. **First**, I believe that every missionary candidate should have a physical examination. Some candidates do not, although most boards require such an examination. I have had patients overseas who had to leave for physical problems which could have been screened out by a proper medical evaluation before leaving the USA. I would like to add a personal observation. One woman with significant asthma had repeated attacks in a tropical environment which was predictably troublesome. I saw a man with neck pain who had not had an x-ray of his neck before going to Liberia. A simple film showed evidence of prostatic cancer metastases to the cervical vertebrae which should have been picked up before sending him.

Spiritual Evaluation

Second, a spiritual evaluation is recommended. My father-in-law, a board-certified psychiatrist, ran a psychiatric hospital in Lucknow, India for ten years. He treated many missionaries with a variety of problems over that time, and felt that many could have been diagnosed and treated by simple psychiatric screening before leaving for overseas. He even designed what he termed a "spiritual check-up," similar to what he used as a physician to look for organic disease, but geared toward psychiatric and spiritual problems.

Because of my father-in-law's experience, before my family went to Liberia under USAID, I contacted a psychiatrist whom I trusted, and asked him to evaluate both my wife and I prior to leaving. I wanted to make certain that I was not making an irrational choice based on emotions. I should mention that I was not saved at the time, and therefore looked more to a psychiatric than a spiritual evaluation.

When we were in Liberia, I became friends with a number of physicians from the Lutheran church. After I was saved, I became aware of the fact that a few of my doctor friends, their wives, and the leadership had no evidence of what we would call being born again. The technical expertise was present, but of course the spiritual power was not.

Orientation

Most mission boards will have some sort of orientation program for their missionary candidates. Some orientation programs are short, limited to one or two weeks, while others may be several months long. I had orientation programs each time I went overseas. The first program was about 4-5 weeks long and was run by the Department of State of the United States government. It was really quite good in terms of dealing with cultural adaptation and culture shock, as well as a number of classes teaching the ropes of government policies. They also tested us for language learning ability. Theoretically I did not need any language, because the language of Liberia was English. But in terms of impact,

CHAPTER 8: MISSIONARY ADJUSTMENT

virtually all Liberians spoke Liberian English, a sort of creole mixture, and once I learned it well, my ability to communicate was vastly enhanced.

My second training period was a combination of two training programs. First, I had about 10 days of training from our former mission. Although there was a little bit of training in cross-cultural adaptation, the major emphasis was on mission policies and finances, and on deputation. Much of the information was helpful. Then my wife, my daughter and I had a one-month special course in linguistics and cross-cultural adaptation. It was intensive, a challenge to me, and a major challenge to my wife, especially since we were both 48 and out of formal education for a number of years. The linguistics program was interesting, but we were trained in recognizing and making all sorts of sounds, including such things as Bantu clicks. A short time learning how to recognize the specific sounds in Dutch and Sranantongo and to be able to accurately reproduce them would have been more helpful. However, in teaching a course for missionaries heading into a multitude of locations, it would be difficult to focus on each of several languages.

An Effective Training Program

An effective training program will include teaching the student to avoid ethnocentrism, so that the individual can better adjust to other cultures and customs. It is very helpful to be able to understand and recognize differences in culture, and also to avoid some pitfalls which can create barriers for the new missionary. I have given several illustrations in the first section of this book. For example, it is important to recognize that many cultures do not appreciate the American informality and apparent lack of respect for elders. It is possible to offend the host nationals without meaning to do so. In Arab countries, the women need to recognize what is considered appropriate behavior for a woman, which is radically different from that of the USA.

It is difficult for a mission board to be able to give country and task specific training, but this is extremely valuable. One way that I prepared myself was to purchase books on the country from the United States government. The one on Liberia was quite accurate and comprehensive, and helped me anticipate what I would find on arrival. Some boards which concentrate on working with remote tribes in primitive settings use a jungle camp as their training location so that they are able to reproduce many of the limitations which the missionary will face, including lack of running water and electricity.

There are a number of topics which can be addressed which will help the missionary tremendously. Here is one list of suggested topics:[36]

1. How do I relate to the home office?
2. How can I manage my daily living requirements?
3. How can I take care of my family?
4. What ministry skills do I need?
5. How can I be effective in my new culture?
6. How should I relate to other missionaries?
7. How should I relate to the national church?
8. How should I relate to non-Christian philosophies, practices and forces?

Financial Support

Denominational Board

Both my parents and my wife's parents were sent out under a denominational board. The board approves the candidates and their assignments, and may ask them to speak at various churches, but the denomination provides the finances involved. This arrangement allows the denomination to determine how many persons it will assign overseas, depending on the financial resources as well as the candidates which apply.

It is an advantage to be able to deploy the missionary without spending much time raising support. On the other hand, the outreach of the board may be limited because the finances are dependent on the total amount the denomination has available, and they may not be willing to spend extra for an expanding ministry. Furthermore, you usually pray

CHAPTER 8: MISSIONARY ADJUSTMENT

more for persons where you have a personal interest, which is more likely when the missionary personally raises his support.

Non-denominational Board

My wife and I went out under an independent non-denominational board. It was our responsibility to raise the necessary funds for our ministry. This arrangement has a number of advantages, but some disadvantages as well. The major disadvantage is the increasingly long time required for the missionary to raise support on deputation. It is no longer unusual for a missionary to spend three to five years raising his support. If the missionary then goes overseas for a single term of four years or less, and does not return to the field, this is a tremendous loss of time and finances. Some candidates do not speak well, or are unable to organize themselves, or have difficulty calling pastors. Such candidates are at a distinct disadvantage.

"Faith" and Deputation

On the other hand, the "faith" method has several advantages. It is not necessary for the individual to take several years. My wife and I were on the field 13 months after beginning deputation. It is a great time of learning, and a time of bonding to a number of churches which provide not only financial support, but also prayer support for the ministry. I visited 160 churches during our 13 months on deputation. The broad exposure to a number of churches was also invaluable.

Deputation is an opportunity to grow in faith, as well as dealing with a variety of different sorts of individuals and churches. The number of missionaries on the field is not limited by the finances of a denomination, and it is much more flexible in terms of raising additional funds for ministry needs after arriving on the field. When the missionary sees how the Lord provides during deputation, it is a great encouragement that He has indeed called the individual and will continue to provide for him on the field as well. It is, of course, also possible for the Lord to block a missionary from going to a field if the missionary is not truly called of the Lord. Without support funds, he will not go.

Getting to the Field

A number of different models have been proposed for the faith mission approach. Some suggest that the sending church cover the majority of the cost of the missionary. Some suggest a "team approach," with a group of like-minded churches banding together and agreeing that anyone sent from one of the churches would automatically be supported by all the churches within the group.

Usually, the sending church will send a substantial amount for the missionary but not the majority of his support. In my case, our home church gave 20% of our required support. It was helpful to get a significant move forward in terms of finances. On the other hand, we felt it necessary to resign from our home church and find another when some significant changes occurred in our home church which we felt that we could not support. Replacing the amount was not as difficult as if it had been 50% or more. The Lord enabled us to see other churches pick up the difference during a single furlough just after we resigned from our home church and arranged for another home church. Thus, we did not experience a shortfall in finances when we switched home churches.

Thought questions:

1. As you evaluate yourself, how do you evaluate your mission call, your Bible training, and practical experience?
2. Do you have the backing of your family? Are there problems there that should be evaluated in the USA before going overseas?
3. What are advantages of a faith missions programs in terms of your own desire to go to the mission field?
4. How is your church able to help you succeed in getting to the mission field?

CHAPTER 9
THE MISSIONARY AND MISSION BOARDS

One of the most important decisions that a missionary makes is whether or not he will join a mission board; and if so, which board he will join.".[37]

The board will have much to do with the sort of missionaries he will be working with. The board will help determine what type of supporting churches he has. The mission board may have quite a lot to do with the exact type of mission programs that he has. This will help determine what type of partnership he has with other missionaries.

Mission boards have been in existence for approximately 200 years. The number of boards has greatly increased in recent years, especially non-denominational boards. Denominational boards have often become liberal because many denominations themselves have become liberal. The actual number of missionaries under denominational boards has been decreasing dramatically over recent years. On the other hand, faith missions have been consistently growing.

In recent years, another option has that has become available in addition to that of the denominational mission board and faith mission board is the clearing house. The clearing house is a cheaper and simpler option to the mission board and seems to be rapidly growing in popularity among those using a faith missions type approach. I will first describe the more classic mission board, and then outline the characteristics of a clearing house. I will mention Central Missionary Clearinghouse because my son-in-law and daughter joined it four years ago after having been in two different faith missions boards for a total of 28, years.

The Functions of a Mission Board

What are the functions of mission board? Here is a list of some of the ways that a mission board may help the missionary.

The mission board seeks, examines, and approves appropriate candidates for church planting and evangelism.

The mission board investigates potential mission fields which have not yet adequately been reached to the gospel.

The mission board sets rules and standards by which the missionary can measure his work and conduct.

The mission board coordinates the work of the missionaries on the field to make the work more effective in meeting spiritual goals.

Why Should We Work Through a Mission Board?

Why should we work through a mission board? Here are some advantages of a mission agency, whether a board or clearing house.

Most governments require an organization to be responsible for the missionary. Many countries grant visas because the missionary is under a mission board, which agrees to repatriate the missionary if necessary. CMC also provides this service.

Furthermore, the Internal Revenue Service recognizes the board in terms of finances and tax-free status. The mission board can handle funds for the missionary. This is often very complex because of foreign currency, banks in other countries, delays in transfer of funds, and fluctuating exchange rates. Again, CMC also provides this service to the missionary.

The mission board may also present previously unknown fields to churches to challenge them to expand their outreach.

The mission board also gives additional accountability to the churches for the missionaries of whom they approve.

The mission board fulfills many practical functions. The board helps the missionary get into churches to present his burden. A mission board with a good reputation can be very helpful when the missionary calls the pastor.

Often the board can give suggestions as to churches to contact.

CHAPTER 9: THE MISSIONARY AND MISSION BOARDS

The mission board can help with missionary presentations.

The board can help maintain communication with supporting churches.

The mission board often helps in emergencies on the field, such as sickness, medical evacuation, deaths, hostage situations, and legal problems.

If we look at the challenge of selecting missionaries from the local pastor's viewpoint, the pastor cannot possibly screen all the missionary candidates applying to him. Thus, a good board is tremendous help. The board does the screening for him, and he may have reasonable confidence that they will steer a good candidate to his church. I spoke to one pastor about how difficult it was to contact him personally. I had never been able to get past th secretary. Finally, a friend of mine helped me to get into that church. The pastor explained that every week he gets at least fifty requests from missionaries trying to present at his church. If he personally spoke with all the missionaries, he would not have time to be a pastor anymore.

Are Mission Boards Scriptural?

Are mission boards scriptural? The apostle Paul eventually functioned like the missionary leader of a board. Paul had direct influence on these twenty-four or so additional men whom he directed throughout the known world. But Paul was really sent out by the church of Antioch and reported back to that church on multiple occasions after completing his missionary journeys. A mission board does not replace the church. The primary responsibility to reach the world is given to the local church. However, it is a very unusual church that has all the expertise which can be assembled at a mission board and the board can handle situations which might challenge especially smaller churches operating basically alone.

The fundamental scriptural justification of a mission board is to help the church and the missionary to work effectively. Ideally the mission board should be an extension of the local church and not usurp the authority of the church. Unfortunately, this is not always the case. From the beginning of the modern missions movement, there have been conflicts between the mission home base and that of the missionaries on the field. Both the "father of modern missions" William Carey and the founder of the initial faith mission, Hudson Taylor, had significant clashes with their missions from the home country. Often, the missionary will look to the mission board who is handling his finances and maintaining contact with him more than his pastor. Sometimes it is not the fault of the mission board because some churches may abdicate their primary role in missions and transfer the primary responsibility to the missionary from themselves to the mission agency. Although we have not had such conflict directly ourselves, we have seen similar situations arise.

Independent or Under a Board?

What about going totally independent instead of being under board or clearing house? When the missionary does this, he lacks the backing of a mission board experienced in meeting many problems which he never faced, or perhaps even thought about. How many missionaries think through the question of the legal aspects of having an accident a foreign country? Or what to do a hostage situation? Or what to do in a life-threatening emergency? When I had a heart attack and needed emergency stents to be implanted, I was grateful for the mission board to arrange the emergency medical evacuation. The missionary may also have difficulty finding meetings, as pastors usually want accountability.

I remember going to a very mission-oriented church. They felt that they were the sending board. A huge sign in front of the church listed all their missionaries and their mission fields. My wife and I happened to be present when they were having thek commissioning service of the previous pastor, who was now going to the field as a missionary under his church. This small church was giving partial support to well over 60 missionaries. When the new pastor gave the missionary challenge, his message suggested that mission boards were unscriptural. However, a few months later, the missionary and the new pastor had major differences in philosophy. The new pastor actually visited the field. I understand that they dropped the support of the former pastor who had become a missionary, and I believe that he left the field.

Financial Guidance Needed

An independent missionary usually lacks experience in terms of finances. It is very easy to under-estimate the amount of finances required. A mission board can help with appropriate medical insurance, often with medical coverage both in the United States and overseas. The board can help in setting up an appropriate savings plan and an appropriate budget, as well as a retirement plan. A missionary going to the field independent or with a clearinghouse would be wise to find a veteran missionary on that field who can counsel him about his support level and possibly mentor him when he first arrives.

The mission may be needed to get into the country. Most countries are reluctant to allow a missionary to come into the country unless they have some sort of income, and a guarantee that if necessary, they can afford to return to the USA. The country does not want to be stuck paying for the repatriation of the missionary. These can be very difficult problems for the independent missionary, especially if this is his first time on that field. Even though we had a missionary organization recognized by Suriname, we also had to come into the country with return tickets, which demonstrated that we had the resources to go back to the USA if necessary.

Financial accountability is necessary for a good testimony not only to the nation where we are now located, but also for our supporters. I believe that we must be very careful accounting for God's money given by God's people for a mission ministry overseas. I want financial accountability both for my own sake and for the protection of the mission. I appreciate accountability for the direction as well as the cost of the ministry. Usually, a mission will support any reasonable direction of the ministry, but the mission may help you avoid going off the deep end and making a foolish decision. Missions vary in policy. One mission organization allowed their missionaries to use missions funds to purchase a home overseas. In some situations, this may make sense, particularly if you are remaining in the same location for a long time. However, I understood that some missionaries used funds to purchase a home in the USA, which I would not consider appropriate use of money given for an overseas mission. I had one situation when funds for a building project were being used inappropriately while we were on furlough. Had I not been required to maintain careful records I would not have been aware of the situation.

I want accountability in doctrinal areas. You will want to carefully study the missions policy in terms of their doctrinal statement, and try to find out if they actually believe and enforce their official policy. There are often sensitive areas of doctrine where there is a lot of contention in the United States. Often the missionary is totally unaware of these problems. The mission board can be helpful in alerting the missionary to these situations, especially when he has just returned on furlough.

Ideally, the mission board can be helpful to your spiritual life. Our well of inspiration can easily run dry without others stimulating us. Some mission boards will make a real effort to help the spiritual growth of their missionaries. The mission representative may make regular visits, not only to see how the work is going and can be improved, but also to encourage the spiritual growth of the missionary and be available for spiritual counsel. In a practical sense, however, this is hard to accomplish. Many of the mission representatives are responsible for fifty or more missionary families, for raising more support for themselves, for trying to recruit new missionaries, and to personally visit families in multiple countries and cultures. This may be an overwhelming task, and it is difficult to maintain such a schedule and provide consistent counsel and encouragement. I found my own greatest encouragement from one of my visiting pastors who was able to sit down with me and discuss our ministry in detail.

Why Do People Go Independent?

Why do people go independent? Sometimes, they may have personal problems which led them to be rejected by a board. There may be issues of health, doctrinal stance, immorality, or divorce. Furthermore, the missionary may have had difficulty working with other missionaries. As an independent missionary, he may lack the close

CHAPTER 9: THE MISSIONARY AND MISSION BOARDS

fellowship that he needs. He may also lack legal help, representation, and accountability. Some independent missionaries may ride on other missionaries' coattails and look to them to bail them out when there are difficulties. They may arrive on the field with inadequate support and then expect others to help them financially. The pastor may legitimately raise questions in his own mind concerning a missionary going out on his own. I realize that many have read Bruchko, the story of Bruce Olson who did go out on his own as a 19-year-old with no stateside support. I would consider Bruchko as the exception rather than the rule. If you do read his story, you will also realize the great testing that Bruce Olson underwent beginning with his arrival in South America.

What about a clearing house?

A clearing house such as CMC can be a solid option to a mission board or total independence. They have a solid doctrinal position and require the missionary to abide by their position. The missionary needs to have three churches who will serve as a board to care for the missionary. These churches are to be independent Baptist churches. Otherwise, the pastor needs to submit a statement to the effect that the doctoral position of the church is baptistic. These pastors are to handle any personal problems such as moral issues, problems with drugs or alcohol, unbiblical doctrinal positions, etc. The clearing house will handle the finances for the missionary, recording gifts, sending out receipts, etc. The clearing house is usually much cheaper than the mission board. The board may take 5-10% or perhaps more of the support of the missionary One of our boards required 10% of your total receipts, including those for special projects. For the average missionary requiring about $6000 per month, the cost would be $600 monthly. Were you to raise $200,000 to buy property and build a church, there was an additional $20,000 cost! The same situation would occur if you needed a new vehicle. In one instance of which I was personally involved, a mission house burned to the ground, and the missionaries had to raise an additional 10% of the cost of rebuilding the home for their board's percentage. Another mission had a set monthly fee. This was more economical when your income was large, but more expensive if you had a smaller income. When we arranged for our support to drop to about 25% of our on-field cost when we left the field, they did drop our expenses to the mission by 50%.

CMC has also given more flexibility to other expenses, including a major cost for most missionaries, their medical expenses. Many of the missions will have an across-the-board requirement to use a certain medical insurance policy, which may prove very expensive. When my son-in-law was with his last faith mission, their cost of their medical insurance was around $1000 per month. However, there is an adequate insurance in Suriname which costs them about $1500 per year for a savings of about $8500 from the price of the US insurance. They also took out US insurance through a Christian cost-sharing group, Christian Healthcare Ministries. This group plan fit their needs better. They kept a very minimal insurance but raised the coverage during their short furloughs in the USA. During a brief visit to the USA, he went to the emergency room in the USA, and after evaluation, was hit with a bill of $10,000. When the hospital found out that he did not have regular US style insurance, they immediately gave him a 50% discount. Although my son-in-law had to initially pay the remaining $5000, When he contacted the group insurance in the USA, the insurance used the 50% discount as a way to cover his deductible cost. The entire $5000 was sent to them a few months later so that their total cost was zero. With their old USA insurance policy, they would have had a deductible of a couple of thousand dollars.

The possibility of more flexibility can extend beyond just the cost of health care insurance. CMC will allow a missionary to set up sub-accounts for special projects or funds such as furlough expenses, retirement, etc. My daughter and son-in-law have been with CMC for four years and believe that they provide all the services they need. They were able to find other organizations to provide such services as prayer letters and communication with excellent service at a minimal cost.

In terms of prayer letters, when we were first on the field, it was a great benefit for the mission board to help with communication. The board would often assist in quarterly or more frequent prayer letters. The entire process of sending out prayer letters was expensive both in terms of money and time. If we sent letters from the field, the postage was

CHAPTER 9: THE MISSIONARY AND MISSION BOARDS

exorbitant. It was still expensive even sending letters from the USA by purchasing US stamps and sending the letters with a missionary returning to the USA. To send 100-200 letters would cost between $100 to $200 each time. Now with email, these costs are minimal. One can send emails with pictures or even video clips from the field.

As mentioned above, the mission board is to be an extension of the local church, but sometimes oversteps its bounds and dominates the decisions on the field. Sometimes this occurs because the pastor abdicates his responsibilities. The structure of the clearing house, I believe, should markedly reduce this danger. Instead of having a board consisting of a dozen to perhaps thirty or more pastors, the missionary must deal with only three pastors, one of whom is from his home church. Thus, the church and two other churches are intimately involved in the ministry of the missionary. He will relate to his home pastor and the other two pastors rather than a board.

A Mission Board's Doctrinal Stance Is Vital

What are some of the considerations in terms of selecting the right mission board? The doctrinal stance is absolutely vital. There are certain major beliefs of Christians which are very important, including such topics as eternal security, the virgin birth of Christ, and the inspiration of the Scriptures. There may even be questions on what is necessary for salvation.

Our former board had let a very experienced and successful missionary go when he rejected his former belief in pre-millennialism. I believe that the board members spoke personally to him, but he would not alter his stand. These situations are sad and difficult. When you know in advance that there is a doctrinal difference, it is far better to talk over the situation to avoid future problems. Each mission has its own ideas about which doctrines are vital and important enough to separate from the missionary. Some doctrines such as the virgin birth, the death, burial and bodily resurrection of Jesus Christ, the indwelling of the Holy Spirit and the inspiration of the scriptures are without dispute in independent Baptist churches, but such things as the timing of the rapture are not.

The mission's stance on both ecclesiastical and personal separation is also very important. These issues may create tension between missionaries. They may also raise problems when short-term missionaries or visitors come to the field with different standards. When there are differences in standards between missionaries, especially in their practice on the field, this also causes confusion among the nationals. We also had problems a couple times when our standards were different from that of students coming from colleges for short-term missions. We tried to strive for consistency to avoid confusion among our national believers.

Another important consideration is the position of the board on the charismatic movement. One large mission group changed its policy to include charismatics. The number of missionaries grew dramatically, but some problems also grew. I know of a situation where one missionary returning to his home country radically changed the direction of the Bible school which he now directed. He had gone for training from a Baptist church, became a Charismatic Christian, returned to his home church, and took over their Bible school. This led eventually to a church split when he instituted charismatic teaching and practice into the Bible school and also the church where he held a prominent position.

Important Knowledge for the Missionary

If possible, it is most helpful if you have a clear idea of which country and or people group you will be working with, and also the type of ministry you believe that the Lord would have you do. Then you can check to find out if the mission board has missionaries already in that field. This is especially important to know if this is the mission you will be working under. Occasionally you may have a mission with multiple boards and no problems, but this is unusual. My original board, Independent Faith Mission, had started our mission in Suriname, Independent Faith Mission en Bijbel Gemeente. For a variety of reasons, some missionaries remained with the original mission, and others ended up joining two other missions. Despite the fact that our mission in Suriname had representatives from three mission boards, we continued to work well together, and really pretty much forgot that we were under

CHAPTER 9: THE MISSIONARY AND MISSION BOARDS

different boards. Of course, we had been working together already for many years, and several of us were from the same family.

Important Questions for the Missionary

Would I fit into the team there? Can I work with them, and can they work with me? Remember the board will have much to do with the type of missionaries with whom you have to work. If this is a new field for the board, are you prepared to open a new field?

When I was still in medicine, about five years before going to Suriname, I was already feeling the call to go on the mission field. Because I was a doctor, and further, an internist-cardiologist with a special interest in teaching, this limited my choices. I was in an independent Baptist church with an emphasis on church planting. The number of independent Baptist mission boards with medical works was quite limited. Later, when we came to Suriname, it became apparent that I would not be opening a new field completely, but that I would be opening a work in the capital city, whereas all the other works were in the bush. So, it very helpful to have some idea about where you will be going and what you will be doing.

As you consider the mission board that you consider joining, ask yourself several additional questions. Do I agree with their doctrinal position? This will influence yourself, your fellow missionaries, and also the type of churches that will be supporting you. I have found that with more than fifty supporting churches, every church has its own idiosyncrasies. One church did not accept a missionary because he had a moustache. Another dropped a missionary when he wore shorts in the tropics while on a recreational activity. If you have differences with the board before you are accepted, you can expect that this will result in problems with supporting churches in the future. I have known of situations where the church dropped the missionary, not because of his personal stance, but that the church disagreed with the stance that they perceived that the mission held.

Do I agree with their financial policies? I was shocked to hear that one missionary left our former board because he did not believe in paying taxes to the US government. He obviously had problems with their financial policies.

Missions do vary in how they approach finances. Baptist World Mission, our current board, is very strict about finances. Not only must you be careful in your finances, but everything must be documented. We send electronically scanned copies of all expenses above $75.00 per month to our home office. Personally, it has taken time to adjust to working so minutely, but I am happy to have very careful financial accounting. I mentioned above that I faced one situation in Suriname, there were financial management problems on the field while I was in the USA on furlough. If I had not been required to maintain careful records, I would not have been able to detect what was wrong and correct it. My daughter relates about the expectations of CMC concerning finances: We don't have to send them receipts because we are considered "self-employed," but we do have to send a monthly financial report which shows how the funds received that month were used—personal, household expenses, or business expenses, or held at the home office for future expenses.

All missions have administrative expenses. They vary as to how they cover those costs. Some charge missionaries for their services, some charge a percentage of the missionary's support, and some have their administrative staff raise their support in the same way that the missionaries must raise support.

Further questions include the following: Am I happy with the type of missionaries they are recruiting? Do I have the same position as the mission on separation issues? Separation issues may seem minor, but they can have long-term effects. They may determine the Bible school your children will attend and the sort of person they may meet and marry. Can I work with the administrative methods and/or administrative personnel of the mission? Are there communication problems between the field and the board? This can result in many problems. Where does the board stand on the charismatic movement? What do they feel about ecclesiastical separation? How do they react to the mega-church seeker-sensitive movement? How do they feel about nationalization of churches and national leadership? Even in a small country like Suriname, South America, I have faced all these problems.

CHAPTER 9: THE MISSIONARY AND MISSION BOARDS

How Does a Board Work With Missionaries In the Field?

Mission boards vary in the way that they work with their missionaries on the field. There are some mission boards which are board-controlled, with the board deciding which missionaries are assigned to a field and deciding what types of work need to be done. Other boards allow the missionary much more freedom to be led by the Holy Spirit. Some mission boards allow the missionaries on the field to basically make the decisions for their individual field. Some mission boards have field representatives who come regularly to inspect the field, to encourage missionaries, to make constructive suggestions, and possibly recruit additional missionaries. Note again that in theory the board is an extension of the local church, but that is not always demonstrated in practice.

What About Single Women and a Mission Board?

What is the mission's approach to single women missionaries? Some missions will not permit a single woman missionary to work alone. Others will. There is great variation in the amount of leadership permitted to women and what role is expected of the missionary wife. Another consideration for the unmarried missionary is the marriage policy of the board. What does the mission believe about marriage on the field? Are missionaries permitted to marry nationals or not?

What Are the Priorities of a Mission Board?

It is very important to understand the priorities of the mission board. For example, in my mission, Baptist World Mission, there is a strong emphasis on church planting. Baptist World Mission will study other ministries to see how they contribute to the planting of national churches. Some mission boards have very specialized outreaches. Mission Aviation Fellowship is geared to mission aviation. Other missions are geared to radio broadcasting, medicine, agriculture or teaching. How much of the priority is towards evangelism? How much is towards the training of national teachers? I had a rather broad-based ministry. I was involved in radio and television broadcasting, translation and publication, Bible Institutes, and church planting. Although I was originally involved in medical missions as well, after five years I was no longer involved in medical missions. Now I teach missions in the USA. Our mission views my activities as related quite directly to the ultimate goal of planting national churches which are self-supporting, self-governing and self-propagating.

For over nine years, I have been working at The Crown College of the Bible, where I teach many of the mission courses. I also teach a Bible course and Human Anatomy and Physiology. Because I am training future missionaries, although I am not overseas, I am still able to remain active at Baptist World Mission. Our radio and TV ministries still continue unto this day. We do provide funds for the broadcasts. For seven years, we were able to return during the summer to encourage our churches and to assist in the ministry of our son-in-law in the town of Moengo, located about two hours from our ministry in Paramaribo. The last two summers we have not returned to Suriname. However, the radio station in Moengo is running 24/7, and broadcasts much of our recorded materials, sometimes more than once per day.

Mission Boards and Supervision

Another consideration is that of supervision. A mission board may assign a field director to help challenge the work in a particular field. This director may open new areas of ministry, see what can be done to increase the impact of the ministry, and also encourage the missionary himself. I have personally found it very helpful to have a field director available when I have a difficult problem to discuss. Some mission boards basically leave all local mission decisions to that specific mission field. Of course, when you have veteran missionaries already on the field, they can take the lead in training new missionaries. They are on site and can usually be more effective than someone from the outside in terms of teaching the specifics of the country and people group to whom you are ministering.

Mission Boards and Financial Policies

What about financial policies in terms of raising support? Some missions provide all funds, and simply expect the missionary to report to some of their churches while on furlough. This is typical of mainline denominations. I remember my wife's parents had to go to a number of churches from their denomination to report to the churches and

CHAPTER 9: THE MISSIONARY AND MISSION BOARDS

encourage missions. However, their support remained unchanged. The faith mission boards require you to raise your own support, including support for your ministry. Some boards want you to simply pray the amount in, and not to mention it to others, while others allow you to ask specifically for your needs.

While it may seem simpler to accept the salary of the mission board, the board is often very limited in their financial resources. If your ministry expands and you need to build buildings, for example, you have more flexibility in raising support. As our ministry expanded, so did our financial need. We ended up building four church buildings and two houses for pastors. We recorded materials for broadcasting, published printed and audio materials, and maintained multiple vehicles. We had to pay for broadcasting on radio and TV stations.

Conclusion: Mission Boards and Support

Finally, in concluding this section about mission boards, I will make a few general comments concerning deputation, but go into detail in the following chapter. I have had the privilege of joining two different faith missions. These require that you raise your own support both on deputation and during furloughs. Many people find deputation difficult. I found it a challenge. It was an eye-opening experience. I had thought that my church was the only serious church in the area, and our way of doing things the best and most Biblical approach. I was surprised to find many churches, both large and small, who were serving the Lord effectively. I had a more balanced view of our home church but continued to have great appreciation for it.

Thought questions:

1. Which services do you consider essential for your ministry when you go overseas? Can a mission board provide them better, or a clearing house?
2. Which arrangement do you find preferable for your own situation? A mission board vs. a clearing house? Why?
3. Which preparation steps must you begin to take now before going overseas?

4. Do you see any doctrinal issues in the board or clearing house of your choice that will hinder or create problems for your ministry?
5. Are you planning to work with another missionary already on the field? Which mission board or clearing house do they use? Can you use the same one?
6. Do you anticipate any clashes in your future mission related to issues on personal issues with other missionaries?
7. Do you have a problem with your mission/clearinghouse stance on the role of single missionaries?

CHAPTER 10
DEPUTATION FOR THE MISSIONARY

Introduction

Deputation was a time to stretch my faith. There was no way that I could make the churches support us — God had to do that. I learned to be careful about judging churches and supporters. God raised up people and churches in ways that constantly surprised me. Through deputation, our prayer base grew much larger. We made friendships which are still a joy to us today. Deputation is not easy. It is indeed a school of faith. It is a time of growth. It is a time of blessings. I am grateful to have been privileged to go on deputation.

Deputation has been a major obstacle for the new missionary for many years. For the missionary with a denominational mission, deputation is usually not much of a problem. The mission board decides whom they will accept. They may schedule the missionary to speak in some churches before going to the field, and also ask him to speak to some churches on his return on furlough. However, the board usually sets up the schedule. The board provides the financial support for the missionary. He does not have to set up his own schedule or raise support. This was certainly the situation with my wife's parents who went to India as missionaries under the United Methodist board in 1961, as well as the situation for both my wife's parents and my parents under the United Presbyterian board when both sets of parents went to China before World War II.[38] The situation is dramatically different for the faith-missions missionary. Usually, he is required to make his own contacts, set up his own schedule, and raise his own support. The missionary may struggle on deputation for a number of years.

When my wife and I went overseas, it seemed as if the average missionary was on deputation for two to three years. Now that time seems to stretch on much further, often three to five years! Many consider the whole system of deputation a colossal waste of time and money. Some advocate doing away altogether with deputation. Others suggest that a group of churches meet to pool their resources, and a missionary accepted by one will be supported by all. A few have suggested placing the missionary on staff as a staff position for the church. Some faith missions depend strictly on prayer to raise support. Their needs are not mentioned. Others may seek support and inform about the needs but make no solicitation. Some will do solicitation of funds also to a varying degree. What are we to think of the current system of deputation for the faith mission board candidate?

Deputation is a School for the Missionary[39]

Deputation is not just fund-raising. Deputation is not just selling yourself. Deputation is not begging the churches. Deputation is a ministry. It is a way of transmitting a burden for a particular field to the churches involved in supporting the missionary. It is also a way of developing faith and spiritual maturity in the missionary.

Biblical Basis of Deputation

Dr. Harold C. Loucks, in *Mission Deputation: A Biblical Ministry and a Classroom of Learning,*[40] gave a very helpful analysis of deputation which put the entire thrust of deputation in another light for me. **The basic concept of deputation is one carrying out the responsibilities on behalf of another.** In this case, the missionary is God's representative to the church. He is a follower of the Lord who is joining with the church to carry the gospel to other lands. The missionary will eventually realize that the expense, time, and travel involved in deputation is worthwhile. To explore the implications of this concept, Dr. Loucks explored the relationship of a variety of different individuals in the Old Testament who were given specific responsibilities to Israel. In particular, he looked at the prophets, priests and kings of Israel to see what lessons are pertinent in their lives which could be applied to the life of the modern missionary.

The Missionary is the Servant of his Master

It is helpful to realize that the missionary is the servant of His Master, the Lord Jesus Christ. In some countries today, the ideal social arrangement is that between the master and the servant. The master is responsible to care for all the servant's needs. The servant is to be totally

CHAPTER 10: DEPUTATION FOR THE MISSIONARY

loyal to the master, and to do what is asked of him. This, of course, goes directly against our individualistic concepts of western society. Some in the USA seem to have a "Lone Ranger" mentality, or a "Rambo" mentality of the individual against the world.

But the master and servant concept is really not so far afield for a proper relationship between the believer and our Lord. Our Lord provides all our needs and promises to do so. *Psalm 23:[1] The LORD is my shepherd; I shall not want.[2] He maketh me to lie down in green pastures: he leadeth me beside the still waters.[3] He restoreth my soul: he leadeth me in the paths of righteousness for his name's sake.* He promises to guide and direct us. *Psalm 32[8] I will instruct thee and teach thee in the way which thou shalt go: I will guide thee with mine eye.[9] Be ye not as the horse, or as the mule, which have no understanding: whose mouth must be held in with bit and bridle, lest they come near unto thee. Psalm 25:[9] The meek will he guide in judgment: and the meek will he teach his way.*

A Missionary's Responsibility: Be Yielded to Him

Our responsibility is to be **totally** yielded to Him. *Romans 12:[1] I beseech you therefore, brethren, by the mercies of God, that ye present your bodies a living sacrifice, holy, acceptable unto God, which is your reasonable service.[2] And be not conformed to this world: but be ye transformed by the renewing of your mind, that ye may prove what is that good, and acceptable, and perfect, will of God.* When we yield to Him, then He can do His work through us.

Thus, God works through His man. We can say that God deputizes His person to represent Him and to do some task in His name. God's first representative was Adam. God told Adam what to do. He was to maintain the garden, name the animals, and ultimately to subdue the earth. Furthermore, God provided Adam with everything that he needed. God used other mediators. For example, Moses was God's mediator with Israel. Moses not only represented God to Israel but represented God to Pharaoh and Egypt. God calls Moses "My servant" rather than "My chosen leader." The same term "My servant" is used for Joshua, David, Jeremiah and others. Isaiah describes the coming Messiah as "the servant of the Lord." (Isaiah 42:1 ff). We often consider the title "servant" as a low title. God does not. Serving Him is the highest honor a human can have!

God's Three Specific Roles

God chose three specific roles for individuals who would represent Him to His people. (1) The prophet was primarily to represent God to the people and to communicate His commands to them. (2) The priest was to represent Jewish people to God and to pray for them and make offerings on their behalf. (3) The king was to administrate the country for God. Each individual was specially chosen and set apart for his work. Further, no single individual could hold all three offices. Two kings tried also to do the work of the priest, and both were punished by God (Saul and Uzziah). Power corrupts and having both positions was too much power for any human to handle properly.

Jesus Christ was the ultimate mediator between God and all the people of the world. He alone was able to be the prophet of the Lord, is now our high priest, and will be our King. No human could hold that much responsibility. The concept is that one in authority can choose someone to represent him in a particular task or function. The servant works in the name of the individual whom he represents. The idea is that the missionary called of God is to represent a people-group to the church in the name of the Lord. He is God's representative to God's church for that people. He is not speaking on his own or promoting his own ideas or plans. He is representing the Lord and what he believes is the Lord's plan for that people.

The Concept of Ambassador

A second concept is that the person who has been chosen (or deputed) can also transmit some of the responsibility on another in his name. For example, the king can send an ambassador to perform a particular responsibility to another nation. The ambassador is not independent; he represents the king. The king is not independent either, but he is ultimately responsible to God. *Romans 13:1] Let every soul be subject unto the higher powers. For there is no power but of God: the powers that be are ordained of God.[2] Whosoever therefore resisteth the power, resisteth the ordinance of God: and they that resist shall receive to themselves damnation.[3] For rulers are not a terror to good works, but to the evil. Wilt thou then not be afraid of the power? do that which is good, and thou shalt have praise of the same:[4] For he is the minister of God to thee for good. But if thou do that which is evil, be afraid; for he beareth not the sword in vain: for he is the minister of God, a revenger to execute wrath upon him that doeth evil.* God, who is, of course, ultimately responsible for all peoples, can transmit some of His responsibility onto the missionary to reach and serve a particular people as His representative.

We find a number of examples of this in the Bible. Moses was chosen by God to represent Himself to Egypt and to Israel. However, when Moses stated that he could not speak well, Aaron was chosen to speak for Moses. Aaron was not to speak on his own. Later, twelve spies were to be the eyes and ears of Moses as they sought out the Promised Land. And when Moses complained that the task was too heavy to bear, God empowered 70 individuals with the Holy Spirit to help him. Jesus chose (deputized) twelve of the disciples, who were also called apostles. Barnabas later chose Paul to help him. And Paul had a number of persons like Timothy and Titus who assisted him, traveling to many parts of the known world. We believe that when God gave the commission to the apostles, it was not confined to them, but was given to the church. The church, in turn, can choose specific individuals to represent herself in other lands; we call these individuals missionaries. The church is responsible to God. The missionary is responsible to the church as well as God.

Deputation is a Call to Present Needs to the Church

If we accept this concept of deputation as Biblical, then this changes the whole concept of deputation. We will see that deputation is a God-given call to present certain needs to the church. We will realize that we are responsible to present the needs clearly, as from the Lord, but that the support is really the responsibility of the Lord. We will not look at ourselves as "begging," but as fulfilling a God-given task which the church needs to hear. We can depend on the Holy Spirit to guide us, and for God to meet our needs. We can also study the lives of many whom

God had chosen to see how they fulfilled their tasks and whether or not they were faithful to their calling. We can ask the Lord to work in our lives to avoid the pitfalls we find, and to reproduce in our lives the successes of those faithful servants who have gone before us.

Lessons Learned from H. C. Loucks

I would like to highlight just a few of the lessons which are outlined in the book by H. C. Loucks. First, we see the disaster which occurred when the first man, Adam, failed in his task to represent God. He fell to the deceit of Satan, and he received a sin-nature which was passed on to all of us. Thus, as a missionary, I can learn that I need to listen and heed God's word and not try to live independent of God and His Word.

The Example of Noah

One of the striking examples of faithfulness in the days before the patriarchs is Noah, the preacher of righteousness. He faithfully persisted in building a huge ark on dry ground at the command of God. He was faithful to the task for more than a century despite the comments of those around him. Obviously, the missionary needs to be faithful to the task to which God has called him, even if others ridicule, and he should not become discouraged and quit. Noah's reward was saving his own life and the lives of his family. He also is the father of us all in terms of our human ancestry. Unfortunately, he became drunk later, and we do not find God using him further, although he lived nearly 350 years after the flood.

The Example of Abraham

Another example is Abraham, the father of faith. Abraham left Ur of the Chaldees to go to an unknown land. He believed God's promises. He offered his son Isaac up as an offering to God, who stopped him before he actually killed his son. Abraham was greatly used of God, although he lapsed in faith concerning Sarah, calling her his sister both to Pharoah and to Abimelech. We learn from Abraham that no sacrifice is too great to do the will of God. Abraham left his family and traveled to a strange land. The missionary may be asked to do the same. Abraham gave up his most cherished possession, his son Isaac. The missionary may need to be prepared to give over things which he cherishes as well. The Lord removed a nursing career from my wife, and my medical career from me.

The Example of Joseph

Joseph proved an outstanding example of someone used by others to do God's work. God chose Joseph as a young man and showed him in his dreams that he would have a special task. Joseph was also chosen a number of times by others in responsibility, including his father Jacob, his master Potiphar, and Pharoah. Joseph demonstrated integrity, loyalty, and competence. Joseph grew in faith through all the trials which he experienced and learned to trust the Lord even in the most difficult circumstances. The lesson to the missionary is also obvious. We can expect many trials throughout life. There may be disappointments and delays. But even in the delays, God is doing His work in our lives to prepare us for His tasks. We must be faithful and patient and forgive where forgiveness is needed.

The Prospect of Failure

As I mentioned previously, Moses was God's deputized spokesman for Israel. He spoke to Pharaoh in Egypt, and also to Israel for God in the wilderness. Moses was incredibly faithful to Israel. Moses also deputized twelve spies, but ten of the twelve proved unfaithful. They died as a punishment for their unfaithfulness to their task and for undermining God's plan. When the people lacked food, Moses prayed, and God sent manna to them. When the people lacked water, God told Moses to strike the rock, and water gushed forth. Later, however, Moses also failed to follow God's specific directions on a second occasion, not to strike the rock, but to speak to the rock. When Moses struck the rock in anger, God stopped him from completing the task of leading the people into the promised land, and gave that responsibility to Joshua. I look at Moses as the greatest leader in the Old Testament. The lesson here is frightening. If Moses can fail because he failed to follow God's directions in detail (even though understandably provoked by God's people), what about us as missionaries? We need to do His work His way — including deputation. We must surrender to His Word and the leading of the Holy Spirit.

Our Responsibility is to the Lord

When we evaluate the work which has been placed in our hands, we need to remember that we must allow the Lord to evaluate the worth of our endeavors. Others lack the Lord's viewpoint. Like the soldier is responsible to the one who is over him, we are responsible to the Lord, who has chosen us as missionaries. We are also responsible to our sending churches, who have deputized us to represent them. We are also responsible to our mission board, if we have one, which has taken the responsibility to provide support facilities for us in our ministry.

Examples from the Book of Judges

In the book of Judges, we find a number of lessons for the missionary on deputation. Othniel demonstrated that the Holy Spirit can come on you for specific ministry. Like Othniel, the missionary must be filled with the Holy Spirit to be effective. Ehud demonstrated that God can raise you up for specific ministry using the talents which you have received. The fact that Ehud was left-handed helped him complete his task. Shamgar demonstrated that one man can do much with the Lord's help. He simply used an ox goad. Deborah showed that ladies can have a significant ministry and service for the Lord. Gideon demonstrated that the Lord can turn small faith into great faith and accomplish great victories even when greatly outnumbered. Jephthah showed that family heritage is not a hindrance for the ministry. Samson gave a warning that there is great danger when you compromise with the world. His tremendous talents failed when he allowed earthly lusts to dominate his life and failed morally.

The Examples from the Kings of Israel

The kings give us many lessons as well. Saul was chosen and anointed by God. He began well, but then began to work independent of God. His initial role in Ramoth-Gilead was exemplary; he gave God the glory and forgave those who despised him. But as time went on, he lost faith while in a difficult situation fighting the Philistines and made an

CHAPTER 10: DEPUTATION FOR THE MISSIONARY

offering which only Samuel should have offered. He was not patient. He made a foolish vow which almost cost Jonathan his life. He failed to eradicate the Amalekites as ordered. Instead, he listened to the people and kept the best of the animals as goods when they were under the ban and must be destroyed. He failed to kill Agag, and Samuel had to kill him instead. Later, he became jealous of God's anointed choice of David. He ended up dying along with his sons at the hands of the Philistines after seeking information through the witch of Endor. The missionary is warned against self-will, jealousy, and doing things his own way like Saul did. God will not be able to bless such behavior.

David, on the other hand, shows how God can work against incredible odds in his fight against Goliath. David shows that God can use you to defeat His enemies. David shows the power of forgiveness and respecting the chosen of God when twice he spared Saul's life although Saul sought to kill him. David was exemplary to the missionary in many ways. He demonstrated courage against great odds, being convinced that the fight was the Lord's. This is a lesson we as missionaries need when faced with problems which threaten to overwhelm us. David trusted the Lord even when his life was in danger and demonstrated the power of forgiveness. We as missionaries need to forgive others; other missionaries, our nationals, and our supporting churches as well as others opposing our ministry.

On the other hand, David also warns the missionary about the danger of abandoning his duty. When he should have led Israel in battle, he remained home and ended up having an adulterous affair with Bathsheba. He tried to cover his sin by making her husband drunk, and ended up having him murdered. David's life and ministry were damaged from then on, and the effects of his sins passed on for generations. So too, we need to stick to our duty as missionaries, and be very careful in terms of sexual sins.

As we go further in the times of the kings, we see how God blessed the nation when they put Him first and obeyed His rules. We see how God chastised the nation when they went into idolatry and immorality. Although David did not engage in idolatry, his son Solomon did. David's immorality had a negative influence on Solomon, who took hundreds of wives and concubines. These women led Solomon into idolatry, which persisted in Israel until the captivity of Israel in Assyria and Judah in Babylon.

A Missionary's Trials and Temptations

The missionary must take heed not only for himself but also for his people. He will have many trials and temptations on the field. Many have fallen due to immorality. This was as big a problem in the missionary outreach in the South Sea Islands as was being eaten by cannibals. Others have fallen for idolatry, primarily placing other things before the Lord. They may seek the idols of money, position or prestige. We need to remember that the majority of the kings were poor leaders and unsaved, but that there were some shining positive examples such as Asa, Jehoshaphat, Hezekiah and Josiah. By faith, both Jehoshaphat and Hezekiah saw the Lord's power in winning great victories. We missionaries need to avoid the temptations of position, prestige, or power. We missionaries need to walk close to the Lord and walk by faith.

Examples During the Captivity

During the difficult time in the Babylonian captivity, God raised up such individuals as Ezekiel, Daniel, Esther and Mordecai. They all demonstrate how God can work even in situations where we are under foreign rule. This situation may occur also for the missionary. My own parents and I were in a concentration camp for three years. They had not chosen to be there; however, God can work in our lives in any circumstance. Their faith and steadfastness was a great example to me. Often in the darkest times, even a small light shines brightly. Daniel showed the importance of integrity, faith, and prayer. He rose to great prominence despite being a foreigner. God also uses women as well as men, as we see in the example of Esther. He may even use physical beauty if the person is totally committed to him, as Esther was, who declared: If I perish, I perish.

Examples of Deputizing in the Three OT Roles

In the Old Testament, God deputized three roles. The prophet spoke for God to the people. The priest spoke to God for the people. The king administered for God.

The King

We have considered the kings briefly above. When people think about kings, most think of money and power. The kings of the earth use earthly weapons to fight earthly battles. But for the missionary, we need to remember that we are engaged in a spiritual battle and must use spiritual weapons. We have been placed in Christ, placed in an invulnerable position if we use all the weapons He provides and stay in Him. I have outlined more details about spiritual warfare in *Issues in Missiology Volume II*.

The Prophet

We as missionaries also have roles which resemble the prophet. The prophet was the representative of God to the people, and also anointed the kings. The prophet would say to the people: "Thus saith the Lord..." Thus the missionary's speech in life should be Biblical both on deputation and on the field. Like the prophet speaks to the people for God, it is the missionary's responsibility to speak to the church for God both in the USA and on the field. He is to present his field, to preach, and to give testimony. It is the Lord's responsibility to work in the hearts of his people to work together to give the necessary support for the missionary so that he would be able to represent the church and the Lord to a specific people group.

The Priesthood

The priesthood worked as God's representative of the people and represented God to the people as he taught the people and demonstrated in his own life and in the sacrifices about the holiness of God. We need to remember that as believers, we are all priests of God, and have a representative function. Like the High Priest needed to live a holy life, the missionary also needs to live a holy life. Like the High Priest carried the names of the people on the breastplate, the missionary should carry the names of his people on his heart. We can be encouraged also to know that God will care for us. God arranged for the support of the priests so that they could accomplish their work. He will supply also for the missionary He calls as His representative.

Examples of Deputizing From the NT

As we look at the Gospels, we are first aware that Jesus Christ, as the second person of the trinity, was deputized by the Father to come to earth as the first missionary and to give His life for our salvation. Although we cannot provide salvation for others, we have a direct responsibility to bring the message of His salvation to others.

Jesus deputized twelve men who were His disciples, whom He taught intensively for over three years. Then He sent them out as His representatives, calling them apostles, or sent ones. In their time with Jesus, they saw that He was victorious over all obstacles; He performed many wondrous miracles, preached marvelously simple and powerful messages, and prayed in such a way that He was always heard.

When Jesus died, they were devastated, but then they were totally transformed when they met the risen Christ. They soon realized that He was not only **with** them, but now lived **in** them. After His ascension, the Holy Spirit now gave them the boldness to witness and the power to do what was necessary for the task of evangelization to go forward. Some have contended that Jesus gave the task to evangelize only to the apostles. This contention seems rather strange to me, because the same individuals do not make the same contention about baptism or teaching — all of which are a part of the Great Commission. They will baptize and teach even now. Then why not reach the lost? I look at this argument as a convenient excuse to avoid doing the task which God has called us to do — evangelize the world.

The Called Missionary is Empowered

Like the apostles, the missionary needs to realize that he has a calling from God, who will empower him to do what he is called to do. The Holy Spirit lives in him and will enable him to witness in the power of the living God. The disciples were so convinced that they were

CHAPTER 10: DEPUTATION FOR THE MISSIONARY

willing to lay down their lives for this truth. According to traditions of the church, all the disciples except John died a martyr's death. The reigning Caesar, Domitian, apparently tried to kill John by boiling him in oil, but John was not hurt and continued preaching. He was sentenced to prison on the island of Patmos, where he had the vision which he related in the book of Revelation. He lived on after the death of the Caesar.[41] The missionary will not usually be required to witness by his death, but that does occur on occasion. Missionaries have been captured and tortured to death, shot, and even clubbed to death and eaten by cannibals. But their work went on with great power. As Tertullian is attributed saying: "The blood of the martyrs is the seed of the church."

Called to a Particular Ministry

As we study the early church in Acts 13:2-4, the church recognized that Paul and Barnabas were the God-chosen men for a particular ministry. The church sent them out as their representatives. The church has the privilege and responsibility to identify with those whom the Holy Spirit ordains and to send them. Actually, there are two Greek words that can be associated with the church's responsibility. *Apostello* speaks about sending the person out, and *propempo* speaks about accompanying the person part of the way. We learn also that those who preach the gospel should live of the gospel. (I Corinthians 9:14) We have Old Testament examples of support for both the prophets, and especially the priests. Thus, we can have confidence that God Himself will supply what we need at the right time.

Paul carefully chose men to train. He outlined the qualifications in *II Tim. 2:[2]. And the things that thou hast heard of me among many witnesses, the same commit thou to faithful men, who shall be able to teach others also.* In the same way that Timothy was representing Paul, the missionary must represent godly churches, who send him to win souls, build up the saints, and defend the faith. We need to remember that we are under authority. God ordains and also enables the servant to do His will. The churches have a responsibility to see that the person is dependable in his work and unswerving in his beliefs. The missionary needs to remember that one day he will stand before the judgment seat of Christ. Thus, we remain focused on the cause of Christ.

Deputation is a Call to Spiritual Maturity

Deputation is a call to spiritual maturity. As we study the above examples and apply the lessons to our lives, we will mature in faith. Deputation is a school of faith in a classroom of learning to prepare for ministry on the field. Although we have already seen many examples of men used greatly used by Him, such as Noah, Abraham, Joseph, Moses, David, the prophets, and the saved kings, we have other examples of servants who were not faithful in executing their duties. King Saul was willful and proud. Eli was unwilling to control his own family, and allowed his unsaved boys to remain in the priesthood.

We should be developing spiritual maturity during deputation. As we see how God meets our daily needs as well as support on the field, our faith should grow. Not everyone will be enthusiastic in supporting our dreams. Some may even oppose them (remember Joseph's brothers). We must not allow that to discourage us but continue working together with our churches. Working together can accomplish more than working apart. We as missionaries must not only follow godly examples, but we must also set a godly example for others to follow.

Deputation is Ministry

Once again, we must remember the deputation is ministry. We do not desire a gift for ourselves, but we desire fruit, that it may abound to the account of the churches. We must remember that deputation is a person or people representing others. Before Nehemiah left on a deputation to Jerusalem, the burden showed on his face. The king of Babylon was able to see his burden. Does our burden show on our faces? Do we transmit our burden to the churches we are visiting? The missionary is not primarily to present himself, but his call, his field, and his burden. However, who you are, and what you have done, does demonstrate that you are truly a servant of the Lord.

World Missions is the Heartbeat of God

World missions is the heartbeat of God. If God has called us, we are doing His work as His servants. The master of the servant was responsible to care for his servant. We do not need to focus on raising support. Focus on ministering and allow God to raise the support. The support that God raises will continue because God Himself raised it up.

In summary, deputation is a school in which God has many things to do in the heart of the missionary. There are many spiritual lessons to be learned while on deputation. We must learn to walk by faith. We must learn that God does supply. We must learn to have a more personal relationship with the Lord. We must learn to transmit a prayer burden for our people to our supporting churches.

Small or Big Church for Deputation

I would like to relate one experience of many which shows that God's power and knowledge far exceeds ours. When I attended a meeting of pastors, one pastor asked me to present our ministry at his church. He even asked: Do you go to small churches? Indeed, the church was small. They started our support at $25.00 per week. However, that church developed a tremendous burden for our field when a new pastor came to the church. Their men made mission trips to Suriname. One of their men came three times with a team from the church, and then a fourth time himself, and a fifth time with his wife to celebrate their 50th wedding anniversary. They developed close relationships with some of our people. When I would report back to that church, the men would ask me all sorts of questions about specific persons in our Suriname churches. They gave generously, and at one point, they actually gave the largest amount of support of any of our churches to our ministry. God knows the future, and He arranges us to go where He supplies our needs, to His glory. That church is now the home church of our son-in-law and daughter. Their support has been incredible and is extending to one or two of our grandchildren.

Thought questions

1. How does this description of deputation challenge your thoughts about your responsibility to raise support vs. God's promise of supply?
2. What role of God's three primary roles of His servants did you find personally the most challenging?

3. A number of Biblical lessons were outlined in this chapter. Which is the Lord challenging you to undertake in a new way?
4. After studying the use of deputation in the Bible, are you more encouraged about the entire process of deputation as a ministry for the missionary?

CHAPTER 11
PREPARATION FOR DEPUTATION[42]

Scheduling meetings
Meet with Your Home Pastor

After you are certain of your call to missions, you should meet with your home pastor. He is a key to your successfully getting on the field. Your sending church and your mission board are very important. You will greatly benefit from the support of both of them. The pastor will want to speak with you to discern your call, as well as the appropriate time for you to go overseas. He will know about your spiritual preparation for missions and can advise you. He may also advise you on a particular mission board or give a selection of boards that he might recommend.

When my wife and I joined our home church, we pretty much knew that sometime we would go back overseas. But we did not know the timing of our departure, or where we would go. At that time, I was convinced that I would use my medical training in missions. When our sending church held a mission conference, during the challenge, both my wife and I wondered about going back overseas. Our four children were in high school and doing well. My practice was doing well, and I was deeply involved in the ministry of our church. I was the deacon chairman, a bus captain, adult Sunday school teacher, choir member, and the counselor for the church. Our pastor said that he expected us to go overseas, but he thought that it would be wiser to wait until our children were through high school. He was right. Five years later, after our youngest child had completed a year in college and our oldest two girls were married, we went overseas with our youngest daughter joining us as a single missionary. A year later she married, and returned to Suriname with her husband, where they have served the Lord for more than thirty years.

If you are attending a solid biblical church with a solid pastor, I would hesitate to go against his well-considered advice. If he has objections, I would look at them very carefully and not simply ignore them. The same consideration should be made from a mission board, if you are going under a board. Someone I know well was advised to wait and get additional experience before going overseas. That advice helped them avoid what would have proven a real disaster. There may be personal considerations, financial considerations, family situations, or additional training which would be helpful — and the delay to meet those situations will be worthwhile.

When you meet with your home pastor, there are number of questions that you should ask. What are the mission policies of the church, and who decides who are supported? If there is a missions committee in the church, who is the chairman? How often and when and where does the mission committee meet? What does the church expect from a missionary candidate? What type of qualifications do they expect for candidates? What application procedures does the church have for missionaries from its membership? What is the support amount by the church? Are there any deadlines involved?

Your pastor will also be able to help you find opportunities to present your needs in a variety of ways. Perhaps you will have an opportunity to speak in Sunday school, Sunday services, youth activities, midweek services, retreats, vacation Bible schools, women's meetings, or other meetings within the church. In addition to the contacts of the home pastor, I was fortunate to have two evangelists who used our home church as their own home church. Both were most helpful in giving me additional contacts. Each of them also gave me a recommendation. I might mention that one of them grilled me before giving any recommendation to make certain that I was going as a church-planting missionary and not just as a medical missionary. He has remained a good friend and even came to serve us as an evangelist for ten days in our churches in Suriname a number of years ago.

Your Home Church

Be certain to use all your contacts which are appropriate. After you have met with your pastor and have given him your vision, your church should be prepared to support you as a candidate. Your pastor may have

CHAPTER 11: PREPARATION FOR DEPUTATION

many valuable suggestions and may also help you gain support both inside and outside the church. My home pastor was a tremendous help. He gave several suggestions which were most helpful in terms of my deputation presentation. He told me to develop a presentation and then illustrate it with appropriate slides instead of having a slide show with a loosely attached presentation. I had been very heavily involved in the ministry of our home church, and he recorded a three-minute recommendation with illustrations of our ministry to be used during the presentation. Thus, he was recommending me, and I did not need to explain my current ministry involvement. I wrote out my presentation and read it into a recorder, and then timed slides to accompany the presentation. This has been basically replaced by videos, most of which are between five and ten minutes long. However, multiple length presentations are often useful, with presentations for different purposes depending on your venue. My colleague Bob Rasmussen had a separate longer presentation involving his children which included the animal life and interesting foods of Suriname. They used it especially for Sunday school for children.

Here is a comment from my daughter from Suriname: We have found it very helpful to have three different lengths of our presentation to use depending on the situation. Our shortest was 10 min. and rarely used. ☺ We had a 17 min. one that we used most of the time and a 26 min. one that Ethan used when he had the whole Sunday school hour—would show the long presentation and have Questions & Answer. If you figure that one of your major goals is to get the people to gain a real burden and understanding of the field, then the more details you can give in churches where the pastor isn't "constrained" by time is helpful. We made our longest presentation first, and then omitted sections that were interesting and helpful but not "essential" to cut down to the shorter lengths.

In addition, my pastor gave me a number of contacts. He wrote a general letter of recommendation for me, but also a personal letter to each of his contacts. We worked out a system where I would mail this letter to a prospective pastor, wait approximately a week, and then call the pastor shortly after the letter arrived. I was able to present our ministry in most of the churches which my pastor recommended. I believe that he called a few friends as well. Now most people prefer email contact, but the principle is the same. Personal contacts make a great difference, and our pastor helped me get into a number of supporting churches.

Contacts

There are many sources of contacts. Your pastor may have personal friends. If you have attended a Christian college, that is an excellent source of contacts, and often they will provide a list of alumni, which is very helpful. I looked at churches advertised in several Christian news magazines. The mission board may also have contacts, although naturally they are happiest for you to find new contacts. If you join a mission, you might contact the various mission board members.

Another possibility is to accompany your pastor or another pastor friend to their pastors' monthly meetings. I went to one meeting, and of the eleven pastors present, I was able to schedule nine meetings, several of which ended up being supporting churches. I also offered to speak in chapel at Christian schools; they are often happy to have an outside speaker. They will usually provide a meal and may give a small love offering. While eating after the meal, the pastor asked me to speak to the church, but we were close to the end of our furlough and could not do so. But that would have been a great contact.

I had the opportunity to speak in several Christian colleges as well; perhaps because a medical specialist leaving his medical practice to start a church-planting ministry was a bit unique. These opportunities are especially helpful between meetings and may provide food and/or housing. Remember too that sometimes your contacts may not yield fruit initially, but they will later. Those men who are students today will be pastors in the future. My son-in-law was also directly supported by a Sunday school class in a large church where he spoke. A few times we were placed in a home when presenting to the church. The church did not support us, but the family of our hosts did.

It is not easy to find enough churches to support the missionary going overseas. Most fundamental churches had three services per week when I started on deputation more than 30 years ago. They would usually have a mission conference once a year, often lasting a week. This is no longer the case. Some churches are doing away entirely with Sunday

CHAPTER 11: PREPARATION FOR DEPUTATION

night services and/or Wednesday night midweek services. They may be replaced by small group meetings, or simply cancelled. Some will have two services on Sunday back-to-back, with a pause for lunch in between services. On my most recent furlough, I had great difficulty finding any church with a Sunday night service in the Washington D.C. area. Our deputation was 13 months long. I was able to get into 160 churches during that time despite being on call as a doctor every fourth weekend for almost the entire year. That would be much more challenging now.

Many missionaries are finding the majority of their support from personal contacts rather than from churches. If you are going to work on raising support from personal contacts, one effective method is to place the 10 best contacts on a list. These may be from work, school contacts, family or personal friends. As they are positive, remove them and put new people on. We were asked by a missionary from Missionary Aviation Fellowship to join their support team. This was long before the most recent changes in church services. They had "shares" in their ministry for $10/share/month and asked us if we would consider taking one or a few shares.

Look for prayer support, interest, and financial capabilities. An initial prayer letter is also helpful. Give a brief summary of your life up to date. Be careful to share burden for the field. Mention that you must raise your own support, and speak about your mission board. You can provide brochures including information about the field and country, support letters from others, and a letter from the mission board about your ministry.[43, 44] There are a number of books referencing this type of personal ministry. A number of mission agencies have been using this approach for some time.

What about using contacts in a church to get support individually? I would be cautious about asking individuals in a supporting church for support. The pastor may not be happy with you soliciting support outside their mission program. In our days, soliciting individuals was unusual. We did have personal support, but ours was not solicited. Individuals approached us and took us on. Some missions seem concerned that individuals are not as reliable as churches, but that was not our experience. We still have had personal supporters on occasion for over thirty years. We did have a few friends support us whose family situation changed after the death of a spouse. In those situations, we had written telling them not to feel obliged to continue support, and at least one wrote back thanking us for our understanding.

A grandson went with a mission which focuses primarily on individual support more than church support. I was skeptical, but he raised his support in under nine months, and has been serving in Zanzibar. I noted that he had come back a year plus later, partially to solidify his support. His mission recommended the best single book that I have found thus far is *The God Ask* by Steve Shadrack, CMM Press, 2013. Their system is well thought out, answers most questions one might have, and challenges the individual to work hard on organization and aggressively make appointments. His system requires a lot of hard work. Remember that your full-time job is to get your support. You should put in 40 hours a week making calls, appointments, scheduling meeting with friends and presenting your ministry.

Setting up Appointments

Set up appointments to meet with potential supporters. Try to set up a definite time to meet. Prepare carefully. Dress neatly and be clean. Pray much. Present your ministry clearly and concisely. Know what you need. Answer all questions concisely but accurately. After meeting, write down all information immediately. If you happen to have a good relationship with the individual, especially a pastor, ask for referrals to others as well.

Do not be overly discouraged when people cancel. This may be Lord opening a door for better meeting or better contact. This is true for church schedules as well as personal appointments. I had a pastor cancel me for Wednesday meeting on that Monday. I called a supporting pastor for suggestions. He recommended one man, and my wife and I went there for the Wednesday service. Not only did they take us on for support, but the man and his wife remained dear friends for many years, and they opened other doors for ministry in a Bible college as well. Over thirty years later, although we are now in the USA, the church continues to provide some support to help our radio and TV broadcast expenses in Suriname. My daughter related similar experiences: Several times we have gained support from a "filler

CHAPTER 11: PREPARATION FOR DEPUTATION

meeting" after a cancellation including the church in Tampa, FL that was arranged by another pastor the night before our meeting. They took us on for support and an individual in that church donated $10,700 toward our radio towers. Ethan never just "accepts" a cancellation without making a real effort to fill that service. ☺

Planning and Organization

Be well organized. Keep good records. Many people use one of many programs available for computer, or a telephone or personal organizer. Thank your supporters. Keep in contact. Work on developing friendships. If your church has a monthly newsletter, or if it has a radio broadcast, these are other possibilities to present your ministry. You may gain other contacts through your schoolmates, and through your mission representatives. This can occur either by traveling with him, or through contacts that he may have. Sometimes it is necessary to make visits to pastors before you can be scheduled. Tell the pastor that in six months you'll be in this area and would like the chance to present your burden.

I was impressed by a young Filipino couple when I was on furlough several years ago. I was scheduled to present our ministry and to preach. This couple drove two hours to the church to attend the midweek service and meet the pastor. When we went out to eat after the meeting, he included them with us. The young man had an opportunity to present his burden for his country and was able to schedule a meeting at the church, which might have been impossible if he were not so enthusiastic.

The Importance of Communicating

Be faithful in your communication with pastors and personal supporters. I worked very hard to get into as many churches as possible. Because I was in private practice of medicine, my situation was a bit unique. My normal workweek prior to deputation was 55-60 hours per week. During deputation, I dropped my medical work schedule down a bit, but was still working more than 40 hours per week in addition to deputation. I tried to schedule three speaking engagements or more per week. We started as soon as my youngest son started college, and most of the time, I traveled just with my wife. My youngest daughter, who was called to Suriname just before her last year of college, went to Suriname with us. She accompanied us on some of our trips if they did not interfere with her college schedule.

The Importance of Scheduling

Ideally, I scheduled the Sunday morning church farthest away so that I could drive there on Saturday. Then the evening church I tried to put closer to my home base to allow me to drive part-way home in the afternoon. I cancelled my clinics on Monday morning, Wednesday afternoon and Thursday morning to allow time to drive to meetings and then back home. Although I still had in-patients and a busy practice, as well as being on call every fourth weekend, I was able to schedule 160 churches in 13 months, and then left directly for the field. I made a circle about 250 miles from home (four to five hours drive) and tried to keep most of our meetings within that radius. We did make one trip east where we had a number of personal contacts and picked up several churches on that trip. We made one trip south in conjunction with a month-long course in linguistics, and I was able to fill virtually every Sunday and Wednesday during that course. I was still on call as a doctor every fourth weekend that year. Because it was difficult to schedule churches on certain holidays, I volunteered to take medical call on Christmas, Easter, and Mother's Day. My partners loved my weekend schedule!

Although the church schedules are different now, the basic principle is the same. Work hard. Schedule as full as you can within the framework of your family. It is important to have a long-term view and think about your furloughs. If your churches are scattered across half of the United States, your furlough will be spent largely on the road. I tried to consolidate my locations as much as possible. When several supporting churches are in the same area, it gives much more flexibility when you are scheduling your return visits during furlough. Because it is expensive to eat out and stay in a motel, I looked especially for churches with prophet's chambers where we could stay for a few days or perhaps one to two weeks. We were able to buy our food much more cheaply than always eating out and did not have any cost for overnight

CHAPTER 11: PREPARATION FOR DEPUTATION

accommodations. On at least two furloughs, we were able to set up a series of prophet chambers so that we would visit two or three churches from each area. We rarely paid for overnight housing.

You may use a pocket organizer, a computer program, or other method to keep track of your appointments. Record your schedule promptly, and have a hard copy of your schedule. In terms of speaking, be prepared to speak in several areas. It is vital to remember to stay within your given time limits. Be prepared to teach on faith promise missions. You may be asked to speak in Sunday school, to other groups, and sometimes at the spur of the moment.

Do not be lax in pursuing meetings. Remember that supporting churches are supporting you to do your missionary work, and that includes scheduling meetings. One mission director told a future missionary, when you are on full-time deputation, you are to work full-time. You worked forty hours a week on your secular job. You need to work forty hours a week now, especially on scheduling meetings and preparing for them.

Organize Your Time

One of the adjustments when you do go on full-time deputation is to organize your time effectively. This is one area which the missionary must be careful to develop. You must learn to discipline yourself without someone else determining our schedule. We also have an opportunity to spend extra time in God's word and prayer to solidify our spiritual life. It may take as many as ten calls to get a single meeting. Stay at it. Sometimes a pastor will set you up with other pastors. I called a pastor who was a good friend about meetings in Florida. He gave me two numbers and told me to call them about an hour or so later. In the meantime, he called both men. I got both meetings. Another pastor taught in a night school for a pastor of a large church. I had tried for years to contact that pastor without success. This pastor arranged for my wife and me to go to lunch at Cracker Barrel with the other pastor and himself, and even paid for our lunches. That pastor told me that he gets at least fifty calls per week from missionaries. They had to build in a strong screening program. Routinely they sent a questionnaire, and then might contact the missionary on basis of what was written. We were able to present on a Wednesday night at that church as well. By the time I was there, I was no longer actively seeking personal support, but we have been able to use their prophet's chamber since then.

These principles also are true for seeking support from individuals rather than churches. Both are worthwhile. The advantage of working with individuals is that you can make more contacts than with churches. Usually with churches you are limited to church services, including weekly services, missions conferences, or special meetings. You want to schedule as heavily as possible. When meeting with individuals, you may have more opportunities. Often the missionary will drive into an area where he has several potential personal supporters and stay for a few days. He might see one person for breakfast, another for lunch, one in the afternoon, and one at night. The advantage of individuals is that you are not limited by the schedule of churches.

My own thought would be to use both. Even thirty years ago we were advised to seek personal support, although not so aggressively. I did pick up several individuals. Our single lady missionaries have the majority of their support from individuals. Many churches are reluctant to support a single missionary lady. However, I do believe that the task of world evangelism is given to the church, and we should not bypass the church and rely simply on individuals. From our experience, both churches and individuals are usually faithful in supporting missionaries long term.

Adequate Support

Adequate support on the field is extremely important. Take the necessary time to get adequate support. I recommend that you ask God to show you a date for departure, and once you know that for certain, tell everybody that date, to pray much, and be constantly scheduling. My good friend Dr. Bob Schindler, now with the Lord, gave me that helpful advice when we started on deputation. I followed it, and God supplied. Dr. Schindler gave the same advice to my daughter and my son-in-law. Her comment: He asked us when we were leaving for the field and we told him, "We hope in a year...." He said "what do you mean you hope? You pray and then do what the Lord shows you."

He had been on deputation for a number of months and in April, his support level was about 50%. He told people that he was leaving in August and made plans to do so. He even scheduled his flight to Suriname. He had heard the Lord correctly and left on schedule with full support. Her comment: we learned of our last supporting church when we were in Florida preparing to leave. We arrived on the field exactly one year and one day after our first deputation meeting—only because there was no flight on our "one-year" anniversary.

Using the Telephone

Plan on using the telephone for scheduling meetings. I have made many hundreds of telephone calls. Only a handful of people have ever responded just to a letter. There are certain basic principles to use when making telephone context. Always be polite and have a good attitude. Keep complete records. Record the pastor's name, address, phone number, date and the time of the meeting, and the pastor's e-mail address. Also, record any special suggestions or requests. Confirm by writing within two weeks. Carry your cell phone with you at all times. The last years that I was in Suriname, I actually preferred to call from Suriname using Skype on my computer. It was quite inexpensive to do so, and made an impression, since most missionaries were from the USA rather tha calling from their field making an international call. Unfortunately, it was not cheap calling to Suriname from the USA.

I spent a significant amount of time preparing my telephone conversation. I worked on getting the key information to the pastor in two-three minutes so that he could decide if he wanted to pursue our conversation further. I tried to give enough information on the phone so that he would know my mission board and my basic goals. I gave a bit about my background, including my time in concentration camp with my missionary parents; I mentioned leaving a lucrative position as an internal medical specialist, our goals, and dates which were open for us to come.

I also prepared a sharp portfolio and mailed it to the pastor on the same day of our conversation. However, I would no longer suggest a portfolio. Most pastors prefer email or digital contact for your materials. Some individuals have really exploited the possibilities with setting up their own website, providing their video presentation online, and even their calendar as well as recommendations. In today's digital world, shorter is usually better.

Talking with the Pastor's Secretary

I might also mention that many pastors use their secretaries as screeners to prevent them from being overwhelmed by calls from missionaries. The pastor does not want to be unkind. I have found that it is very wise to be extremely courteous to the pastor's secretary. I will often give enough information that they themselves become interested in our ministry. The secretary is often the key to being able to reach the pastor effectively. I have had the secretary "on my side" in several cases and she has made extra effort to help me get through to the pastor. But ultimately, you will need to talk directly to the pastor, or to whomever he has assigned to make these decisions.

Specific Financial Planning

It is also important to have financial planning. Get information from your mission agency over the cost of passage, shipping, and customs, including return passage costs if required by the country. Many countries want a guarantee that someone will pay the cost for your repatriation if necessary. Learn about the costs of a vehicle and cost of household goods. Also, when you are on deputation, it is best to have a decent car, care for it and sell it and use that as part of your vehicle fund. Do the same with your household goods, unless it is very difficult to find things at your new location. One new missionary came with a twenty-foot container (paid for by friends) with beds, bikes, books, and all sorts of things. I wonder what the nationals thought. By the way, his family stayed less than a year.

In planning for your deputation, often you will want to keep some sort of job initially. Schedule your deputation meetings in an area where you live, a distance which you can drive back on a Wednesday or Sunday night and still get back to your job. As the support builds, the time will come when you can go full time. I worked full-time as an internal medical specialist until about six weeks before departure. Because I was in private practice with a group which had a number of missionaries in the group, they allowed me to flex my schedule to permit me to go to churches both on weekends and Wednesdays. The extra income was very helpful in raising funds for overseas shipping, including a twelve-passenger van. However, each individual should pray and ask the Lord for His guidance. The sooner that you can go full time, the faster you will get to the field.

How Many Meetings Are Necessary For Funding?

It is also possible to get an idea of approximately how many meetings you will need to schedule. We went on deputation in 1985 with a projected support was approximately $2500 per month. Of course, 36 years later, the costs have risen considerably. At that time, the average church was supporting from $40-50 per month (when we left the field 26 years later, our average support was twice as high). On the average, our mission estimated that approximately 25% of churches would take their missionary on for support. In my own case, when I left for the field of Suriname, I was supported by 42 churches of the 160 churches I visited. My son visited 200 churches and was supported by 72, or 36% of churches. However, many of his meetings were with smaller churches and smaller offerings so that the total amount was about the same as ours. My daughter and son-in-law gained <u>36 churches out of 165 meetings.</u>

Thus, if you anticipate approximately $50 per month as the average support level, and 25% of the churches will take you on, then on the average you can expect about $12.50 of support per church visited per month. To raise support for $2500 per month, this would require approximately 200 churches. Of course, you may have some exceptional churches which give much more than the normal, and you may have additional support from personal supporters. This was very similar to the experience of my son, who went to Hungary about five years later.[45] Today's figures will be higher, but the basic principles remain.

When I checked with Baptist World Mission in 2020, the figures were indeed substantially higher, but the number of churches needed remained about the same. The average church support was about $125.00 per month, and the normal requirement for many fields was about $6000.00 per month

We had 100% support just before we left. It was difficult to schedule more than 12 to 14 churches per month. However, I was still working as a full-time physician, and although I was on call covering my partners' internal medical practice every fourth weekend, I was still able to visit 160 churches in 13 months. It helps greatly to begin scheduling several months before actually beginning deputation. Both my son and I were able to get off to an excellent start on deputation by scheduling meetings several months in advance so that we had a full schedule from the beginning of taking meetings.

I am adding my daughter's note: Ethan (my son-in-law) started scheduling meetings his last semester of college so that our first meetings began as soon as we were approved by our board. Of course, he had tentative approval from the director to schedule before meeting with the board. Otherwise, it would have taken us at least six more months to really get going on deputation. I have heard of some young couples joining a board their last semester of college (some while engaged before marriage) so that they could be "ready to go" as soon as they graduated and got married. I'm not sure I would recommend starting deputation immediately after marriage, but some do it. (Kim and Ethan Champlin had married the June before his senior year in college).

The individual who schedules only one or two meetings per week is in for a long deputation. Of course, it is necessary to consider the limitations of your family. It may be difficult to pack your schedule like our three families did, especially if you have several small children. I remember seeing one family with four small children. They had to be at one church Sunday morning after staying overnight at someone's house. The children were all neat. After church, they went out to eat with the

CHAPTER 11: PREPARATION FOR DEPUTATION

pastor. Then all the children were packed into the car and off for a few hours ride to another location. The children were to be on their best behavior, although perhaps they had no naps or chance to play. Then they heard the same presentation and sermon as in the morning. Finally, after eating after the service, it was a long trip home. There is a limit to how hard you can push your family and your wife in these situations.

The Need for Housing on Deputation

It is also important to seek housing while on the road. We tried to locate prophet's chambers in various locations, and then worked out of them as a base. We were able to save considerable money in terms of housing and food between meetings. This is an additional advantage of scheduling at schools and colleges. It is helpful to try to schedule when the church is having mission conferences. There is often a better than normal chance of support, even if you cannot be there for the entire time. I can think immediately of two places where I was only able to be present on a Friday night of a mission conference. Both churches took us on for support. In fact, when seeking support, my general policy has been to avoid being tied to a mission conference for the entire time.[46] We have gone rarely, usually if the pastor insists on our staying the entire time. I have given up some conferences, because the pastor wanted us to either come for the entire time or not at all. If possible, I try to schedule additional times in other churches. Of course, it is helpful to have a mission conference cover your food and lodging expenses for the entire duration of the conference. My son Marc Patton had a similar experience. He analyzed the statistics of going to missions conferences versus going to several churches during the same time. His results are in the addendum which is included in this book. He concluded that one could usually do better by going to multiple churches versus spending an entire week, or even Wednesday through Sunday, attending a missions conference. He also tried to go just for the meeting days in the middle of the conference.

Preparation for Your Presentations

I am including my original description of what to have for communication on deputation. However, now much is digital, and has pretty much replaced paper. Still, clarity, neatness, and concise materials are important.

You need to have a quality presentation for effective deputation. When we first began on deputation, there was no internet. Written communication was by letter. Thus, I advised the following: Begin with well-prepared, well-printed stationery. A good, personalized letterhead is better than using the standard missionary stationery. The letter should include the return address of the missionary, his field of service, his home or sending church, the name of the pastor, his mission agency, and the mission agency address. The prayer card should have the same information. It is best to have a four-color professional photo printing. It's good to have a verse. First impressions are important. I believe that it is also good to avoid having so much material on the card that it appears cluttered. Now of course email and electronic illustration and communication is standard, but the principles of neatness and clarity remain important, and give a professional appearance.

I now ask the students to call their pastor to request what methods they prefer for communication. Almost 100% prefer email to written letters. One even stated that it is safer to use email, because written letters can be lost or forgotten, but email is easier to access. All the pastors make the same statement about prayer cards. All advise not to clutter up the card. The missionary's name, the mission board, the field, and the basic type of ministry are important. It is also important to give information as to where to send any funds. On at least one or two occasions I found that our funds were sent to the account of another missionary. This is particularly likely to occur when the church is supporting multiple missionaries from the same location.

A Field Brochure

It is also helpful to have a field brochure. Ideally it should be printed in color. It is good to have an outline map of the country, and something that symbolizes the culture and the country. Include a picture of the missionary family. A brief description of your sending church, where you went to Bible College, and a brief background of both husband and wife are helpful. Initially I would send this brief information in my information packet. However, now I believe that a website would be ideal. You could put a link into your email letter to the pastor for easy access.

A few pictures of the country and a brief explanation with information are also useful. In the field brochure, include information on the people, culture, customs, cost-of-living, problems to be faced, and plans to meet the needs of reaching the people. Have well laid-out plans. Some have written the philosophy of ministry and missions. List your goals and plans to meet those goals. Again, be clear and concise. Avoid clutter.

Now I would certainly go digital. I would have a website with information on the field. I would include a link to my personal testimony and recommendations from my pastor. I would have a link to go to my mission board or clearing house if I have one, and ideally one or more links to the country itself. I My brochure which I sent more than thirty years ago had a lot of information, probably too much even then. By using a website, you can make all access quick and easy, readily available, and not overwhelming. The interested person can then dig into the information if he is really interested.

It is also feasible to put your video presentations available for the pastor to review. My daughter made a significant comment. They put their videos on a private channel on YouTube. That way it did not appear on a search engine. Their concern was that perhaps something would be considered negative in the eyes of some nationals, and this gave a bit of privacy by restricting the views to the pastor.

Items Representing the Field

If you have access to some small items representing the field, that is ideal. One of the missionaries to the interior of Suriname was able to catch a tarantula and a scorpion and encase them in plastic. One of the typical curios from Suriname is a mounted piranha. I cannot count the number of little fingers of children who feel the teeth of the fish to see if they are really sharp. (They were at first, although ours were now dulled by hundreds or perhaps thousands of little fingers feeling them.) We also had a small kaiman (a small species of alligator) on display, along with some wooden items. My son-in-law had samples of cassava bread (I thought that it was pretty tasteless) available for children to sample.

Equipment Needs

DVD Projector

In terms of equipment, most people now use a laptop and small speakers. In former days, most missionaries used slides, but now most missionaries are showing video presentations using a DVD projector or computer. Most churches have their own equipment for multimedia projection, but some smaller churches do not, and if you are presenting to a smaller group, such as a Sunday school, you may want your own equipment. Your own equipment also serves as a backup in case of some technical problem with the church's equipment. When I went to a mission conference in a large mission-oriented church, I was scheduled to speak in a small conference room in their basement. Although the church had great equipment for the auditorium, I was most grateful to have my equipment for the basement room. The church did take us on for support and later even printed our Sranantongo Bible, which is now in its fifth printing.

I would suggest getting a projector with sufficient lumens to project even in daylight, at least 2000 lumens or above. It is difficult to get a church room dark, especially in a morning service. The price of projectors has dropped incredibly. When my first one was purchased, it was nearly $3000. The same quality projector is now below $400, and by the time you read this, the price may have continued to drop. Usually it is successful to use a wall, or a larger church may have its own screen. I did carry a screen with me, but would not recommend it; I did not use it enough to justify its occupying so much space in our car trunk.

It is very helpful to have your own extension cord with various adapters and outlets. I have an extension cord with three outlets far enough separated so that I can put in three different plugs which have a safety third prong. I use my computer not only for presentations but also for PowerPoint presentations, e-mail, etc.

Direct Box Connection to PA Systems

CHAPTER 11: PREPARATION FOR DEPUTATION

I also bought a direct box connection which can connect directly into most PA systems, along with a 25-foot audio extension cord as needed. I was given a direct box which also had a volume control on it; this has proven very helpful, because I have control over the volume, even when using the PA system of the church. If the church has someone in charge of their audiovisual equipment, he is usually most helpful.

Spare DVD's, Speakers, and Extension Cords

Have a few back-up DVDs or flash drives of your presentation. If you happen to leave them in the church projector system, you don't have to turn around and drive back. This is very disconcerting, especially if you need it for a Sunday night service and you left it after the Sunday morning service several hours drive away. Have I done this? Yes, but fortunately had a spare. I have also had requests from pastors or persons in the audience for a copy, and I am happy to give them one. I also carry small speakers with a volume control which can be hooked up into my projector. In some situations, they have proven a lifesaver, especially in rooms with no PA equipment such as Sunday school rooms. With an extension cord with three outlets which are usable, then I can plug in my projector and, if necessary, my sound system.

Now I would consider that flash drives have pretty much replaced DVDs. The flash drives with small capacities are adequate for your presentation or presentations (if you have more than one), and you can leave one behind if necessary. If you have the presentation on the computer or website, you have an additional backup. Here is an additional comment by my daughter: We also had our DVD presentation on both DVDs and flash drive, depending on which a church preferred. **The digital file needed to be saved on the flash drive in both Mac and PC format so that it can play on either.** I carried copies of all different forms in my purse, and then we also had copies in Ethan's briefcase and a flash drive in his suit coat pocket. Twice during our furlough our DVD stayed behind in a church's player to be mailed to us later, but we always had extra copies. (bold – my emphasis. (Alternatively, you can set your disc for a program called *ExFAT* which can be used by both Mac & PC.)

Cold Weather and Equipment

One additional piece of advice: think about the effects of cold weather on your projector. It is best to allow it to warm up before projecting. You may want to be certain that the projector is not left in the back of the trunk of the car during the winter season. Bring it inside if you stay overnight. You may want to keep it in the front of the car while traveling, and bring it inside promptly when you arrive for the service. Otherwise, the lens is steamed up and the quality of the program suffers. (I had that problem with a Sunday morning Sunday school presentation. After a few moments, it finally was no longer steamed up. Think about your glasses if you are outside in the cold and come into a warm room)

An Attractive Table-top Display

A good attractive table-top display is helpful. It should be attractive, lightweight, compact, and portable. You should include information about you and your family. Have some pictures of the country, some information about the people of the country, the spiritual needs of the country, and curios typical of the country. One of the major things to consider is quality. A few well-chosen items are better than many of poor quality. Have a quantity of quality prayer cards available. If you have younger children, they are wonderful at passing out prayer cards. When you purchase your cards, get plenty. The prices drop dramatically when you order 3000-6000 at a time. On the other hand, if you have young children or your family is expanding, you will have to replace them the following furlough. My wife and I have been able to use the same prayer cards for a number of years, and so a volume was helpful.

My advice is to consider anything on the display table as likely to get broken, taken, etc. I had several Chick tracts as well as other tracts in Sranantongo to demonstrate how they could be used. A number disappeared – I suspect that small children may have picked them up. Display items may be damaged – so choose those which will not be a problem. Alternatively, display them under plastic so that they will more likely remain.

CHAPTER 11: PREPARATION FOR DEPUTATION

Some individuals have a photo album of their ministry and people available on their display table. My son-in-law came up with a neat and effective solution. For about $100 at the time, he bought a small projector and desktop screen which he set up to show many pictures of the ministry in rotation on a continuous basi

Literature Can Have an Impact

Literature can have an impact. When Dr. Darrell Champlin preached at our home church one Wednesday night, I felt called to Suriname during the sermon. My wife passed by their display and picked up some of their literature. It was while reading their brochures the following day that the Lord confirmed her call in her heart. When I spoke to her the following night about what I was thinking, she felt that the Lord had already called her to Suriname as well.

Prepare a Variety of Messages

You need to have a variety of messages prepared for a variety of different settings. Both you and your wife should be prepared to give brief testimonies of 1-5 minutes. You should be prepared also to give testimonies of varying length and stay within the time framework. I have presented and preached hundreds of times, but two times I overstayed my time, and I remember it with shame even until today. Fortunately, both times, people were forgiving.

I would advise having several sermons to preach, and also prepare Sunday school lessons. When I spoke at one church on Sunday morning and Sunday evening, I was prepared to preach three times. But the pastor wanted me to preach four times. Fortunately, he gave me time during the afternoon to prepare the fourth message.

Wife Should Prepare Also

The wife should be prepared to teach Sunday school, or to speak to wives or children. In teaching children, it is handy to have some artifacts from the field available, and perhaps some illustrated missionary stories. Although the church may want your wife to speak to the ladies or in children's church, it is best that she be brief when she speaks to the congregation. My wife had prepared very brief greetings varying from one to five minutes maximum for the main service. Before she was married, our daughter Kim accompanied us on some of our meetings and went overseas as a missionary in her own right. She also was prepared to speak briefly during our presentations.

Contact the Pastor Again Shortly Before Going

Prior to your meeting, it is very important to contact the pastor about one to two weeks ahead of time and reconfirm the meeting. A rare case occurred when I had clearly scheduled the meeting, but apparently the pastor had either forgotten or lost his information. It would have been 4-5 hours' drive in each direction, and that call saved me a great deal of trouble. Give the pastor the estimated time of arrival, and the number of people coming with you. Let him know if you need a place to stay overnight, and especially if you need to stay more than one night.

Allow Enough Time to Travel

I normally plan to arrive at least an hour before the church service, and preferably I allow about an hour and a half. When driving across Chicago, I routinely allowed an extra hour above that because I had experienced long delays on multiple occasions.

Extra time allows for car problems, as well as traffic problems. The situation is much better with the availability of GPS, but I have had two experiences where the GPS left me in a very difficult situation in a remote area. It may seem a waste of time to allow so much time before a meeting, but sometimes you will be very grateful that you did so. Once, I arrived at the church between three and four hours early because I crossed Chicago with absolutely no delays. However, another occasion I drove my wife to a meeting an hour northwest of Chicago, and we ran into heavy traffic. Even with the extra time, we made it with only five minutes to spare.

Another time a major accident closed I-85 just before we were to arrive at church in Greenville, South Carolina. I was lost as I went off the interstate because I had no alternate directions (this was before the days of GPS.) The Lord allowed us to find our way five minutes before the meeting. On another occasion, I allowed 2 hours extra to go to north

CHAPTER 11: PREPARATION FOR DEPUTATION

Chicago to meet a new pastor and eat at his home. The traffic was incredible. My borrowed cell phone did not work in that area, and I was locked into a huge traffic jam on I-94. Finally, I got off the interstate and drove through downtown Chicago, arriving at 7:25 for a 7:30 meeting. The poor pastor's wife had prepared a delicious meal, and the pastor was trying to put together a sermon. It was my first contact with a new pastor. Fortunately the church had supported us for years, and the pastor became a good friend. These things happen occasionally even when you deliberately leave early. Allow extra time.

Accept Accommodations Provided

Accept the accommodations which the pastor provides you. It is courteous to contact him on arrival if you arrive the night before a meeting. Sometimes the Lord Himself will help you in difficult situations. In one situation, we were staying overnight in a pastor's office. The office was in the front of the church behind a large window. After showering and changing to our bed clothes, we returned to the office to find the door had an automatic lock. We were locked out of the office with our clothes and sleeping accommodations inside! Of course, the telephone for the church was also inside the office, and this was before the days of cell phones. However, I noticed that the office wall only extended up about nine feet, and there was a space open above it. We prayed much. We hunted through the church and found an extension ladder. We would have made quite a sight coming down the center aisle in our bed clothes carrying the ladder. I climbed up to the top, but saw that the drop down was far, and that the bed was spring-loaded and I could easily get hurt.

I climbed back down, and we prayed some more and hunted again. Believe it or not, we found a second ladder. I climbed up, my wife passed up the ladder, and in a few minutes we were safely inside. The Lord does provide. That night He helped us in a number of ways. I had just picked up my suit from the cleaners and had forgotten a tie when we left. But we were able also to find a correct color tie for the suit in the church and mailed it back to the pastor after the morning service. I bought another tie at K-Mart for the evening service.

Questions a Pastor Will Ask

It is worthwhile to consider how the pastor will evaluate you as a missionary. What will the pastor ask himself about a missionary candidate? I would suggest that he will ask the following questions: Does he have a clear call to the field and people where he will serve? Has he had the opportunity to visit the field? Does he have a clear testimony of salvation? Does he win souls now? Will he be able to get along with other missionaries? Does he have what it takes to stick to the job? If there are children, are they under control, and responsive to their parents? Is he well-trained, ideally from a good Bible college?

What has he already done in his local church? What does his own pastor say about his going to the mission field? What mission board or clearing house is he going out under? Is he devoted to the word of God, both in understanding and in personal application to his own life? What about his wife? Is she supportive of his decision and dedicated to Christ? What kind of church does he attend now? Is that the kind of church he will duplicate? When you meet the pastor, plan to be able to answer any questions which he may have, including the above. I tried to answer the questions without him having to ask them when we conversed on the phone as well as in the materials about our ministry.

Ask the Host Pastor What He Desires

In planning for a meeting, ask the pastor what he would like you to do. You are his guest. Ask about time limits and stay within them. If there are no time limits, ask when the service normally stops, and aim to stop then. Arrive early enough to have all displays and your equipment in place prior to when the people arrive so that you can greet them and answer questions.

Once again, prepare several different messages ahead of time. Be prepared to preach on a variety of subjects, including faith promise missions. Be prepared to give Sunday school lessons. Be prepared to teach children if you are asked to teach them. Also, have two or three different length testimonies. Remember your main goal is to present the burden of the field and be careful not to exalt yourself. Do not be critical of the church. Do not be critical of another missionary or mission board.

CHAPTER 11: PREPARATION FOR DEPUTATION

Be thankful, be grateful, and be yourself. Be knowledgeable and enthusiastic about your field. Remember, it is God's job to work on hearts. Our job is to be faithful and exalt Him.

Be Interested in the Pastor and Church

Be thoughtful and interested in the pastor of the church where you minister. I like to know as much as possible about the pastor and the church and try to ask questions about the church without prying into personal business. After all, if the church chooses to support us, we are in a partnership relationship. I always pray for my supporting churches and knowing about them helps me to pray intelligently.

Proper Dress, Appearance, and Behavior

Proper appearance and behavior is important. You need to be clean in terms of your clothing, and, as much as possible, your car. You need to be careful about your nails, shoes, suit, and breath. You must behave like a guest with a sweet attitude. You must attempt to be friendly and as helpful as possible. It is important to have your children under control. Do not allow the children to handle or pick up things, place their feet on the furniture, or run all over playing tag. If there are toys, have the children put them back when they are finished playing. If you have a child in diapers, find a private place to change the diapers. Likewise, nurse children in private. Advise people of your schedule ahead of time, especially if someone is taking you out to eat. Make them aware of what time you need to leave for another service if that might be a problem. Be careful about staying longer than overnight without previous discussion. Also be considerate of the pastor's time.

Express Appreciation

While in the service, express appreciation to the pastor and the church for the privilege of presenting your burden. Give a brief testimony of your salvation, your service, and your call to the mission field. Your burden should be clear. If you and your wife sing; sing. Having a visual presentation is usually very helpful, but make sure that you get clearance from the pastor before the service. Keep your visual presentation under 10 minutes. When you prepare your presentation, ask one or two persons who do not know your ministry if the presentation is clear.

For the veteran missionary, thank the churches for their support. Report on the work. Give them your plans as to when you are returning to the field. Give them a challenge for missions. Remember to stay within your time limits. Be careful that your visual presentation and your sermons do not become old in your heart. Get alone with God before each service, and let God do his work in your heart. (Even on deputation, it may be difficult to maintain enthusiasm after the same presentation 200 times. I found that I needed to be careful in preparation. When I had a new message, I would always spend time praying and reviewing the message. But when I had given the message multiple times, it was difficult to maintain that concern. I needed to remind myself that if the Lord does not empower it, no message in and of itself will do the supernatural work which it should do unless it is empowered by the Holy Spirit.)

Furlough Meetings

Furlough meetings from supporting churches are usually easier to schedule then getting into new churches. The church is already supporting you, and thus you are not seeking new support. Nevertheless, it is important for the church to maintain personal contact and to understand your ministry which they are supporting both by finances and prayer. My mission requires that you report back to your supporting churches a minimal of every six years. I try to remember that my coming to the church does cost the church money. In addition to a love offering, they will often take you out for meal, and may put you up for overnight accommodations. I try to be considerate and grateful. When I am on the field, I tried to start scheduling nearly one year in advance. Many larger churches need to work on that sort of schedule. In terms of presentations, in addition to being prepared to preach, it is important to let the church know how the work is progressing. As they are better informed, they can pray more intelligently for your ministry.

CHAPTER 11: PREPARATION FOR DEPUTATION

The Two Biggest Problems on Furlough

When on furlough, the two biggest problems for the missionary are normally transportation and a place to stay. I know that many missionaries stay for a number of months at their home church. My personal ministry and schedule worked out much better with a shorter time back in the United States. On my first furlough, I was back for about four-five months, and tried to see almost all of our churches. This was also true for the next two furloughs. Later, it became much more profitable for the ministry if I stayed about two months during the Suriname summer vacation during August and September. I saw approximately half of my churches each time and came home more often. When I started teaching classes and courses in Bible colleges, I stayed in the USA approximately three months. Of course, each person's situation is different, and ours has changed as we aged and our ministry in the USA has changed. I arrived on the field at age 48. As we approached and passed 70 years of age, we came more frequently and for a shorter time. This schedule allowed me to stay on the field seven years after a heart attack before relocating in the USA at age 74. I was also enabled to have yearly cardiac follow-up.

In planning for furlough, the first thing I tried to do was to schedule the use of a prophet's chamber in each of the areas of our churches. Once that schedule was set, then I would work on scheduling the various churches around that prophet's chamber location. Otherwise, one is confronted with a great cost in terms of hotels and eating out. Usually I have been able to work out the schedule, but sometimes it has been quite difficult. Occasionally I have had to reschedule a church for another year. I rarely had to overnight in a motel which I paid for personally.

Writing Letters

Regular communication is important. Writing letters (now usually email) is also part of the missionary's task. When writing letters during your deputation, give a brief opening, report about meetings, and mention any who have been saved or surrendered to preach or go on a mission field. You may thank the Lord for any churches which have taken you on for support since the previous prayer o. Mention the scheduled meetings for the next two months, and request prayer. Include brief goals and plans for the future. And once again thank your supporters for their prayers, concern, and financial support. Many churches and individuals prefer e-mail, which is both faster and much cheaper than "snail mail." Some now communicate via their website.

Letters from the field are somewhat different. After greetings, you can mention people saved, churches planted, and baptisms. You can mention future evangelistic plans. It is important to outline the progress of the work, including buildings, new programs, and progress towards church organization. Request prayer for your people and for the work. Give a brief report of the welfare of your family. Give appreciation for continued prayers and support. Acknowledge the support you have received.

I would also mention that it is important to be personal. People do not connect emotionally or relationally with statistics as much as with personal stories. The people saved are real people with real problems, and not just numbers. I have tried also to give some information on local customs and culture from time to time, as well as notes about my wife and myself. My daughter in Suriname had a real advantage. With nine children, some still small, she usually had at least one amusing story to relate! One of our missionaries has a real talent for conveying stories of the culture of Suriname in most of their prayer letters.

You will want to build long-term support through your relationships with your personal supporters as well as your supporting churches and pastors. Send emails out to inform them of what is happening. Be sure top pray for your supporters as you want them to pray for you faithfully. As you build relationships your prayer support will grow, and often your financial support will grow as well.

Expect a Certain Amount of Lost Support

I was told before going overseas that I could expect to lose 10% to 15% of my support over my first four years. I doubted that would happen, but it was true. Some churches closed, and other personal supporters either died, or were unable to continue support. However, we maintained a regular contact with our supporting churches and personal

CHAPTER 11: PREPARATION FOR DEPUTATION

supporters. I prayed for them on a daily basis. When we arrived on the field, we had 42 supporting churches. Approximately one year later, I believe we had 52 churches. I strongly suspect that some of these ten additional churches picked us up for support because of continued good communications.

The Lord was very gracious. God has always supplied support for the programs which He has called us to implement. It is possible at times that the Lord may direct you not only positively by support, but also negatively by lack of support, indicating that something is wrong. Perhaps your goals are wrong, or your attitude or priorities. I certainly would rather stop a program that the Lord does not want than to press forward with my own program that will not bring His eternal rewards.

A Realistic Budget

Your home mission office can help you set up a realistic budget. You should be debt-free before going on the field. Sometimes this requires that for a time, you continue working when you begin deputation. Your monthly needs should be estimated. The mission will also need to estimate your passage costs (usually airline tickets and transporting your personal effects,) cost of outfitting, and cost of a vehicle should you decide to ship one. When you have these figures, it is much easier to see precisely where you are financially at any time. Because I continued to work as a doctor until within about six-eight weeks before going overseas, I was able to save most of my love offerings as well as most monthly support. As these support funds grew, they covered the cost of travel and outfitting, including purchasing and shipping a twelve-seat Chevy van.

Thought questions:

1. What are your plans for your video presentations? How many, how long, and with what emphasis?
2. What are you planning to do for a display board and display items?
3. What has your pastor recommended for you in terms of mission organization and your training through the church to prepare for overseas?
4. What are your anticipated expenses to get to the field?

5. How do you propose to raise the funds for your support and outfitting?
6. What are your planning dates for applying to a mission organization and to begin deputation?
7. How are you planning to build your support team through your contacts?

CHAPTER 12
PREPARATION FOR OVERSEAS

I suspect that most of us as Americans travel with far too many things when we go on the mission field. Nevertheless, it is worthwhile to consider what you will need on the field as well as preparation to make various arrangements in the USA.

Legal Papers

There are important legal papers that you need to have before going. Naturally, you will need a passport and visa. At the time of obtaining your passports, get perhaps twelve passport photos. They will be needed for many other items. Find out if there are any special requirements. In Suriname, one ear must show, and you must not smile! Usually, your mission board can help you know the visa requirements. A travel agency may also help but remember that the requirement for a permanent visa is different from a tourist visa. Many countries require a responsible agency to guarantee that they will repatriate you including return airfare if necessary. Without such a paper, you may have difficulty getting more than a visitor's visa.

When we arrived in Suriname, they required that we had already purchased return tickets. The country will require a passport, and may require a certificate from the police department that you have no criminal record. They may require certain medical clearance as well for physical and mental health. Although some countries will allow an entire family to be on a single passport, I would recommend that every individual have his own passport. Sometimes it becomes necessary for one or two of the family to return to the USA, but not the entire family. Then it is possible to be flexible as to who travels with whom. It is more expensive, but worth it.

There may be additional complications in countries which do not normally permit missionaries to enter. My father-in-law was able to stay in India for 10 years, but as a psychiatrist heading a psychiatric hospital. I doubt that he could have received a visa as a church-planting missionary. Many people have a special skill or trade which they can use to get into "closed" countries. Some have mechanical skills, others have a certificate to teach English as a second language, and others come as teachers, pilots, agricultural experts, etc.

The Importance of a Will

It is also important to have a will drawn up before leaving the country for both husband and wife, and to give certain individuals power of attorney. If you have children, you need to arrange for their care should both parents die. Our mission requires that we provide that information so that in case of a death or medical emergency, or a possible hostage situation, the mission can access the necessary funds and documents to expedite solving the problem. It is helpful to the mission to know where bank accounts, savings, and other sources of income are located. These things should be completed before going overseas. Make several duplicate copies of all important documents, and have the original in a safe place, and copies with you. It may be helpful to have your copies notarized. Sometimes you will be required to present the original documents.

Medical Exams, Documents, and Medication

In terms of medical care, most mission boards will require a physical examination prior to acceptance. Even if you are not required to do so, I would personally recommend that you have a routine physical examination. The examination may reveal something that could be taken care of easily in the USA but would prove a major hassle overseas. You can often receive information concerning the availability of medical care in the area where you will be working. Medical care is improving, even in third world countries, and it is often possible to work in situations which would not be feasible previously. When I was 67 years old, I had a heart attack. They had just opened a catheterization lab the week that I was hospitalized, and I was able to bring my cardiac catheterization results with me. When I went to the USA, they asked me if I wanted stents (4), or an open-heart bypass. I elected to have stents; their concern had been that if a stent closed, no one would be available to replace it. But six years later, the country had five cardiologists capable of inserting

CHAPTER 12: PREPARATION FOR OVERSEAS

stents if necessary, and I lived less than 10 minutes from the hospital. For a third world country, we were fortunate to have that level of care.

Bring all important medical documents with you. Bring all your medications also, and spare glasses. It may be helpful to bring x-rays or other reports (CT scan or MRI, catheterization DVD, etc.) with you as well. Be certain to get all the appropriate vaccinations before going to the field. Before going to the field, if you have medical problems, it is helpful to consider how the new location will affect your health. In an area with malaria, you will need some sort of malaria prophylaxis, which varies from region to region.

One of our physicians from the medical clinic in the USA had spent years in Congo and was contemplating returning to practice there. The hospital where he had worked was deep in the forest. Both he and the people there knew that it was inadvisable for him to return for medical reasons. If you have questions, ask your doctor. I had mentioned above about a missionary with asthma. Had she asked me, I would have hesitated to recommend that she come to a tropical climate.

Have Some Basic Medical Knowledge

If you are going to be working in a remote area, some basic medical knowledge will be invaluable. Two books that can be helpful if you are in a remote area are: *Where There is No Doctor*[47] and *Where There is No Dentist*.[48] There are short courses also available for training missionaries in remote situations to handle relatively simple medical problems. In that case, you will probably want a supply of medicine with you, not only for your own needs, but also to help your people.

Consider Simple Medical Equipment

You may want to bring certain simple medical equipment with you as well, including a stethoscope, blood pressure cuff, otoscope, bandages and antiseptics. Darrell Champlin, who had no specific medical training, asked a dentist to teach him to pull teeth. With some basic equipment, he became quite proficient and had many opportunities to serve his people.

Regional Diseases

You can get more information from the book by Dr. Roy Dearmore called *Biblical Missions*.[49] One problem is that every area has its own specific diseases in addition to the common diseases throughout the world. I was well-prepared to expect the common parasites and malaria when I arrived in Liberia, West Africa. However, there were other diseases which I had never seen. Primary liver cancer, called hepatoma, is extremely rare in the USA. It often presents with a massively enlarged liver, and sometimes with jaundice as well as body wasting. In the USA, these symptoms would almost invariably indicate metastatic liver disease from another cancer, usually from the GI tract, or occasionally from the lung. I ordered a number of studies on the GI tract before I finally realized what I was dealing with. Certain tropical diseases are limited to certain areas. Burkitt's lymphoma was another tumor that I had never encountered in the USA but was common in Liberia. Some of the diseases from Liberia were rare in Suriname, although both were tropical countries. I mention this so that if you are to get involved at all in medical treatment, it is helpful to understand what local diseases are important, and how they must be treated. The spectrum of diseases was very different in Liberia from that of the United States.

Another interesting problem for us in Suriname was skin diseases. My wife had a common skin infection called scabies which she caught from a child who loved to sit on her lap. An experienced dermatologist in Suriname missed the diagnosis, calling it heat rash. He was not used to seeing skin diseases in light skinned Caucasians. When we went to another dermatologist in the USA, he made the diagnosis directly on sight.

Packing and Preparing

Packing and preparing for going overseas can seem to be an overwhelming task. This is particularly true if you have a number of children, whose sizes will be changing. Trying to plan for four years of children's clothing is a major challenge. The more information you have about the conditions of the field, the more intelligent decisions you can make. It is usually preferable to buy things locally if the quality and

CHAPTER 12: PREPARATION FOR OVERSEAS

availability are satisfactory. Arriving with a huge amount of imported goods may have a negative impact on your ministry. The nationals may well view you as incredibly wealthy, and you may have difficulty with a national church accepting responsibility to build their own buildings and pay their own way. They may reason: Why should we sacrifice. Let the American pay for it. After all, he has plenty of money.

I will add a comment by my daughter, who contrasts the current situation in Suriname with what we had met on arrival. She writes: I would add a note somewhere that times are changing, even in third world countries. It is now possible to purchase a lot more things in Suriname than when we first came. We also now have a reliable freight forwarding system to use in ordering things online from the US. So, we no longer pack barrels of things to ship back to the field. We pretty much bring our luggage and then order specific items to be shipped.

We had a rather amusing (in retrospect) situation when we first came to Suriname. At that time, man items were not available, including toilet paper. When I arrived at the hospital, the nurses were all excited about something in a large black paper sack. It was toilet paper! If you worked in a hospital, you would be excited too, even if it was loose and not wrapped into rolls. We used to ask the students which came to Suriname to be sure to bring a sufficient supply of toilet paper with them. When we came, we packed many of our supplies in barrels. So, we covered the bottom of a barrel with rolls of toilet paper and packed on top of it. One of the items which we brought was hair spray, which was also hard to obtain. We were able to find a whole gallon and included it. Unfortunately, the hair spray container cracked and leaked the hair spray on our toilet paper, which was rather stiff, but we still used it.

Electrical Equipment

Remember that electrical outlets vary from country to country and prepare accordingly. You may need adapters. Countries vary as to the type of electricity, including voltage and whether it is 50 or 60 cps. You may need voltage regulators to step down from 220 v. to 110 v. We were in a country that did use 60 cps and 110 volts as they do in the USA. However, all their outlets are different. Some solved the problem when they had a number of electrical products from the USA by buying adaptors for extension cords with multiple outlets. Then they would use the US items in the US extension cord. Be certain that you either can buy the appropriate batteries for various items in the new country, or bring them with you, recognizing that they may spoil.

Baggage Requirements

Baggage is a constantly changing situation which varies from country to country. When we first came to Suriname, it was very cheap to bring extra baggage. They did not control the weight carefully; I even brought a box with me as a single extra bag that weighed over 100 lbs.! We were charged a flat rate of $50 per bag after our original allowance of two bags. On our first furlough, I felt embarrassed bringing ten boxes and suitcases back with me, until a man passed me with a total of thirty boxes! He found it cheaper to bring all his things back to Suriname as excess baggage than to ship them! I saw automobile tires chained together as overweight baggage! In Miami airport, you could easily pick out luggage destined for Suriname. That is no longer true. The airlines are strict with weight allowances; we are no longer allowed 70 pounds per bag as previously. Air freight is often expensive and may be unreliable. Shipments sent by sea are best placed in a container for safety. It is still possible to lose items. My son-in-law lost most of a shipment when a container was broken into while in Guyana before arriving in Suriname. Customs officials may also be difficult, and delays may make storage fees high. Each situation is different, and you must assess the situation at the time. You may want the help of an expediter. We had one helping us getting into Suriname. We became very good friends, he and his family were saved, and joined the church. He even ended up driving a van to pick up children for the church.

Foreign Currency Problems

Bringing in foreign currency can also be a problem. I have used a money belt, and usually split our funds with my wife. I kept a small amount of cash available for tips and food. Some countries make you declare what you are bringing into the country; usually it is not a problem if you do not exceed $10,000 per person.

You may need assistance to open a bank account on arrival in the new country, and you will want to do so promptly. We originally

CHAPTER 12: PREPARATION FOR OVERSEAS

brought in traveler's cheques, believing that they would be safer. However, we found that we were charged a higher exchange rate, and that they were not accepted overall. We no longer use them.

When traveling, be aware of where your bags are at all times. This is especially true of such items as laptops and cell phones. One of our men from our church had his laptop stolen while it was close to him at an airport. He was a very experienced traveler; we need to be alert.

Vehicle Advice

Get the best advice you can concerning vehicles. I was advised to ship an American twelve-seat van. The van was sturdy and worked well for a number of years. However, as it began to need repairs, there was a constant problem of getting US parts, which often had to be special ordered and shipped. We were fortunate that there was another van of the same model in Suriname which had broken and was now available for parts; sometimes we could use parts from that vehicle, but often the needed part was not available in Suriname. Depending on the problem, this might mean that the van became totally unusable for several weeks or even a few months. We were basically without our own transportation for about six weeks when the transmission broke. The longer we remained in Suriname, the more we shifted to rebuilt second hand Japanese cars, which were readily available. Parts were much cheaper and easier to find. Mechanics were used to working on them.

Of course, if the vehicle is used in the bush, you may need to be your own mechanic, and you may need a variety of special tools as well as replacement parts. The entire Champlin family are all skilled in mechanics and repair vehicles, outboard engines, etc. There is a good section on this situation in Dr. Roy Dearmore's book *Biblical Missions*.[50] Dr. Dearmore worked for years in the interior of Zaire and the Amazon as a physician. He gives very specific advice. His advice about trying to avoid native drivers is also appropriate. Your vehicle will often last MUCH longer if you are the driver.

Specialized Training

Certain types of work and living situations require additional training. If you are living in a very remote area, you may have to build your own house, doing your own plumbing and electrical wiring. You may have to build a road, dig a well, etc. You may need special training to do these things well. There are also special considerations in some climates, such as rain forests, deserts, etc. Again, there is a section in Dr. Dearmore's *Biblical Missions* that outlines specific advice, especially if you are living in a remote area in the tropics.

A Few Final Thoughts

Do not be afraid of deputation. When you report to your churches, you are not begging, but you are seeking partners to work together to reach the world for Christ. Focus on prayer. Pray for your meetings. Pray for new churches. Pray for your supporting churches. Pray that you will be a blessing. Pray that you will be able to communicate your burden for the ministry. I still pray through a list of our supporting churches and our supporters on a daily basis, some of whom have supported us for over thirty years. I believe that they need our prayers, as well as we need theirs. I have seen the Lord do great things when God's people pray together for God's work.

When we left Suriname for the USA, I wrote to all our supporting churches (about fifty) informing them that we would be self-supporting. They could transfer our funds to another missionary, or perhaps drop to 50%, which we would use to pay for our radio and TV broadcasts. I expected to drop about 75-80% of my support level. That is exactly what happened. We have about twelve-fourteen supporting churches and a few friends, and cover the cost of the broadcasts and some administrative and transportation costs.

With the advent of e-mail, it is now possible to maintain excellent communications with your supporters. During my time on furlough reporting to churches and teaching in colleges, I ask people who will pray for us regularly to sign up for our e-mail prayer letter. I now have over 600 people on my contact lists. Knowing that we are lifted up to the Lord is a tremendous blessing. And if an emergency arises, e-mail can generate almost instant response. When the house of my son-in-law and

CHAPTER 12: PREPARATION FOR OVERSEAS

daughter burned to the ground, and they lost everything, we were able to contact their churches at once. When I had a heart attack and needed to be medically evacuated, again, prayer support was immediately available.

I am also including an addendum written by my son, Missionary Marc Patton, who has been in Hungary nearly thirty years. He was asked to write a summary of his deputation experiences and advice soon after his arrival in Hungary. His wife Charin also adds a brief section for wives of missionaries on deputation. Their advice is excellent, and I would urge you to take time and read their addendum.

Thought questions:
1. What documents will you need to obtain, copy and preserve for your overseas ministry?
2. What equipment will you need to take with you to the foreign field?
3. How are you planning to ship your goods overseas?
4. How are you going to arrange for finances in an overseas situation?

CHAPTER 13
ARRIVING ON THE FIELD

Culture shock

Culture shock is common. It may occur to anybody living in a new culture. Some people think that this just happens to missionaries, but this is not true. Many government and business organizations have ways to help you cope with culture shock. When I went to Liberia, West Africa, I went under the United States Agency for International Development. I received a month's training in Washington prior to being sent overseas. Much of that training was to help alleviate culture shock. The training proved helpful.

Rules for Normal Living Change

What happens in culture shock? The rules for normal living change! You cannot communicate normally. It will take much practice and many mistakes to learn a new language and a new way of thinking and doing things. Routine things take much longer to do. Suddenly there are many changes in our relationships with other people, and our own identity changes. When I first came to Suriname, I remember the humiliation of realizing that any young grade-school child could communicate better than I could. Here I was, Professor of Medicine and highly trained and highly skilled, but I could not communicate easily to those around me.

Stress from Culture Shock

It is important to recognize that culture shock bring stress into our life.[51] Some have developed ways of scoring points for stress. For example, they assign 50 points to language learning. They find that 50% of those who have accumulated over 150 points were sick, and 80% of those above 300 points were sick. Many missionaries may have over 400 points! Physical illness is common. Psychological and spiritual depression is also common.

Here is a sample list of points causing stress in one's life:[52]

1. Death of spouse — 100 points
2. Divorce — 73
3. Death of close family member — 68
4. Personal injury — 53
5. Marriage — 50
6. Change in health of close family member — 43
7. Pregnancy — 40
8. Gain of new family member — 39
9. Change in financial state — 38
10. Change of work — 36
11. Change of responsibility at work — 29
12. Change of living conditions — 25
13. Etc, etc. — and this does not include the points for language learning!

The Cycle of Culture Shock

There is a well-known cycle of culture shock. The first phase lasts several days to a few weeks, and is often called the tourist stage. Others call this the honeymoon phase. Everything is great. We love the food. We love the sights. We love the people. We love the music. We can say that we are in love. But the honeymoon does not last forever.

After a few weeks, we move into disenchantment. We are no longer outside visitors. A visitor is here for a short time and then goes home; but we are here for "the long haul." We cannot just return home after a brief visit or go hide in a western style hotel. At this point, the frustrations began to climb. Language is a challenge. The adjustments and the culture that seemed so quaint now becomes annoying. Many people resign at this point. But as we move ahead, there is resolution. We began to learn new cultural ways. Sometimes, however, we think our old culture is still superior. This is a key time for proper adjustment. Ideally, we will not simply reject the new culture, or reject our old culture in favor of the new one, but integrate the two cultures.

CHAPTER 13: ARRIVING ON THE FIELD

The Need for Positive Attitudes

We need to develop positive attitudes of appreciation and acceptance of the culture. If we remain aloof, we will probably never come truly into the culture. We want to be bonded to the culture. I have seen people build walls around them to adjust to culture shock, and never tear down the walls. When we were in Liberia, some people had all their associations and friendships among the American Embassy people. All their social contacts were with other Americans. Their only contacts with Liberians were at work. They ate American food, went to the American Embassy to watch American movies, etc. Such an attitude will preclude ever adjusting to the culture. One lady from the embassy refused any close friendship, even with fellow Americans. She had to move often, and found it too difficult to make new friends, and then to part from them. So, she built an emotional wall around herself to insulate herself from others. How sad.

Reverse Culture Shock

And strangely, there is reverse culture shock. Those going back to the United States are often shocked. I remember a good friend of mine returning to the United States. We were living in Liberia, West Africa, a poor third world country. When he returned for a visit, he was shocked at the affluence in the United States. In Liberia, you were fortunate as the man of the house to own a bicycle. It was your transportation. But in the USA, he saw bicycles sitting unused in the garage, often one for each child. He experienced reverse culture shock.

It is not surprising that those with excellent adjustment to the new culture are most likely to develop reverse culture shock.[53] They have adjusted well to a new culture. Now the old culture seems strange. We need to approach returning "home" as if we were learning another culture, and to learn from the "natives," although the "natives" may well be our own family. More than one missionary on returning "home" has longed for the time when they could return to the field. (My daughter's comment is telling: We never refer to the US as home.... returning to the country of their birth or citizenship might be better for those of us who don't think of America as home. ☺)

Other Problems Facing a First-term Missionary

Another list of problems facing the first-term missionary includes the following:[54]

1. Loneliness
2. Pressures adjusting to another culture
3. Constant time demands
4. Lack of adequate (by US standards) health facilities and care
5. Overwhelming workload in difficult circumstances
6. Pressure to be a good witness to the nationals
7. Confusion of role in the national chu
8. Lack of privacy
9. Difficulty in recreation and vacation.

Lack of Security and Safety

Another thing which could be added to the above list is the sense of lack of security and safety, with burglar bars, etc. The lack of safety can be unsettling. I remember being amused at first to see the burglar bars on the houses. I thought that it looked like everyone was in a bird cage, trapped on the inside. I was too casual initially in our safety precautions, until we had uninvited guests one night. They had cut the rope used to hang clothes outside, and somehow looped the rope around an open window on the second floor, and then climbed up the outside wall, removed the windowpanes, and came into the house. When I awoke in the morning, I saw that the door to our bedroom was closed, and found it locked. My keys were gone. Many things in the house were ransacked. Fortunately, they had not cut the phone line, and we were able to call for help. Later we found that items had been stolen from our bedroom while we slept. We were told that there was some sort of spray that could be used to keep you asleep while you were being robbed.

The following day I repaired a light that was burned out in back of our house, started using an alarm system faithfully, bought watch dogs, and had bars put on the windows that lacked them. We were fortunate that we were not harmed and that our vehicle was not stolen. Our co-workers were not so fortunate, when they were robbed at gunpoint and

CHAPTER 13: ARRIVING ON THE FIELD

the missionary hit over the head with a gun butt. These situations are unsettling, but it is possible to adapt, take precautions, and leave yourself in the Lord's hands, as you do what you can do.

Lack of Conveniences

Some find it difficult to adapt to lack of conveniences. My wife always tried to assume that things were going to be a bit more difficult than they actually were. Then it was a pleasant surprise to find that things were better than expected. We were fortunate to have electricity, running water, and many appliances including a refrigerator, stove, washer and dryer, and vacuum cleaner. Many lack some of those amenities.

Getting Over Culture Shock

There are several things that can help getting over culture shock. One of the first is to get into the culture early, before you have developed so many routines that you shut the culture out. Remember that you are a learner. The nationals will be helpful if they see you as someone in need who would welcome their friendship and assistance. It may be very important to take time out periodically and just get away from everything for a short time.

The amount of adjustment depends on the difference between our original culture and the new one. We need to recognize our anxieties, identify them, and learn solutions to them. Furthermore, we need to have a true interest in our people that we are ministering to, to accept them, and to build trust. It is very helpful to set realistic goals. You cannot do as much in a foreign culture as you can in your own culture. Avoid burnout. And remember, you are not indispensable.

The Key to Getting Over Culture Shock

Our attitude is key in helping to recover from culture shock. We need to be flexible. Humor is especially helpful, and the ability to laugh when we make mistakes. We are certain to make cultural blunders because we are from another culture. We will make language mistakes, and some of them will be very amusing. You might as well join them and laugh. We need to be free to forgive, and thankful for all that is done for us. We don't need to carry the entire burden ourselves; it is good to share burdens with others.

Marjory Foyle, who replaced my father-in-law as head of Nur Manzil Psychiatric Hospital, gives a number of practical suggestions.[55] She emphasizes that at times, it may be necessary to get away for a short time and recoup. It may be necessary to get into the culture in steps rather than plunging into the culture at once. People vary in their toleration of stress.

Resolving Culture Shock

In terms of resolving culture shock, it is important not to remain "stuck" at one point in the resolution process, such as in anger or depression. We need to be patient and allow time to form deep personal relationships. As time goes on, relationships will deepen. My wife and I were in Suriname for 26 years, and have been with a number of families through many trials and victories. The hardest part of our relocation in the USA was leaving a number of our friends there. Have patience, and let the Lord love through you, and the bonding will come if the Lord has truly called you.

Here are some practical suggestions from Marge Jones:[56]

1. Recognize that a rupture is taking place
2. Accept negative responses as normal
3. Talk out and pray about negative responses
4. Select positive responses to overcome negative ones
5. Do not expect instant bonding
6. Remember why you are on the mission field
7. Be prepared to laugh at your mistakes

Thought Questions:

1. Have you already experienced culture shock? If so, what did you do to resolve your problems.
2. Is there a big difference in the culture of the people to whom you will minister and your own culture? If so, how are you preparing yourself to cope with culture shock?

CHAPTER 13: ARRIVING ON THE FIELD

3. A number of areas to adjust were mentioned. Which areas do you expect may be most difficult for you to handle?
4. Are you prepared to laugh with the nationals when you make mistakes, or will you react defensively or take offense?
5. Are you prepared to gear back your expectations as to how much you can accomplish in a foreign setting compared to the USA?

CHAPTER 14
LANGUAGE ADJUSTMENTS

The individual will remain basically an outsider in the culture until he develops real facility in the language. This is a major challenge for new missionaries, and often the mission board has specific criteria which must be met, sometimes within a specified time frame. I know that this was a major challenge for both myself and my wife.

People do differ in their ability to learn language. There are tests that can be used to determine language aptitude. When I was tested in a group of about 50 foreign service applicants, I did well, but the best grades were obtained by two men involved in computer work (and this was fifty years ago, when computers were in their infancy.) It also seems that one's ability to learn a new language drops rather abruptly around age thirty-five.

Thus, my wife and I were quite concerned when we came to Suriname and were confronted with learning two languages beginning at age 48. My wife had not done well in the language learning program which we had taken at Bob Jones University for a month prior to leaving. (Incidentally, she was a top student throughout all her schooling, including a masters' degree in Nursing Education.) However, she reasoned that if God called her, God would also enable her to learn. My daughter, who had graduated from college at the top of her class at age twenty, had no difficulty, and my wife depended on her to carry the conversations. However, when our daughter left Suriname after less than a year on the field to get married, my wife was amazed at what the Lord enabled her to learn.

Accuracy in Pronunciation Is Important

Accuracy in pronunciation is important. We were fortunate that in Sranantongo, there are virtually no sounds which did not exist in English. That is not the case in Dutch, which has a number of different sounds as well as changes in language structure which were difficult for us to learn.

Some sounds that did exist in English do not exist in Sranantongo, and this is especially true in the local tribal language of Aukaans, which many of our people speak. It is important to hear the differences, because otherwise you will not be able to pronounce words accurately. In many non-European languages, there is no difference between the "r" and the "l" in pronunciation, and they are substituted freely for each other. Thus "rice" can be pronounced "lice," and "clap" can be pronounced "crap." In Aukaans, the "r" sound does not exist, but the "l" does. Thus one of our preachers, whose name is Carolus, is shortened to "Carlo." But since the "r" is not pronounced, his shortened name is pronounced "Kalow."

Another sound that does not exist in Sranantongo is the "th" sound. It is usually pronounced as a "t." And there is very little difference between a "t" and a "d" although actually one should be voiced, and the other unvoiced. I decided to call my dog "Thor," correctly assuming that people would have trouble pronouncing his name. They would usually pronounce it "Tol."

In Chinese, there is a difference between the "p" in spin and pin. In the former, there is no puff of air with the p, but in the latter, there is. The Chinese hear the difference, but we don't. Our pronunciation of some words would be as amusing to them as their difference in pronunciation between rice and lice is to us.

At times, we can pronounce the sound, but we are not accustomed to its occurring in a particular place in a word. The word cats ends with a "ts" sound. We pronounce it with no problems. However, no English word begins with the "ts" sound. My sister-in-law is married to a Japanese, and her married name is Tsuyuki, a very common Japanese name. After a bit of practice, we could pronounce it without difficulty. My wife's elderly maiden aunt, however, was never able to pronounce their name, although she lived with them for some years. She would invariably say "Tasuki."

Methods of Learning a Language Differ

People learn by different methods. I like to systematize my learning, but many do not. Our missionary language teacher in

CHAPTER 14: LANGUAGE ADJUSTMENT

Sranantongo was excellent in the language, but insisted that the first month we spend our time memorizing phrases to use. I found that difficult and boring. I was much happier when we added grammar and I could "make some sense" out of what I was learning. Others may find memorization the best method.

Patterns in Languages

After some time, one can also begin to learn patterns which help anticipate the changes in speaking between languages, especially between Sranantongo and Aukaans. In Aukaans, the "r" does not exist, but the vowel is lengthened instead. This probably was adapted from Dutch, where it is common to lengthen a vowel and create a different word. The word "stad" means a city, and the word "staat" means a state. The difference in pronouncing the "d" and "t" is minimal; the primary difference is between a single "a" and a double "a," which is pronounced longer. Here is an example: In Sranantongo: "waran brede," which means warm bread. In Aukaans, both letters "r" will be dropped, but the vowels lengthened to "waan beele." Notice that the "l" has been substituted for the "r."

Learning patterns of change can be most helpful. When we were in Liberia, the official language was English, and I was told that virtually all Liberians could understand me. However, the common trade language was Liberian English, which is a sort of creole corrupted English. In truth, I found that the national Liberians did not understand me. One day an Episcopal priest came to the hospital and taught some expatriates the difference between regular English and Liberian English. My doctor friends rushed me off to hear him. Within two hours, I was given enough information to dramatically change my communication. During the following days, I decided to imitate exactly what I heard, much to the amusement of the national doctors and nurses. But within a few days, I was able to communicate much better with everyone, and my bonding with the culture was greatly enhanced.

Total Immersion Versus Language School

A number of different options are available to learn the language. One method is total immersion within the culture, where the missionary actually lives with a national family, hearing and seeing the nationals throughout the day and night. It is a wonderful way to learn the culture as well as the language, and also to pick up the clues of communication through non-verbal means. It is estimated that about two-thirds of the communication between persons is actually non-verbal, emphasizing not *what* is said as much as *how* things are said. Of course, this may or may not be taught in a formal language course. Many people use their hands and body a lot while speaking Sranantongo.

Total immersion is effective for those who can manage it – particularly young people who are single, or perhaps a young married couple without children. It becomes more difficult with a family or comes to the field older. Hamilton College, where I went to undergraduate school, has developed a program to learn the Chinese language and culture. The students go for a year to China, and there they promise to use no English, even among themselves. By the end of the year, as you would anticipate, all the students are fluent in Chinese and adjusted to getting around on their own in China.

Formal Language School

Another option is a formal language school, which ideally is within the country where one will serve, but sometimes is elsewhere. I mention this, because in many countries which were formerly colonies, they will speak an European language. However, the pronunciation of the language will be different in the former colony. There will be the influence of pronunciation of the languages used by the former colony. When I was learning Dutch in Suriname, I attended a week of church services in which a native Surinamer was preaching. However, he had lived in Holland for many years, and had the pronunciation of a Hollander. It took me two or three evenings listening to him preach before I was able to follow his messages well.

My son and daughter-in-law went to language school in Hungary shortly after their arrival, and did extremely well learning Hungarian. On the other hand, their children, all of whom were born in Hungary, have gone through the public school system. Of course, they are totally fluent in Hungarian. However, the family speaks English at home so that

CHAPTER 14: LANGUAGE ADJUSTMENT

they are also very comfortable in English, although their vocabulary is a bit limited. Since they were born in Hungary, they never had a problem in Hungarian schools. However, missionary children who grew up for some years in the USA can anticipate having problems if they attend a school in a different language and may lose a year while learning the language.

Learn One Place and Travel to Another

Although some people learning French, Spanish, or other European languages may actually learn the language in Europe and then travel to their country of ministry, you may sound like their former colonists. You should expect that the language will be pronounced differently in such countries that were former colonies. Guyanese have a form of English which I do not understand, and at first, I did not understand Liberian English. If you listen to those from the Caribbean, they sound different from those in the USA. There are differences even in English from England or Canada. You can imagine how this may present problems to some of the nationals from former European colonies.

Hire a Local National?

It is also possible to hire a local national to teach the language. In many cases, the missionary must structure the class, but the national can give the necessary information about the language. This is especially true if it is a small tribal language. It is also possible to have a combination of methods. I took formal lessons in Dutch, and had a medical student tutor me. In Sranantongo, I did a number of things. I listened to a broadcast of the news in Sranantongo, and then went over the broadcast with my language helper. When I began to preach, I recorded my sermons. At first, I filled two legal size sheets of paper with my mistakes. But I noticed that gradually the number of mistakes dropped to one legal sheet, then a half a sheet, and eventually I did not require that exercise any more. And my wife and I spent a lot of time calling and soul-winning as an additional opportunity to speak with nationals.

Linguistic training:

Linguistic training can be a real asset before arriving on the field. This is especially true if you are going to be working in a remote area with a new tribal language which has not been broken down and analyzed linguistically. Baptist Bible Training Institute, for example, emphasizes proper pronunciation and the ability to write accurately in phonetics. This training may prove invaluable for the missionary. I went to a one-month training program at Bob Jones University along with my wife and daughter prior to leaving for Suriname. I did find many things helpful. They also taught cultural anthropology, but most of the information I had already known from our time in Liberia. What would have been ideal was for someone to listen to our languages, Sranantongo and Dutch, and analyze the sounds and how to produce them. Of course, with people heading in multiple directions, this is not easy to do.

The most fascinating class I remember was during linguistics. The teacher had spent about a year in the Philippine Islands and knew a local language there. She brought a student from Southeastern Asia into our class who spoke a tribal language which she did not know. Neither was permitted to speak English. Our teacher just had a very few props to help. It was amazing – you could just see her first go after nouns, then verbs, the adverbs and adjectives, and before the end of the hour class, our teacher was conversing with her in complete sentences. That was a foretaste of another month's classes, but I could see the great value of this type of training when working on a new language which had not been already studied.

Conclusion

I would like to conclude with a few observations. Language learning is difficult and takes a lot of discipline. Although age and natural ability are important, the self-discipline and motivation to work on the language are more important. Even more vital, the Lord will help if He has called us to the task. Jonathan Goforth, the great evangelist missionary to China, had great difficulty learning Chinese. Another missionary from the same college he attended had a quick grasp of the language, and the nationals would always ask him to speak rather than

CHAPTER 14: LANGUAGE ADJUSTMENT

Goforth. One day, after his school had learned of his struggles, the school had a special time of prayer. Goforth returned from preaching to tell his wife that the back of the language seemed to have been broken. All the strange sounds and structures suddenly made sense. When he spoke and then turned it over to his friend, the nationals asked him to keep on speaking. And months later, another missionary asked him how he learned to speak as he did. He said that he could be understood by many Chinese of different dialects. It was of the Lord.

Second, it is important to become really competent in the language, and not just "get by." There are a few people whom I have seen with real problems. One was a nurse with hearing difficulties, who never really learned to speak Sranantongo. Another was a man in his late 30's with a hearing disorder; he was also very quiet and tended to be laid back. Yet both were effective missionaries, bonded with the people, and were successful in their roles. However, for the majority of missionaries, given time and patience, it is possible to learn the language. You are otherwise cut off from meaningful conversation with the nationals, and your ministry is limited. The wife of a missionary in Hungary went to the country when she had a teenage daughter. The girl learned the language, but she never succeeded and ended up depending on her daughter. This greatly limited her ability to counsel the women of the church, who would be reluctant to share personal problems through the translation of a teenage girl. This problem may occur especially for the missionary who has moved to a second or third field and is no longer young. To learn an additional language is a real challenge.

Thought questions:

1. It is key to be confident of the call of the Lord; that certainty will help you during language study. Are you certain that the Lord has called you to a certain people group?
2. Do you have any plans to work on the language before you get on the field? Have you considered taking any linguistic training?
3. How do you anticipate working on the language after you arrive on the field?
4. Have you determined in your heart to become competent in both understanding and speaking the language?

CHAPTER 15
BONDING WITH "YOUR PEOPLE"

We recognize that bonding is a very important aspect of effective relationships. A newborn infant is handed to the mother directly after delivery, perhaps even before the cord is cut. There is a virtually instantaneous bonding between mother and child. The initial opportunity appears to be key. I remember a nurse during our training who gave birth to a trisomy 21 (Mongoloid) child. The doctor came in to speak with her, and said bluntly: "You are a nurse. You might as well know that we believe that your child is Mongoloid." The nurse never really bonded with her infant. Later, we learned that she would leave the child in her car unattended while shopping, and eventually, the child was placed in a state care facility.

I believe that God Himself allows the missionary to bond to the people to whom he is called. This bonding should occur early in the missionary career, when the missionary identifies with "his people." However, the missionary needs to remember that his primary identification and loyalty is to the Lord. Otherwise, his people may expect him to stick with them, even when they are engaged in what is clearly unbiblical behavior, and they may consider him disloyal if he protests their unbiblical actions.

Identification with a Missionary's People

The identification of the missionary with his people is shown particularly with his openness and love for them. He does not hold himself apart or consider himself superior to them. It is important not to withdraw, and retreat from involvement with them. The missionary should not isolate himself from his people, having minimal contact with them. I have seen this situation on a number of occasions when I was working for the US Agency for International Development in Liberia. The contact between the US individual and his Liberian counterparts was limited to business, but otherwise, all contact was limited to other

Americans. Insulation and isolation are not productive ways to handle problems.

Work with Your People Rather Than as Boss

As the national church develops, the missionary may find himself in the situation of working for the national leadership rather than being the "boss" of the ministry. The missionary must be willing at some point to turn over the ministry to those who have been trained, and not to hang on to his own rights or privileges. This is also not a time to spend in fantasy, imagining how things could be different, but working together with the national church.

Developing Independent Churches

One of my goals was for our churches to be independent. I wanted national leadership to develop and take over the ministry. However, even with that as a goal, it is sometimes difficult to relinquish the reins and take a back seat to the national leadership. That was my role over the last three years in Suriname, when I functioned primarily as an advisor, and as an assistant to the nationals. They needed the responsibility to lead, as well as the authority to do so. They needed the opportunity to learn by both their successes and their failures, just as I did.

Negativism Hurts the Ministry

Negativism hurts the ministry. It is easy to criticize and see faults in others, and that is especially true when the individuals are from a different culture, language, and educational background. But if God has called us to a ministry, we do need to look at the positive. Rejection is another unproductive attitude. It is difficult to remain objective, especially when nationals criticize or reject your behavior, but it is important to be able to face reality, and accept your faults, and change where necessary. This approach will greatly enhance your bonding to your people.

CHAPTER 15: BONDING WITH YOUR PEOPLE

The Right to Privacy

Americans love their privacy. We have our mountain cabins and retreats. We place fences around our property. We are willing to pay extra for a private room in the hospital. This is not true in many other countries. In Suriname, for example, the patient may be afraid to be in a private room with no other patient. Many would feel that it is cruel to have a child isolated to his own room. This may well lead to problems for the missionary, who may have difficulty adapting to a lack of the privacy that he is accustomed to having. Some privacy is indeed necessary, but it is helpful to realize that you may have less than you might wish.

Sharing

Sharing is also expected. Many parts of the world have families in large kinship groups. They may live with minimal resources, and they expect all the members of the clan to pitch in to ensure the survival of the group. I have mentioned this earlier in the book. The same sharing attitude may come as far as a vehicle is concerned. In America, we are accustomed to having our own vehicle, and going where we want with whom we wish, but we usually feel no real obligation to help others with transportation. That is not the situation in some countries, especially where transportation is limited.

When we arrived in Suriname, we brought a twelve-passenger van with us, fully expecting that we would transport people to church and other activities. That was indeed the case, and for many years, my wife and I drove separately so that we would be able to help transport people. Sometimes they would abuse the privilege, as far as I was concerned. I remember stopping for some children going to church. In jumped a couple adults as well with bags of produce. Partway to the church, they asked me to stop and jumped out with their produce, happy to have a free ride.

Situations Change

In our final years on the field, the situation changed for us. My wife and I no longer provided major transportation for the church, both because of our age (both over 70), but also because many of our people had their own vehicles. However, we still try to help people going home from church by dropping off those traveling in our direction. It is a part of ministry. One missionary couple's family resented having nationals in their vehicle, and the children's resentment became obvious. The family had a number of personal problems and lasted on the field only a single year. Their attitude had a negative effect on the ministry which lingered after they left.

Dealing with Disappointments

Most missionaries are highly motivated and have high expectations for their ministry. Many have had successful ministries in the USA before going overseas. Moreover, they have the expectations of the sending church, the mission agency, their supporters, their missionary colleagues, and the national church to contend with as well. Yet things seldom go as anticipated. Inevitably, things take much longer to accomplish on the mission field.

Expectations Are Often Not Met

First, the expectations on the field are often different than they had anticipated. The nationals are not always delighted to see their arrival, and in some cases, they may be resented or even rejected. The problems they face are new and seem intractable. The spiritual standards of the national church may be below that of the church from which they came in the USA. This, of course, is not unreasonable to expect. The nationals may be coming out of a heathen culture, with only a few years of opportunity to grow as Christians.

The young missionary may be disappointed in the senior missionaries on the field. They may seem to be out-of-date and set in their ways. They may be impatient, lacking sympathy for the newcomer, or, on the other hand, they may feel threatened by the competency of the new missionary. Both may need to adapt to each other and to meet the other's needs. The new missionary may feel abandoned and without someone to relate to, and he may believe that the senior missionary is tied up with his own ministry.

Reasonable Goals

Here are some reasonable goals for a first term missionary:[57]

1. A good foundation in the language
2. Satisfactory adjustment to the culture, climate, customs and people
3. A good working knowledge of the mission
4. Understanding of the field, its problems and demands
5. Awareness of his gifts and place in the work
6. Confirmation of his call, and bonding to his people

Reasonable Ways to Handle Disappointments

Here are some reasonable ways to adapt to disappointments and have a realistic assessment during the first term:[58]

1. Set reasonable goals
2. Don't take your job description too seriously (although a good job description can help)
3. Be committed to joy
4. Maintain good emotional health
5. Remember that you are human, and have limitations
6. Don't be afraid to be a little eccentric
7. Be flexible
8. Don't take yourself too seriously
9. Reduce stress where possible
10. Make your cultural change gradual
11. Forgive both yourself and others
12. Establish some close friendships with the people of the host culture
13. Be thankful
14. Encourage others
15. Take courage, because He understands

(minor adaptations by rdp)

The missionary who follows the above advice and is realistic in his assessment of his call and ministry, is much less likely to leave the field after only a single term. The cost of training and sending missionary is extraordinary, and to lose him prior to his most effective years is a great tragedy for all concerned.

Thought questions:

1. Do you have a clear idea of a people group?
2. When you have an idea of them, would you start praying for them and ask the Lord for the right burden?
3. What kind of time frame are you looking at in terms of overseas service?

CHAPTER 16
CONFLICT RESOLUTION

Conflicts with the Mission Board

There are multiple levels of conflict possible for the missionary on the field. One of the basic areas of conflict is between the missionary and the home office. There are many ways of setting up a program for the missionary. Some home offices want to determine the field, and even the job, for the missionary. Others leave those decisions to the other missionaries on the field. Some want to "micro-manage" all the details of the mission, whereas others leave the field to do pretty much what it wishes to do.

My first mission board had no experience on the field, and never visited the field; our current board has field administrators who do visit the field. The first situation worked out in our situation because we had an extremely capable and experienced senior missionary on the field. We had a good team effort and he was able to do some of the counseling we needed, as well as give advice on the field. Also, I am pretty well organized and a self-starter by nature and appreciated having some free rein to develop our programs. However, a young individual (I was 48 when we started in Suriname) who lacked organizational skills, or who was struggling with culture shock would have been in a difficult position.

The goals of the home office and the missionary on the field may be different. The missionary may feel that the mission board simply uses the missionary to further its own goals of expansion and covering their financial expenses. They may focus primarily on recruiting missionaries, opening new fields, and securing financial and prayer support for the missionaries. On the other hand, the mission board may believe that the missionary is focusing just on his small ministry, without seeing the broader picture of the mission needs overseas.

Both sides need to recognize some of the problems facing the other individual. We were blessed with a wonderful field director, who was totally supportive of our ministry, involved in giving prayer support and advice, and any other service that he could provide. I am amazed at the load that our field directors must handle. This particular man is responsible for overseeing over 60 missionaries, including their finances (he must approve any purchases over $500 which are not already budgeted,) their ministry needs, and any health issues. He attempts to visit each missionary on a regular basis as possible. This involves raising funds for travel, and traveling long distances, often over a number of time zones, and sometimes involves tiring trips into remote areas. This is exhausting even for a young man, and our field administrators are all seasoned missionaries. We were most fortunate. He understood and could give advice. I did not have to explain "how it is" in a developing country, as he had personal experience with the various limitations of living overseas.

Pastoral Care for the Missionary

Many missionaries feel the lack of pastoral care. They are "giving out" to the nationals, but need care themselves, especially if conflict situations arise. It may be difficult for the field director to be able to devote the necessary time to do pastoral care, or he may lack any training or experience in doing so. When I was with our former mission, I especially appreciated one of our supporting pastors coming to preach for us. He did an excellent job, but what was more helpful to me personally was being able to sit down with him and develop a biblical perspective on some issues that I was facing. On that visit, he was my pastor, and I appreciated his ministry. Apparently, the lack of pastoral care is a major problem for many missionaries.

Financial Conflicts

Financial issues can also present problems. I know that one missionary left a field because he refused to pay any taxes to the US government, which was, of course, against mission policy. The missionary should understand the financial arrangements and agree with them prior to going to the field. Our first mission chose to cover its administrative costs by charging a percentage of the missionary's income. However, there was a big discussion about what should be done with special project money. The missionaries opposed any

CHAPTER 16: CONFLICT RESOLUTION

percentage to be taken of funds raised for special projects, while the home office wanted to use funds to help defray their expenses. Other missions may bill directly for their services.

There may also be discrepancies between the earning power of the missionary on the field and the mission board staff. For example, the mission staff may have wives that work. But, in many fields, this is not possible, either because of the workload involved, or the regulations of the mission or the country itself. Some sort of equity is advisable. However, I must add that the Lord has amply provided for us as His servants, and we have more than enough. May His name be praised.

Conflicts in Philosophy

Another more difficult area of conflict is difference in philosophy. This difference became marked after many denominations were taken over by liberal philosophy. The older missionaries on the field were often conservative and held to the fundamentals of the faith, but the new missionaries coming on the field did not do so. As I mentioned in my testimony, I was disturbed by my visit to the Presbyterian Board of Missions USA when I was in training for medicine. They were not at all concerned that I questioned the deity of Christ or the inspiration of the Scriptures. At that time, I was a typical liberal church member. Actually, it bothered me that the board was basically indifferent to my beliefs. It was not until 1974, while I was serving in Liberia, West Africa under USAID, that I received Christ, and became a Bible believing fundamental Baptist.

Conflicts with Charismatics

At this time, the philosophy of the charismatic movement has entered many mainline denominations, and the "seeker sensitive" and contemporary approach to services is becoming more prominent throughout the evangelical churches. We can anticipate that there will be many clashes, and indeed we have seen them in sister mission boards in Suriname. As I mentioned elsewhere, one Baptist church member went to Holland for training. He fell under the training of a fellow Surinamer in Holland who was Charismatic in philosophy and had built a mega-church. The man returned to Suriname and was placed in charge of their

Bible Institute and given a prominent leadership role in the church. His charismatic approach ended up splitting the church with a number of members following him to form another congregation when he was unable to change the direction of the Baptist church.

There are other significant areas of conflict between missionaries, especially in mission boards which have a broad base with different doctrinal positions. Some boards like Wycliffe have people from a wide variety of churches.

Conflicts Between Missionaries

I have already mentioned previously some of the problems which can occur between new missionaries and older ones. These types of situations have occurred since the beginning of modern missions. Such venerable missionaries as William Carey and his partners, William Ward and Mr. & Mrs. Marshman, and even Hudson Taylor, had major conflicts with new missionaries coming to the field. We can anticipate that such conflicts will meet us now as well.

I will include a list from Allen over the desires which younger missionaries have for the senior missionaries.[59]

1. A model for the younger missionaries in spiritual, mental and physical life
2. Good communicators
3. Flexible enough to entertain new ideas
4. Open to new ways of doing things
5. Ability to solve personal problems and conflicts
6. Ability to teach
7. Shepherd and nourish others
8. Seek the growth and success of those under them
9. A servant's heart
10. Willingness to train younger leaders
11. Experience as team leaders
12. Understanding the new generation
13. Sensitive to conflicts facing the new workers

CHAPTER 16: CONFLICT RESOLUTION

14. Sacrifice personal ambition to help younger missionaries
15. Help supervise planning

When I read this list, I was shocked, and wondered if the older leader would need to also walk on water. Who can measure up? But it is a good list to challenge every senior missionary. The senior missionary can help the new missionary set reasonable goals and to adjust in order to diminish culture shock. He should pray for them and do whatever is possible for them to have success.

As missionaries, we should be able to resolve our conflicts Biblically. If we are truly born again, we do have the Holy Spirit indwelling us. We have the Bible to guide us. We can seek out passages which help us to understand our feelings. We need to practice forgiveness of others as well as ourselves. At times, we will need the counsel and prayer of others.

Personal Separation

A further area of potential conflict lies in the area of personal separation. Different standards of dress, music, Bible texts, and other issues can lead to real conflicts. Even in the same denomination or faith group, potential for conflict exists. In most cases, the missionary does not have the choice to decide who works with him or not and there is a real potential for clashes. Openness and transparency can help resolve conflicts, as well as much prayer, and trying to understand the other individual's feelings and point of view.

Family Conflicts

The most crucial area of family conflict is between husband and wife. Not only does conflict exist in the home, but the situation may become open to the national church as well. The constant exposure to nationals may contribute to this situation becoming known, especially when the wife needs household help. The nationals are usually quite aware of what goes on in the house and may understand a remarkable amount of English. They can also read the non-verbal clues that will reveal tensions within the family structure.

Husband and wife conflicts may occur in many areas. They may disagree on the education and raising of their children. They may have financial conflicts. A particular problem is in the area of vocation. Do both marriage partners feel called to the field? One situation arose when the wife had felt called before marriage, but it was never clear that the husband was called. However, prior to their marriage, he had promised to go overseas as a missionary. When they finally went overseas many years later, there was considerable conflict, which eventually resulted in their return to the USA without completing their first term.

Dr. Marjory Foyle emphasized that when the couple are being evaluated by the mission board, it is very helpful to interview each member apart to determine how the individual feels without being under pressure from the partner. She found that the missionary wife was often freer to "open up" when speaking to her privately.[60] The situation may especially be true in the situation of the wife, who may have little to do if her children are no longer in the home, either because they are away at school or they have left the home. She may have additional problems in a Muslim country because of the restrictions placed on wives, who are expected to stay at home and rarely appear in public without their husbands.

Conflicts Between Parents and Children

The family may have additional conflicts between parents and children, especially during the teenage years. The teenagers are often "third culture" children, a mixture of the home culture and the culture of the host country. Children often feel more at home in the host country, where they have grown up, than in the USA, which was the childhood home of their parents.

The children's education is one of the key areas to address. The parents need to come to a decision about which of three basic options is best for the education of their children.

Home-school

This, of course, demands a great deal of time from the mother, who needs to be well organized and capable of teaching in this framework.

CHAPTER 16: CONFLICT RESOLUTION

There is a proliferation of materials which allow the parents to do this effectively and efficiently. For example, my daughter in Suriname has nine children, and has home schooled all of them. All have done well, and the four oldest have gone to college in the USA and done very well academically. She has used the A Beka DVD system. At least in the past, they allowed missionaries to keep the materials; those in the USA are supposed to return them at the end of the year. Of course, A Beka is upgrading with some new materials every few years, but the basics remain the same. When she started teaching her children, there were three families with children in Suriname of school age. The three worked together to be able to share the materials. They also ordered multiple copies of the workbooks so that if there was an upgrade, they still had copies of the workbooks which correlated with their DVDs which they shared.

Local Schools

Some parents decide to have their children attend local schools. Sometimes, these schools are in English, and are basically day schools, perhaps run by a mission, or an embassy or other group. Others send their children to the public schools. My son in Hungary had all four children attend local Hungarian schools. All four have done well in Hungary and have done very well in the American system as well. The teaching is usually in the national language, and the system of teaching is that of the host country. These students may have some adaptation challenges if they attend college in the USA. His children are all good students, but we notice that their vocabulary in English is a bit limited. Because they are relatively close to German-speaking countries, they also have German as a second language, and are quite competent in German too. Their youngest daughter, now in her second year in college, was ranked number two in German in a national competition. She is currently studying international communications in the USA and doing very well. The older three children finished college in the USA with very good grades.

Boarding School

Some parents use a boarding school. My son-in-law's parents sent all four children to a variety of different boarding schools. Most work out well, especially if they are well run, and have good dorm parents. The schools are often geared to allow the parents more extended times with their children than would be true of a standard school schedule. Years ago, Rift Valley boarding school had a schedule, I understand, with three months of instruction and one month to go home. My son-in-law attended a boarding school in both Suriname and Brazil, and also stayed in other Christian homes, at times, for schooling purposes. He has maintained contact with several of those people through the years. He stayed also in a few places he stayed other than boarding schools – with Kathy Young in Moengo, Suriname, with the Jenkins Sr. in Paramaribo, Suriname after the boarding school closed, and with the Baneys in the US.

All three systems have both advantages and disadvantages. It appears that the main factor is a good relationship between husband and wife, and a good relationship with the children. Often the parents have more difficulty adapting than their children. However, it seems that more parents are opting for home schooling now that internet communication opens many options for teaching.

The Missionary and His Own Parents

Perhaps here is a logical place to mention that the relationship between the missionary and his own parents is also important. The person having difficulty with his parents in the USA is likely to bring those adjustment problems with him to the field. We have had personal experience dealing with situations where missionaries had unresolved problems with parents which adversely affected their relationship with senior missionaries on the field. It certainly is preferable to have such problems resolved before the individual arrives on a foreign field, although this is not always possible.

It is not uncommon for a single woman missionary to be tapped by her family to care for an elderly parent, returning from the field to do so. One single lady missionary who once was a co-worker in Suriname ended up coming off the field twice – once to care for her father, and

CHAPTER 16: CONFLICT RESOLUTION

another time to care for her mother, after they had divorced years before. I suspect that the attitude in many families is that a single woman missionary can come off the mission field more easily than they can adjust to caring for an elderly parent and expect them to do so.

Conflicts with National Workers

Many of the areas of potential conflict revolve around where the national church believes that the missionaries should work and the type of work they should do. For example, the church may need someone to work in a remote area in the interior, but it may be difficult for the missionary to handle such a location. They may also try to place a missionary in a job position where there is a need, but it is outside the individual's real talents and interest.

The missionary may have problems allowing the national to lead, especially if he or she had had superior training before coming to the field. I made a deliberate choice to place myself under a national pastor for the last three years of our time in Suriname even though my training was superior, and indeed, I had trained the pastor. Our goal was strong national churches. The nationals need the opportunity to develop leadership skills. It is important to give responsibility and also give the authority to fulfill the responsibilities.

A very sad story of conflict with both other missionaries and with nationals was related in the life of Dr. Helen Roseveere (known also as Mama Luka.) She had taken over a medical work in Ibambi which had been started before by the famous missionary C. T. Studd. She built an entire nursing program and ran it well. When the Congo was in turmoil, she left for England for a few years. She returned and the Simbas overran the hospital, she was captured and raped, and again returned. During these years, she was replaced by a male doctor who was placed over her. After her return, the students rebelled and refused to listen to her, apparently a reaction to a strong-willed woman from England after they had been freed as a colony. However, she was able to let the Lord deal with her hurt, her emotions, and the destruction of her pride in her accomplishments, and the Lord used her greatly to speak for Him during the last years of her life. She had experienced great conflict both with other missionaries as well as with the nationals whom she was serving, but allowed

Conflicts in the Area of Finances

There may be conflicts in the area of finances. Although the churches are to be self-supporting, there is often a tendency to look to the expatriate as a source of funds. Another very difficult situation is when individuals, especially pastors, in the churches, come requesting funds from the missionary. The contrast between the missionary salary and that of most nationals is great, and this situation places the missionary in a difficult position. Furthermore, what the missionary considers real hardship may not be seen in the same light by other nationals living in the country. In one situation, the national church had a stated policy that nationals were not to request funds personally from missionaries. The church told the missionaries to refer any such request to a group of nationals to handle the request.

I was approached a number of times. I finally decided to ask the individual to approach those who had control of the finances to see if the church could help them, and that I would be happy to help through the church. That meant that the nationals would be assessing the need. Their perspective on real needs was better than mine. I do not remember being approached for a need specifically after that decision. Of course, if it is an obvious need or emergency, I would help.

The Need for the Missionary to Work Himself Out of a Job

The relationship between the national leadership and the missionary is important. My contention was that I needed to work myself out of a job and develop national leadership. There is a tension between doing the job the way that you want to see it done, and to have things done by the national leadership. I have concluded that it is usually better to have things done by nationals, even if things are not always done as professionally as if you did them yourself. This is, of course, the way we train our children as well. And ultimately, I have found that often the

CHAPTER 16: CONFLICT RESOLUTION

national do things much better than I can do them. We made training national leadership a priority.

We need to recognize that there are many ways to approach one's work, and many ways to solve problems. What works best for me is likely to be different from many of the nationals. Also, as a foreigner, I was likely to make more mistakes because I was not as competent in the culture as a native.

It is also important to be willing to give not only the work to a national, but also the authority to carry out the work. For years, I had provided much of the funds for the churches, and people came to me for financial needs of the church. When the funds were completely turned over to the national church, for a few weeks, people kept coming to me, and I kept referring them to the national leadership. Eventually they stopped coming to me.

Openness, love, and prayer are needed to maintain open communication between the missionary and the national churches to resolve some of these problems. It does help to be aware of common problems so that you can be pro-active.

Thought questions:

1. Do you have any family conflicts? Do you have problems with your parents, your spouse, or your children which have not been resolved?
2. What kind of expectations do you have for the missionaries on the field? How do you anticipate working with them successfully?
3. Are you willing to have a national in a position over you? Will you be willing to follow his/her leading?
4. Have you considered what you will be doing in the area of finances, especially in terms of your ministry among the nationals?

CHAPTER 17

SPECIAL ADJUSTMENTS FOR MISSIONARY WIVES: THE ROLE OF THE MISSIONARY WIFE

by Liz Patton and Kim Patton Champlin

Introduction

In doing some study for missions, I found a lack of information from the point of view of the missionary wife. Yet I have seen that often the wife has more adjustments to make overseas than the husband. The husband may have a set position to fill, but the wife must make a home for her family in any situation that the family encounters. Therefore, I asked my wife and daughter to write some of their observations concerning the mission field. My wife and I lived in Suriname as a couple for about 26 years, and after my daughter left for marriage, we were "empty-nesters. My daughter, married a year after arriving in Suriname, has lived with her husband, a missionary in Suriname, for 32 years. She has nine children, with four still at home. I would also refer the interested individual to Charin Patton's notes in the section on deputation. I will place the comments for both Liz and Kim separately, as their views relate to their situation. I will add a few comments on my own.

What Should the Wife's Role Be in Terms of the Husband's Call to Missions?

If My Husband is Called, so am I

Liz:

In my experience, and also looking at Biblical principles, if my husband is called to be a missionary, so am I. I am to be submissive to the head of the home. However, I firmly believe that if we are spiritually where we should be, God will confirm His call in my life too. Bob's call has always been confirmed in my life also, by the Lord.

The Wife Determines Not to Be a Hindrance

Through our married life, I have determined not to be a hindrance to Bob, but to encourage him in his vocation. I made that decision even before his salvation. For example, when he worked as a doctor, it seemed like he would always be called out when I had made a special meal, like a birthday meal for one of our children. I tried never to complain, but to say that it was special that he could be used to help others.

(Dr. Patton comments — This was a tremendous help to me. It kept the kids from resenting my work. Liz would say: "Isn't it wonderful that your father can help people with real problems." I remember one day when we were to go out on our anniversary, and instead, I went to donate blood for someone who needed my blood type.)

Surrender Our Rights to the Lord

As Christians, we must surrender our rights. Our rights all belong to the Lord, and my life should be lived to please Him and glorify Him. It is sad to hear a husband say that he can't go to a foreign field as a missionary because his wife is not willing. Sometimes we forget that we are to be a helpmate and not a second head of the family. It is sad to see that today many women are seeking their own careers, which may separate a family. Sometimes they make a move to accommodate the wife's job.

A Good Relationship Between Husband and Wife is Necessary

If a wife and husband have a good relationship, they should be able to talk and share feelings about both his call and the wife's hesitancy to support it. I know that my husband looks to me for feedback. Sometimes wives have a sixth sense. Both partners can share their observations. (Comment rdp: One of our pastors was sick in the lung pavilion where he was hospitalized for several weeks. I was able to lead one of the nurses to the Lord. My wife warned me not to go for follow-up at her home without someone accompanying me. Of course, that is always appropriate. I had not sensed any problem, but she did.)

CHAPTER 17: MISSIONARY WIVES

We knew we would return overseas sometime after leaving Liberia, but when we questioned a call five years later, our kids were all teenagers. Bob talked to our home pastor then and he felt the timing was not good. Our kids were all teenagers and doing well.

Five years after that, we were called to Suriname, and both of us knew that it was the right timing and our pastor said he had been expecting it. We waited a year before going on deputation to be home for our son's senior year in high school. He was the youngest child.

Pray Together

The husband and wife should pray together and ask for God's will. If one is not sure, they can write down the pros and cons of any choice, but the bottom line is God's will. He promises to direct our paths when we honor Him. (Proverbs 3:5-6)

Kim:

I don't really have any input here, as both of us were called while we were single, so I have never faced a husband being called.

What are the Challenges for the Wife During Deputation?

Liz:

Deputation is a challenge, especially with children. Although we did not have children traveling with us, we were able to observe other mothers during deputation. In some ways, it is a good preparation for the mission field, demanding flexibility. After you are called, be sure to teach your children about the mission field Help the children feel a part of the ministry. If they are old enough, they can help with singing or passing out prayer cards. Devise games for the car ride, looking for certain house colors, car colors or animals.

Finances

Finances demand that you be frugal, looking for bargains and sales. Take healthy snack foods in the car which can supplement the meals you buy. If your husband asks you, be prepared to be a bookkeeper, pay the bills, and do the record keeping so that he can focus on teaching and preaching. I have always handled the finances at his request. Major expenses go to him, but the everyday expenses he leaves to me. A wife can be very helpful in that realm if her husband wants it.

Do Not Spoil Your Kids

It is important to show your kids that it is more important to serve God than to earn a lot of money or gain a lot of the world's riches. Do not spoil your kids with the things of the world.

Be Transparent

While on deputation, be willing to be transparent to others about your struggles performing missionary work. If you have a chance to speak to a ladies' group, be honest and share your problems. Be available to answer questions. Show that you are a real person with ups and downs, but by the grace of God, you can do what He wants (Phil. 4:13).

Help with Displays

Help your husband by having an attractive display. If that is not a talent of yours, find someone to help, or work on ideas with your husband. It was not a talent of mine, so I asked for help.

Help with Communication

Good communication with your potential supporters is vital. The wife can often handle routine letters and thank you notes for her husband. Especially with a family, it is a big challenge to remain organized and manage your time well.

Kim:
The Missionary Wife and Deputation

We were a young couple with no children on deputation, so I don't have much to add about schooling of children, etc. Basically, I would encourage the wife to go to as many of the meetings as possible. I think in our 32 years on the field, I have only missed two meetings with Ethan.

CHAPTER 17: MISSIONARY WIVES

Timing and Finances

Since we did not have children, we both worked for the first six months of our deputation and then traveled full-time. The wife should be supportive by living and eating as economically as possible in their travels. Dollar menus at restaurants are boring but stretch the budget tremendously. Since normally you are fed a big meal by the church, eating lightly while traveling to and from the meeting shouldn't be a problem, and might help prevent excessive weight gain.

Preparation of the Children

If your children are well-disciplined and used to obeying, traveling with them should not be a problem. Children should be taught to go to sleep when they are told to do so (regardless of where they are), to eat neatly and quietly whatever they are served with a good attitude, to have good manners, etc. When we had young children who needed naps, we found it helpful to plan shorter trips for nap time so that they would sleep for a large portion of the trip. That helped prevent boredom. When traveling on all-day trips, etc. we planned to stop at a fast-food restaurant that had a play area and allowed 30-60 min. for the children to play to help burn up energy. Then, normally, they would fall asleep as soon as we started traveling again. Whenever one person needed to make a pit stop, everybody was required to go so that we would not have to stop again quickly. Although we traveled with snack foods, we rarely gave the children drinks between meals as that eliminated frequent pit stops.

Organization of Trips

Ethan always organizes his meetings in groups in the same area of the country rather than bouncing back and forth across the country like a ping-pong ball. That saves a lot of money on gas and removes a lot of stress from extra hours on the road.

Attitude

If the wife has a good attitude, then most likely the children will as well. If the wife is complaining, then the children will pick up on that as well.

Ministry in the Churches

Basically, a wife should be prepared to handle whatever she is asked to do in terms of teaching while they are at a meeting. Although Ethan never volunteers me for things if I'm not asked, we also never turn down opportunities when somebody requests me to do things.

Ladies groups

I have found that sharing my personal testimony and lessons I have learned on the field (or deputation) is well-received, rather than just trying to give a general Bible lesson that a non-missionary could give. Also, having time to answer women-type questions about the mission field is good as well.

Children's Classes

We often use a missionary story that is similar to the culture in which we minister. I also take various items of interest from our display table to use in sharing with the children. Teaching a familiar Bible song in the language of your country (like Jesus loves me) is also fun for the kids.

Setting up the Display

Normally, the children and I set up the display while my husband sets up the DVD presentation or talks with the pastor.

Availability to Answer Questions

The children and I always stay by the display table before and after the service to answer questions people may have, etc.

Helping with Administrative Tasks

Ethan is not a letter writer, so I handle all of the correspondence for him, much as a secretary would do. He makes all the phone calls, but then gives me the information (schedule of meetings, etc.) and I write all the confirmation letters, etc. I always have him proofread anything before it is sent to double-check for accuracy. I carry Suriname postcards with me to leave as thank you notes in the homes in which we stay. Ethan also gives me all the checks (love offerings, etc.) which I keep together and send to our mission every one-two weeks. Also, I

CHAPTER 17: MISSIONARY WIVES

have a notebook, in which I record any traveling expenses that are considered business, keep receipts, etc. Those are little details that I can do easily and allow him to focus on things that only he can do, like talking with the pastors, preparing messages and lessons, etc.

Preparation for Overseas Life

Liz:

Suggestions

In terms of preparing for overseas life, a survey trip is very helpful. Also speak with your children about the field, the people, and the country. Be excited about God's call and reinforce it. If other missionaries are from that field, ask them about what you need to bring and what is available.

Your Relationship with the Lord and Heart Attitude

While on the field, the key is really the heart attitude and relationship with the Lord. Are you totally committed? Are you willing to do whatever God wants regardless of the cost? This does not mean that things will always be easy.

You Are Being Watched

Remember, we are being watched by the nationals. They watch how we relate to our husbands and children as well as how we relate to them personally. You must always remember to respect and submit to your husband. This is a must if you want your kids and the nationals to respect him. They pick up not only on what you say but your body language and your attitude. We were thrilled to hear one of our nationals say: I want my relationship to my husband to be like your relationship to yours. I see how you help him and support him. (Proverbs 12:4).

Never Talk Badly About Your Husband

Never talk badly about your husband's shortcomings to anyone, even to other missionaries. The Lord is to meet all our needs, and not our husband. (Proverbs 31:11-12). Also build him up to your children. I have never had nationals come to me complaining about my husband because they know that I will not listen to their complaints but send them directly to him. (Comment: We made a point of supporting each other. I cannot remember having an argument in front of our children. In fact, one daughter was telling her husband that she never saw us arguing. He did not believe it – his parents had a very stormy relationship. We would settle our differences privately. When on the mission field, we did the same thing – supporting each other in front of the nationals. One result is that no national came to either of us complaining about the other. If such a thing might happen, I know that my wife would have said: You need to talk directly to Dominee [Pastor]).

Being Versus Doing

Titus 2:3-5 shows us that *to be* is more important than *to do*. If our marriage had stress in the USA, adjustments on the field will make things worse, not better. What is inside us will come out under stress. And we will have many stresses and adjustments; language (or languages, as we had two) to learn, adjustment to the weather, new area, new foods, new customs, etc.

The Wife Needs to Set the Tone in the Home

You will be exposed to so many needs that you can be overwhelmed and wonder how to manage. Look to the Lord for balance. The wife needs to set the tone in the home. She must help create a good attitude in the children so that the nationals feel free to visit. The home must be a safe haven for your husband. Look at interruptions in your schedule as God-ordained. Be accepting of his schedule and interruptions without complaining. Be an encourager to your husband, and not like Job's wife.

Language Considerations

Language learning can be hard. Suddenly you are an adult, yet any kid on the street can speak better than you can. Accept all corrections graciously. Otherwise, nationals will not correct your mistakes. Be willing to laugh at yourself and be willing to be flexible.

Work as a Team

Work as a team. Avoid working in the flesh. Initially I worked with children and later with ladies. Then I worked with teenage girls and young adults. Now nationals are in charge of those ministries, and I am

CHAPTER 17: MISSIONARY WIVES

able to help my husband more directly since our nest is empty. My husband likes me to attend his Bible Institute lessons both in Suriname and in the USA. I handle the administrative aspects and corrections stateside. I also attend his classes, because he likes feedback. (Comment: This role has continued since leaving the field. My wife tries to be in EVERY class that I teach. She is also with me in the office. She gives invaluable feedback about the classes as well as help encouraging the students. Although my office in the USA has two large windows, I like her physical presence when young ladies come to the office with problems with their courses. This eliminates any awkward situations, and the students are more comfortable. She assists with attendance and other administrative tasks, and works on being available for the students)

Household Help

Household help is an adjustment for most of us. There is a loss of privacy, and we associate household help with the wealthy. However, when you hire household help, you give someone a job, and you free up your time to be able to do something else. If you have children in the home, involve them in cleaning up, doing dishes, and other appropriate jobs. Adapt to the child's age but let everyone have his job. When the children are young, household help can enable you to do some other things so that you are not always tied to the home. Because many of the conveniences of the USA are not available in other countries (for example, dishwashers, sometimes washer and drier, etc.), routine maintenance of the home does take longer than in the USA.

Adapt Your Eating Habits

Try to adapt your eating habits to fit the local produce. Many countries have imported food from America, but typically they are very costly. Kids need to learn to eat what is set before them regardless of being in the USA or on the mission field.

Learning from Nationals

You can learn how to cook with local produce and use that time as an opportunity to get to know the nationals better, and to show interest in their culture and foods. (Comment: My wife is an excellent cook. She is able to cook most of the standard meals of whichever country we are in.

When in Suriname, she also cooked with her language helper and went to the market to purchase food. This way she picked up a lot of the language as well as the culture. Most individuals are delighted when you appreciate their food and culture.)

Ministry

Liz:

Your Children Are Vital to the Ministry

Remember that children are a vital part of your ministry. If you want to reproduce yourself multiple times, begin with your children since you have maximum contact and influence on them. Wives should look for opportunities to work with ladies and children. The nationals will watch your own kids as well as you. Your walk in the Lord, and how your kids behave will speak more than your talk. Make your walk say the same thing as your talk.

In my situation, our kids were all grown, married and involved in ministry or their local churches. The lady who took over as leader of the ladies group in our main church would ask me from time to time to teach on child rearing. She already knew the Biblical principles which I had taught previously, but she commented that her children were still at home. Until they leave and are on their own still living for the Lord, she said that her testimony would not be as strong as mine. She said: Your kids are out of the home and still following the Lord.

(Comment: One of the great lacks in our work in Suriname was for the nationals to have good models for a proper Christian home life. This was especially true when we first arrived in Suriname. The culture is matriarchal, meaning that the cultural line of inheritance and power goes through the woman's family rather than the husband. The most influential man for a child is often his mother's brother rather than his father. Separation or divorce was common. Women often dominate and run the family. Children are often disrespectful to their parents. Therefore, a godly Christian family is a great benefit in such a situation. It may be difficult to change your old ways without a positive example lived out in front of you.)

CHAPTER 17: MISSIONARY WIVES

Work as a Team and Protect Your Husband

Work as a team as much as you can. Help your husband with typing, proofreading, treats for classes or meetings, prayer, and correspondence. Accept his schedule. Often, he may be gone to meetings, or people may come to see him at inconvenient times. Try to protect your husband from over-commitment.

Family and Ministry Needs

It is important to balance priorities of family versus ministry. There are many needs between husband and wife, many needs with the children, and many needs in the ministry. Ask God to show you what ministries He wants in your life. Don't automatically say *Yes* to everything. God does not expect you to do everything, or work with everyone.

Train Someone to Take Over

They may not work like you do, but that is Okay. The national woman knows her people and will be able to minister to them in a way that you never can. Your primary goal should be to teach her to have a close walk with the Lord.

Preparing for Overseas Life

Kim:

List What You Need

Each wife should contact another missionary wife already serving on the field to get an idea of what she might want to take to the field, what is available locally, etc. If the couple has children, then consideration should be taken as to materials for home schooling, clothes for them to grow into or extra fabric, etc.

Packing

Find out what you should take with you and start eliminating whatever is not needed. Each couple will be different as to how they divide the packing responsibilities. In the early years, Ethan insisted on doing all the packing. As our family has grown, the children and I end up doing much of the preliminary packing. Also, find out in what type of containers it is best to pack, such as plastic barrels, Tupperware containers, etc.

The Missionary Wife and Overseas Life
Spiritual Growth and Prayer

It hardly seems necessary to mention this, but every missionary wife should have her own daily devotions, preferably early in the morning before the rush of the day, to help her cope with the day. Whenever I had a nursing baby, I would keep my prayer list by the rocking chair in which I nursed my baby. That way, I could pray while I nursed the baby. Before I had older children to help me with things, that was often the only "down time" that I had during the day. Each couple should also preferably have a daily prayer time together, as well as devotions with their children starting at a very young age. In our family, my husband and I normally have a prayer time together in the morning following our personal devotions, and then family devotions following supper each night, since we don't have many evening obligations.

Relationship with Her Husband

A missionary wife must maintain a close relationship with her husband. A husband and wife should have a "best friends" relationship because they often have no other really close friends on the field. A wife's relationship with her husband should be her major priority. It takes precedence over her children and ministry. She must never allow the ministry to cause her to neglect her own family. How involved each wife is in the ministry will depend on her husband's feelings on the subject. (I might add here that often major tests will come in your ministry as you are encroaching on what was Satan's territory which you are now contesting. One of his favorite targets is the family. He may attack the husband-wife relationship or that of parents and one or more children. My wife was my strongest advocate. When I would question a challenge to our ministry, my strongest consolation was knowing that she was always for me. Rdp)

CHAPTER 17: MISSIONARY WIVES

Adjustment to Climate

I don't know what to say here. You just accept the weather the way it is and learn to live with it. Living in the tropics does have the advantage of being able to wear the same clothing year-round. That makes life much simpler with rapidly-growing children!

Adjustment to Food

It is ideal to learn to cook as much as possible with what is available locally. Normally this is much more economical. Having a few American treats for special occasions is fine, but you should not eat like an American on just imported things.

Schooling for the Children

Each couple will have to make their own decisions regarding schooling for their children based on the situation in their own country. Some missionaries choose to put their children in the local public schools and feel that is an outreach into the community. Although this is not common anymore, some still do send their children to boarding schools.

The Most Common Choice for Schooling

Home-schooling is probably the most common choice in this day and age. There are many home-schooling options available, but we highly recommend the A Beka DVD program. It gives the missionary kid a very high-quality education with a minimum of the mother's time. If the children are well-disciplined, they can do most of the schoolwork on their own, with just supervision and grading done by the mother. This allows the wife and mother to keep up with her own housework and still have some time for ministry. (I would mention that it is a huge advantage to have well-disciplined children as well as a well-organized mother! I have seen major problems in families in the USA who home-school but the children are not disciplined, or the home is disorganized and their education is haphazard. Rdp)

Since A Beka allows overseas missionaries to lease the DVD's permanently, then for those with a large family, it is fairly economical. This option is not available to missionaries in North America, including Canada and, I assume, Mexico. What we personally have done to help cut down on costs is share the cost of the original purchase with co-workers whose children also used the program, had our children use notebook paper for many of their tests and quizzes so that test/quiz booklets can be re-used, and purchased in advance extra workbooks (especially English Grammar and Arithmetic courses) for our younger children so that we do not have to upgrade every time A Beka upgrades a course or grade level.

Purchasing Items for the Home, Food, Etc.

This will vary from couple to couple and field to field. In the Champlin families, the men do most of the shopping while the wives stay at home.

Household Help

There are not as many automatic household devices; so, everything takes longer. Once again this will vary depending on the country and the season of life of the missionary couple. When I had just preschoolers and lived in the jungle with very few conveniences, etc., I had a lady help with laundry a few days a week. This saved me many hours of time, as we re-cycled our wash water, hung clothes on the lines, etc. Once we moved into town where we have regular water and electricity, I am able to get an automatic washer and dryer as well as other modern conveniences My oldest child was close to ten and able to help with chores. Since that time, I have never had hired help, as I prefer to teach my children to work. We start our children doing simple chores while they are still preschoolers. Also, with a large family on a limited budget, we have not had extra funds to pay for household help. Since we live on the church property, my husband does have different teens help with various outdoor jobs when needed, and when we don't have children of the right age and gender to handle the work themselves.

Language Learning

It is essential that the wife learn the language fluently so that she can minister effectively with her husband and interact with the people.

CHAPTER 17: MISSIONARY WIVES

Adapting to the Culture

Once again, this is just a decision of the will. You decide that this new country is now home and adapt as well as you can. There are certain things you will **not** adopt for various reasons, but you should never feel uncomfortable in your new home country. For example, Surinamers do not wear shoes in homes. So, we always remove our shoes in our own home as well as in other's homes. However, I do not let my children run around naked or bathe in the yard (which violates Biblical principles) just because the nationals do. All of our children were born here in Suriname and consider this home, not America. If the parents still consider America home and long for furloughs, this attitude will affect the children's attitudes as well.

Ministry in the Church

The one thing I would emphasize in terms of all areas of ministry is that a missionary wife's primary Biblical function is her own family. So, she should never take on ministry (no matter how big the need is) if it will hurt her own family or cause her to neglect their needs. Over the years, the ministries I have been involved with have varied depending on the ages of my children. However, I have always tried to be active in ministries that did not detract from my family, especially those that took place simultaneously when my family was also occupied. For example, I would teach Sunday School or ladies classes during regular church hours, when all the rest of the family was occupied. I would go on visitation or hold discipleship lessons in the afternoons when my children were playing outside. As much as possible, I have people come to our home for lessons so that my children are still able to play outdoors. I also often have less distractions at home than in the homes of the nationals.

Support of Husband

Basically, a wife should help her husband in the ways that are important to him, which may vary from man to man. (I will comment again because this is SO important. If the husband and wife are not a team, it is hard to see how they can have an effective ministry. When I studied the history of China Inland Mission, I was impressed with their great zeal for souls, but felt that they went too far when they split up couples at times so that the ministry would reach more souls for Christ. It is vital for the ministry to model a Biblical family with the husband and wife demonstrating a godly relationship which the nationals can copy. Rdp)

Helping with Ladies Work

Ladies are more effective reaching women, especially training them in the areas of the home, so most missionary wives will be involved in some aspect of ladies' ministry.

Helping with Children's Work

Working with children is also a regular way that missionary wives can help in the ministry.

Training Nationals

The missionary wife should encourage nationals to work with her in the ministries, with the idea of being able to do the same ministries themselves in the future.

Church visitation and outreach

My husband and I normally go on visitation together. This eliminates a lot of problems in terms of running into women at home alone, etc. When the children were young, we just took them along. It is amazing how many doors they opened. Now that we have older children, the older ones usually babysit the younger ones for us while we go on visitation.

Ministry with Other Missionaries

If you are planning to work in a team ministry, you should spend time together before committing to do so to be sure you are compatible in ministry philosophies, etc. Then, once you begin working together, good communication is a key to maintaining a good working relationship.

CHAPTER 17: MISSIONARY WIVES

The Special Problems of Single Lady Missionaries

A single missionary can be an asset because they have less home responsibilities, but also a difficulty. It is ideal to have two singles working in the same location for companionship and to avoid the second wife syndrome that happens when the missionary husband has to care for the single lady missionary.

Ministry with Other Nationals

Once again, communication is important in maintaining a good working relationship.

Furlough: The Missionary Wife and Furlough
Schedule & Preparation

In our family, Ethan makes all the phone calls and I handle all the correspondence, which may include sending information to new pastors, confirmation letters, follow-up letters, etc. We work together on the schedule in terms of the time we will be in the U.S., planning meetings around special family activities (such as graduations and/or weddings as the children get older). Since most of our family are overseas, we have not based our schedule on visiting family in the U.S. However, some missionaries try to divide their furloughs between the two locations where their families live, so that the grandchildren can have quality time with the each set of grandparents.

Purchases While on Furlough

Priorities will vary for every missionary couple, but it is good to make a shopping list before you leave the field of things you want to bring back with you. I also take an inventory of what I have left of certain items (toiletries, spices, etc.) so I know how much to buy of certain items. Once again, school supplies must be taken into consideration, as well as Sunday School visuals and other ministry materials.

Traveling

The organization while traveling on furlough is similar to the travel plans for deputation. Once again, we schedule our meetings in certain areas of the country at a time. We try to have a home base in each area, even if we are only there for a week or two: either a missionary house in which we can stay, or somebody we have met in the past who always opens their home to us. It is much easier for the family to have a place of their own where they can retreat between meetings. With school-age children, we normally take shorter summer furloughs so that we don't have to handle schooling on the road. Also, since we live in the tropics, avoiding winter weather eliminates a lot of problems such as winter clothing, bad weather while traveling, etc.

We try to schedule some fun activities for the children in our travels. However, in reality, our children enjoy spending time with other like-minded children and families more than actual sightseeing. As your children get older, we have found that it is simpler to travel with one carry-on bag for every two children to share rather than larger suitcases. The older children can help pack for the younger ones so that the whole load does not fall on the mother. Also, older children can take responsibility for younger ones during the trips, such as helping to take them to the bathroom at restaurants (we never send them alone), helping them in buffet lines, etc. so that the husband and wife are freer to interact with the pastor or whoever takes them out.

Thought questions:

1. For the husband: What adjustments will you need to make to help your wife in:
   a. Deputation
   b. Time on the field
   c. Furlough

   I recognize that this is a rather broad question, and perhaps should be broken into three parts. Has any of the advice given opened your eyes to areas which you had not considered?

2. For the wife: What adjustments will you need to make to help your husband in:
   a. Deputation
   b. Time on the field
   c. Furlough

CHAPTER 17: MISSIONARY WIVES

I recognize that this is a rather broad question, and perhaps should be broken into three parts. Has any of the advice given opened your eyes to areas which you had not considered?

3. What areas do you consider especially important or challenging to give a good model of a Christian home to the people to whom you will be ministering?

CHAPTER 18
RETURNING TO THE USA

The Reasons for Returning

Some missionaries never plan to return to the USA. They plan to "die with their boots on" in the country to which they have been called, or perhaps to retire there if unable to continue working. However, the majority of missionaries do return to the USA after completing their ministry in another country. Some return to retire and look forward to retirement and re-establishing contacts with their family. Some return to the USA because they believe that their work in their chosen field has been completed and that the Lord would have them move on and leave the work to the nationals. Some return because of health reasons or family reasons. And some are terminated.

Adjustments

There are a number of adjustments for the returning missionary. The longer the missionary has been on the field and the larger the difference in the culture of the host country and the USA, the bigger the adjustments he can anticipate on return. The missionary may feel overwhelmed by modern technical advances which were unavailable in remote areas. The rapid pace of life may be difficult. If you have been overseas for many years, the USA is not the same country as when you left.

The Biggest Need: Finances

Perhaps the two biggest needs of the returning missionary are finances and the need for meaningful work. Many missionaries have major problems financially, especially if the mission board has not set up a retirement program. A number of missionaries "opt out" of social security and may not have other sources of income. Some faith missions encourage the churches to continue to support retired missionaries at a reduced salary, but many churches do not do so. They want their funds to go to missionaries on the field. A number of mission boards or agencies do provide housing for missionaries at either a reduced cost, or perhaps no cost. This can be a tremendous blessing, allowing the missionary to have a place to stay, and also to fellowship with fellow missionaries.

I had contributed to Social Security since high school and had fulfilled the minimal requirements of 40 quarters. Fortunately for me, my salary before going overseas was that of a doctor rather than a poor medical student. Social security was a big help! It is difficult to set up a very substantial savings program on a missionary salary, but it is important to have some sort of savings.

The Second Big Problem

The second problem listed is that of meaningful work. The missionary has often been in the center of activity. Everybody knows him by name. Suddenly his work, his position, and possibly his profession are gone. For most individuals, some form of meaningful work is still important. Many different possibilities exist. In my own case, in addition to the possibility of teaching missions in college, I was approached about possible furlough replacement for overseas missionaries. Some assist in counseling missionaries on the field. Others may be involved in helping with clerical work, short-term work overseas, serving as translators, church planting in the USA, and a wide variety of other positions.

Returning for Health Reasons

Returning to the USA for health reasons is often a real blow, but again, it is often possible to find very meaningful ministry back in the USA. Sometimes health issues will resolve. Some missionaries return to help their children through high school and/or college, or to care for elderly parents. This is especially true for single woman missionaries. Often her married siblings expect that she will return to care for elderly parents when they are no longer able to care for themselves.

It is important for the missionary to acknowledge grief in leaving the field, but to be realistic and to draw a healthy line with the past. If overseas service at the time is not possible or advisable, one needs to recognize that overseas service is not necessarily the highest calling on the missionary's life at the moment.

CHAPTER 18: RETURNING TO THE USA

Termination

Termination is usually a tragedy. The investment to get a missionary overseas is extraordinary, and one desires to receive the maximum return on such an investment. Frank Allen lists several causes:[61]

1. Lack of gifts - the individual tries to do something for which he is not gifted. One of the more tragic situations is when a missionary is extremely effective in a particular position – for example, as a church planter. Because of his effectiveness, he is promoted to a high executive position in the mission for which he is not equipped nor skilled, and he fails in that new position.

2. Culture shock. The individual is not able to make the necessary adjustments to a different culture. Allen also refers to "culture fatigue" – that it is too difficult to make the continuous adaptation necessary to learn the language, adapt to food, climate, culture, etc. I believe that a good orientation can often assist the missionary in adjusting to culture shock. It may also be possible to move to a different location or take a break from the new culture to allow one to adapt more slowly.

3. Unfulfilled expectations – the missionary was unable to complete what he wanted to do. For example, one missionary went overseas to teach in the seminary, but was assigned to administrative and financial duties. These situations may be anticipated. It is good to address the type of work you are to do before even getting to the field. Of course, adaptability is very helpful, but one may be forced out of his God-given talents by the needs of the mission at the time. This situation can lead to a very dissatisfied missionary.

4. Moral problems, especially sexual immorality: Our sexual nature does not stop when we go overseas. This is probably most common in single men, but single women may also become involved in immorality with men, or even women. Homosexuality is a real risk in some situations. If sexual

temptations are a problem before going overseas, they should be dealt with before leaving for the field.

5. Disagreements with the mission board and its policies. You should study the mission policies carefully before departure to be certain that you can abide by them. I would urge you to pay special attention to such issues as the approach to the Bible, which may include the basic text issue; how freely the individual may pursue his own mission goals versus control from the mission board or mission field director; a mixture of charismatic and non-charismatic missionaries; separation issues, including clothing; the financial policies of the board; and the method of discipline of the missionary.

6. Family problems – perhaps between husband and wife, or parents and children. The best time to solve these issues is before going to the field rather than adding family problems to the already daunting challenges of adapting to a new culture.

7. Language – the individual may never learn the language. People with a hearing deficit are at a real disadvantage because they may never hear the language pronounced properly and be able to imitate it. When we were in Suriname, we had two missionaries with substantial hearing loss. Both had difficulty speaking Sranantongo. However, each was able to communicate well enough to make a positive contribution to the ministry.

It is important to have debriefing and counseling when the individual returns to the USA for any reason. This is especially true for those who have been terminated. Every effort should be made to restore the individual to a position of function and productivity for the Lord. It may be in some situations that the missionary may return to the field and resume his ministry. It may be that he will have a new ministry back in the USA. Or it may be that he retires but continues to serve the Lord in his new life in the USA.

Thought questions:

1. Seven common reasons for leaving the field of your ministry are mentioned. Which, if any, do you see as a potential problem for

CHAPTER 18: RETURNING TO THE USA

yourself, and how can you be pro-active in meeting the problem or solving it?
2. Have you given thought to work that might continue when you are no longer on the field? What are your thoughts?
3. What financial plans have you made for your life after your ministry overseas is finished, if any?

CHAPTER 19
THE INCARNATIONAL MISSIONARY

Incarnation and Enculturation

In the incarnation, Jesus Christ, God the Son, became flesh and blood and lived as a man on the earth. He became 100% man without ceasing to be 100% God. He came as a Jew, was born into a Jewish family, spoke the language of the Jews, was raised as a Jew, and was looked on as a Jewish prophet. Some say that we should become incarnate in our host country like Jesus did when He came as a Jew. Of course, this is not totally possible. When we are born, we have essentially a blank slate as far as our culture and language is concerned. But we are enculturated, especially during the first years of childhood. When we go to another country, that slate of culture is not wiped clean. We carry our language and culture with us. But we can adapt and adopt some of the ways of the new culture. Lingenfelter talks about becoming 150% people, by which he means that we become more than we are now as we accept part of the host culture.[62]

Every culture is an attempt by a people to meet their needs within the context of their environment. We have already looked at a number of different ways that people adapt. Culture per se is not sinful, but all cultures are contaminated with sin because people are sinners. Yet it is possible to live in a culture without sin because Jesus Christ did precisely that. Furthermore, He lives in every true believer. The task, then, is to live incarnate in the culture, reflecting the life of Christ in us, in the context of the culture. We need to see how to live in the context of the culture in a way that is Christ-honoring.

Come as Learners, Not Know-it-alls

We need to come into the culture as learners instead of those with all the answers. This attitude often opens doors to share the gospel. We need to recognize that there are often cross-cultural misunderstandings. We may have a block in understanding the culture. Anything that does not make sense usually means that we do not understand how it fits into the culture. Eventually as we learn and adjust to the culture, we can become bicultural and able to function comfortably in both cultures.

When I lived in Liberia, I worked hard at learning Liberian English. This is a sort of Creole and is spoken by virtually all the natives of Liberia. When I started working in the hospital, they told me that I would have difficulty understanding the nationals (that was true) but that they would understand me (that was NOT true). One day an Episcopal priest gave a lecture on Liberian English. After hearing him speak, I decided to learn. When I first started, everyone laughed, but within a few weeks, I became very fluent. I can remember laughing at some Liberian doctors who returned to Liberia after they had been overseas for a number of years. When we were making rounds on our patients, they would start to ask the patient some questions. Often the patient would not understand them. Then I would ask them in Liberian English and they would understand immediately. Everybody would laugh that the American was speaking Liberian English, and the Liberian natives had forgotten it. Of course, in a few weeks they were much more fluent than I was. I became very comfortable in Liberian English, and usually spoke it in preference to American English when speaking to my Liberian friends and colleagues.

When I returned to the United States after five years in Liberia, I had a sort of reverse culture shock. Because all Liberian national patients were black, I was accustomed to speaking to all black people in Liberian English. This created some real problems for me when I returned to the United States and had black American patients. After a few months I learned not to speak in Liberian English anymore. When I came to Suriname ten years later, I ended up having mental confusion between Liberian English and Sranantongo, and now I can no longer speak Liberian English.

The Problem with Ethnocentrism

As we have seen in a variety of different contexts in this book, Western missionaries have had a major problem with ethnocentrism.[63] This is the attitude that "my culture is civilized and yours is not." It is really more of an emotional response than a conscious rational one. This

CHAPTER 19: THE INCARNATIONAL MISSIONARY

was a major problem during the 19th century, when the missionaries were often tied together with colonialism.[64] Many felt that they had to carry the "white man's burden" to help the poor Africans. They brought western culture mixed with the Christian belief. This attitude created a disaster. Much of Western civilization actually conflicts with Biblical truth. This is especially true as the United States has moved to modernism, and then to secular humanism, and finally to postmodernism. When we recognize our ethnocentrism, we can begin to have more empathy with our people. We need to learn perhaps more than we teach. We need to see others as individuals. And we need to remember that often our reaction to their culture may be defensive in nature, especially as it exposes the faults in our own western ideals.

I have tried hard to avoid ethnocentrism and bond with our people. However, some of the young people in the church, especially those attending the university, reacted against any white man. One of our young preachers who had real problems with me had worked for Amnesty International for a while. He reacted against my taking my position as pastor seriously and reacted against any show of authority. (At the time, I was the senior pastor of the main church.) Later, I turned over that position to a national pastor. After a few years, his attitude toward me changed, and we are good friends today.

Another situation came up while I was in Liberia, West Africa. I was professor of Internal Medicine and had an excellent relationship with the Liberian doctors, especially after I had adjusted to my medical work in Liberia during the first year. Once, the international conference of West African surgeons was held at our hospital in Monrovia, Liberia. I had finished my patient rounds for the morning and slipped into the back of the auditorium to listen to some presentations. It seemed like the entire temperature of the room dropped when the white man entered. I was very uncomfortable. Most of the other physicians had recently been in situations of colonial rule, while Liberia had been a free country for over 100 years. They resented my appearance in their meeting because I was a Caucasian.

Cultural Relativity

We need to respect all cultures, but this is not the same as cultural relativity. Cultural relativity contends that all cultures are of equal value, regardless of their standards or practices. Cultural relativity ties tightly with "political correctness" and postmodernism, but it does not always fit correctly with the Bible. We need to realize that Biblical norms are above all cultures. This contention makes the post-modernist furious. In his eyes, everything is acceptable except believing in absolute truth. (Ironically, he is absolutely convinced that no absolutes exist!) He believes that any claim to absolute truth is an attempt to dominate others and represents a pure power-play. The correct attitude for the believer is to study the values of our own culture as well as the culture which we are trying to reach. Then we need to compare both with Biblical norms. To accomplish this, our own ethnocentric ideas must be shattered.

We do not need to totally reject the new culture, or to become isolated, or to "go native." One missionary couple in the interior of Suriname felt that to reach the people, they needed to adapt to the cultural level of the people. They lived in a hut, and their children ran around naked and barefoot. Naturally, their children were infested with parasites. With their white skin, they had additional problems with sunburn in the tropical sun. The natives did not appreciate their lifestyle. It appeared to some that they were ridiculing them. Others felt they had nothing to teach them, because they were not doing anything different from the natives, and not doing the native things well. The Bible also has principles of decency and modesty that they were ignoring.

I remember that my wife and I had to put aside some of our own ideas when we came to Suriname. The view of most people, when missionaries go to a third world country, is that they are living in a hut and sleeping in hammocks. The senior missionary rented a rather nice house for us. It was not overly elaborate but quite nice. We felt a little bit out of place as if we were living above what we should be. But our people's reaction was different. They felt that the house was highly appropriate. Their attitude was: "You are a doctor, and you are a dominee (pastor). This type of house is the kind of house you need."

CHAPTER 19: THE INCARNATIONAL MISSIONARY

We needed to be willing to accept this house as appropriate, even though it went against my wife's wishes, who wanted to live more simply.

Even after 25 years in Suriname, I was still not a native. I will never be a native. My son-in-law, who was born here, is also not a native, although he speaks like a native. He understands the Bush Negro culture extremely well. However, he was raised in a different culture, because his parents are American missionaries. We can never fully enter into life with a new culture because we do not come into the culture with a blank slate.

However, there are some advantages to this situation. If we are total insiders in the culture, we may be viewed as competitors for leadership and resources. Many oral societies and peasant societies have the concept of "limited good." This means that there is only of a certain limited amount of money, relationships, food, prestige, etc. within the culture. As an insider, I become a competitor. But as an outsider, I am not in competition for resources, but bring resources in from the outside. This is at least one advantage to being a foreigner. Furthermore, we may be able to bridge the gap between cultures and protect our people from being misused.

When I was in Liberia, and later when I was in Suriname, I taught medicine in the academic hospital. However, I never opened a clinic or had private patients. In both countries, the number of people who could afford to go to a highly trained specialist was limited. Had I had a private practice, I would have been in competition with my colleagues. However, I was no economic threat as a teacher. The same situation occurred when some of the doctors we trained wanted to go to Europe or the USA for specialty training and certification. The older doctors did what they could to control how many students or trainees left for different specialties. These are additional examples of the concept of limited good.

Compartmentalization

Some people integrate partially into the culture by what we call compartmentalization. They do certain things in each culture like the people in that culture, and other things they will not do. This may result in a lot of tension, and it may appear that they are hypocritical. A better approach is to integrate into the culture, accepting the things in both cultures that correspond to biblical truth. Some things are fairly easy to identify with. If we make an effort, we can usually identify with the food. I have never had a problem with this. I loved the Liberian food. I loved Suriname food. In fact, I had to watch my diet. Also, wearing some of the national clothing is often not difficult. Hudson Taylor found that it was a great benefit for him to wear the clothes of a Chinese scholar when he moved to the interior of China. Sharing transportation may be more difficult, but quite possible. One of the bigger adjustments is usually the loss of privacy and housing.

Identifying with Certain Roles: Proper Attitude

We can often identify with certain roles. For example, when I was in Liberia, as a doctor, I identified with the Liberian doctors very well. My wife is a nurse and identified with other nurses. The same thing was true in Suriname. And when I became a pastor, taking over that role was not difficult. What was more important than our role was our attitude. Do we treat people with dignity and respect? Are we willing to give them power and position of leadership? Are we willing to trust them with goods? For example, the Suriname nationals now control the finances of our churches. I basically had little to do with finances during our final years in Suriname. All of our churches were also led by Suriname pastors. I was available to help support the work, and available for advice, but they had the position and the power of leadership. Now, nearly ten years after leaving Suriname, they are doing everything in the church, and doing things well despite the challenges of the COVID epidemic.

The Difficult Integration Problems
Philosophy and Worldview

What is more difficult is to integrate our basic beliefs, philosophy and worldview. We western missionaries believe that we live in a real world which really exists outside us. It is a rational world, orderly, and works under natural laws. We believe that science is important. There is a biblical basis for our beliefs. God created the universe which is outside of Him and also depends on Him. God is a God of order, and His creation reflects that order, operating under reliable natural laws. On the other hand, in eastern religion, the outside world is considered imaginary. People may be just projections of the mind of God. Time is cyclical. Truth comes from meditation when we become one with the universal spirit. Appealing to history and science become very difficult with this worldview.

Concept of Nature Versus Concepts of Animism

We find the difference between the concept of nature in western civilization and the concepts of animism. The division of the animate and inanimate universe corresponds to a western perspective. But many cultures, particularly animistic cultures, look at all nature as alive. Animals and even inanimate objects such as stones and trees have spirits. They often worship the spirits under huge trees or on the river or the river rapids. This may even be reflected in the language. For example, Sranantongo is without a passive tense. You cannot say: "I was cut by the knife." You have to say: "the knife cut me (*Da nefi koti mi*)." You cannot say that you were caught in the rain. You have to say that the rain beat you (*Alen ben fon mi*). Everything is alive.

Conquering Differences

If we are to become "150% individuals," then what must we do when our worldviews and basic assumptions are so different? We must accept what the Bible teaches. The Bible does teach that there is a real external world created by our Creator. The Bible also teaches a linear sense of history; that indeed history had a beginning and has a conclusion. The Bible also acknowledges the presence of spirits in the world and that many of these spirits are demonic. However, God, who created both the visible and invisible world, has total power, including power over all demonic spirits, and one does not need to fear them or worship them.

Learning from Anthropology as Missionaries

Americans look at nature as something they may exploit when they dominate it. The Hebrews, in contrast, look at nature as good, and that humans have the responsibility to take care of it. Some folk groups believe that they are basically overwhelmed by nature. It is interesting to look at Chinese art. Look at the size of nature, and then the size of the people in the painting. Often nature totally dominates. Furthermore, some animists feel that you must ask pardon from an animal that you killed or the tree that you chopped down. Again, in their view, all nature is alive. We in the west can learn about respecting nature although not worshipping it.

Western Materialistic Values Versus Sharing

Western values are usually materialistic. We look at what the person possesses. We ask if he has physical health. We do not put as high a priority on his intellectual or spiritual development. In the same way, Americans judge other cultures by their technologic development and material comforts. They emphasize private ownership, and not group ownership. Missionaries may be considered greedy when they practice private ownership. I remember one talented Bush Negro in the interior of Suriname wanted to purchase a new boat, but he did not buy it because his irresponsible brother would use it and break it. It seemed to me that you could just refuse to let him use it. Not so in the Bush Negro culture. Another situation arose when a young man had earned money and bought a bicycle. His friend borrowed it and broke it. However, the friend seemed to feel no sense of responsibility to repair the borrowed bike, and the owner of the bike did not seem disturbed by the situation.

Although it is frustrating that some family members fail to take responsibility, the attitude toward sharing is more Biblical than that of the American who focuses on possessions and health. Other cultures are also more Biblical when they focus on relationships more than on simply doing things. We can learn from them and incorporate these attitudes into our lives.

Differing Views About Control and Planning

The United States missionary often loves to analyze and fix things. In many other places, the belief is that things are uncontrolled and that the person is not to blame when problems occur. However, it seems that with some foresight, it would have been possible to avoid the problem.

CHAPTER 19: THE INCARNATIONAL MISSIONARY

This difference in attitudes makes planning difficult, much to the frustration of the Western missionary. Furthermore, those in the United States love sharp divisions between things, and look at situations as black or white; no gray areas are allowed. There is often a sharp distinction between work and play. This is totally incomprehensible to many cultures. They find it far better to do both at the same time with enjoyment.

Western civilization values planning. We can plan in a rational universe. We have the power of choice, and we have the responsibility to choose and to make a difference. Moreover, we tend to be pragmatic when it comes to solutions. Other cultures feel that is far more important to be a good person and build good relationships then simply to solve problems.[65] The West tends to treat the world as a mechanical source of material goods and human beings. These resources are to be organized and used.

Tasks Versus Relationships

The West views the completion of tasks more important than building relationships. It is important to do and to complete your task. Laziness is viewed as a sin. In many other cultures, developing your spiritual life and becoming a better person is far more important than having material goods. Remember the contrast in how Jesus dealt with Mary and Martha. Which is more biblical? It certainly appears that Jesus focused on people and relationships with them more than accomplishing tasks and setting out a program to follow.

Quantitative Versus Balance and Beauty

Western civilization values things that you can quantitate. If it's bigger, it's better. Many other cultures value balance and beauty much more. They would prefer the craftsman doing the entire work to the assembly line working efficiently. In the West, there is a big emphasis on individual rights and freedoms. In Japan, dignity, harmony, respect, and "face" are very important. In the West, personal identity is often found through material goods and achievement. This gives the individual worth. Again, we need to ask which values are Biblical, and build those Biblical values into our lives and ministries.

Independence Versus Dependence

We in the West are afraid to be dependent on others. The goal is self-reliance. On the other hand, in Latin America and in the Orient, as well is in many animistic cultures, the emphasis is on the group, and not on the individual. In Southeast Asia, the ideal relationship is often between the patron and the client. The patron helps the client in all ways, and the client is totally loyal to the patron. While the individual is important indeed, and salvation is, among other things, for the individual soul, yet we need to seek to serve others, and be willing to be dependent. Jesus Christ was totally dependent on His Father. We in the west can become so independent that we feel that we are independent of God Himself, and when we need Him, we will call Him. How unbiblical!

Rights of the Individual Versus Rights of the Group

In terms of business, in the West, the rights of the individual are considered above the rights of the group. The individual may leave the group if he views it to be personally advantageous. We tend to have superficial relationships, and often leave for a better job. One of our basic organizations is the club, where people come for their own benefit and enjoy fellowship with people like themselves. They are free to leave the group at any time if they wish to do so. Many have the same attitude about the church. They ask: What can I get out of attending this church? What is in it for me? If another church offers more, then I move to the other church. There may be no sense of responsibility or long-term commitment.

This seems very strange to many cultures, where the major tie is kinship, and you are born into the group. Likewise, I remember reading that when a Japanese businessman is accepted into the company, it was often for life. The business dominated not only his work time, but also his social life. Again, the US drive for independence and self-determination is often very self-centered, which is not a Biblical trait. We should be others-oriented, and willing to submit for the benefit of others, as long as we do not violate other Biblical principles.

Americans put emphasis on private property to be used and disposed of as we wish. "It is mine, and I can do with it what I want."

CHAPTER 19: THE INCARNATIONAL MISSIONARY

This came home to me when we were running buses for our church in Suriname. I was able to secure a bus for a good price. Initially I drove the bus and maintained it. Later, we had national drivers who would come to our home and drive the bus from there. One day I sat down and calculated the cost of the bus, the depreciation, the cost of maintenance, etc. and found that it would be actually cheaper for us to rent the bus and driver than to drive it ourselves. That was because we were only running the bus for our church services, while a businessman would be running the bus every day. So, I sold the bus. Our people were upset, not because I made the wrong decision financially, but because I had not consulted with them at first. My thought had been: I bought the bus, I am paying for it to run, and therefore I am free to decide what to do with it. That clashed with a culture which is group oriented. I learned a lesson.

In the USA there is a strong value in humanitarianism, but it is often institutionalized, and often impersonal. We have the government or the church or the social organization take care of the person in need, but will seldom be involved personally. The individual places his own desires above the needs of others. He may not be willing to invest both time and money into other lives unless he feels personally inclined to do so. These traits are not those of Biblical generosity.

Equality Versus Hierarchy

We emphasize equality, and by this, we mean equal opportunities. We favor democracy where the majority also respects the rights of the minority. However, some cultures believe that humans are not equal. They have a hierarchy, which may be based on karma. They may believe that the person needs to atone for his sins, perhaps sins from a previous life. This would be particularly true in countries like India. In that culture, there is little incentive to have social programs, but to let the person "work out their karma." It is clear that the concept of karma goes directly against the Bible, and must be rejected, as is the concept of reincarnation. However, we must not allow pride to enter in, believing that we are "self-made men." We need to look for opportunities to help others to advance, and not just ourselves.

Informality Versus Respect

Americans value informality, and this can create problems. It is good to have kindness, courtesy, and to avoid ostentatious living. One must be very careful not to belittle someone with a higher rank in his own culture. Unless you are very certain, be respectful and maintain a bit of reserve. Also, in America there is a tendency for competition and self-reliance. We may compete for fame, status, and money. In the American system, there is little room for a loser, but we must all "play fair."

I grew up in a culture where there was respect for older individuals, parents, and leaders. One did not easily call someone by their first name. Even though we were fifteen years older than our children's teachers, we normally called them their last name. Informality has occurred in more recent generations. This informality goes very much against a number of other cultures and is a real trap for the unwary. My son Marc Patton tells me that in Hungary, you really need to know three different ways to address individuals. You address children one way, you address your peers a second way, and older individuals or strangers a third way. When I went into a store with Marc, the store owner addressed him using the friendly colleague type greeting but addressed me (I was about 60 or older at the time) with the more formal method. Marc gave me an idea of what the more formal address is like. In asking a lady to take a seat, you would say "Does it please the lady to take a seat?"

I must be honest when I say that I am a bit taken aback when a young woman who I do not know, who may be the age of my granddaughter, addresses me by my first name when she calls me to see the doctor. I am, by the way, also a physician. But my reaction, I suspect, is very mild compared to those of cultures where respect is extremely important. If you are operating in a shame culture, you do not want to cause someone to "lose face." My wife was in a hurry to find a child to go to church one day, and quickly asked a man sitting in a house if the child was there. He looked at her and said: "I am a human too." She had failed to address him courteously first, but just asked the question. She recognized her mistake and apologized. As Christians, we need to afford those in the culture the respect that is appropriate for their culture, even if it goes against our American egalitarianism.

Direct & Confrontational Versus Private Decisions

Americans tend to be direct and confrontational. The Japanese, on the other hand, prefer to make their decisions privately. They use meetings simply for making public announcements. Some groups prefer to use a third-party. We need to learn the appropriate methods of dealing with situations to allow the best possible result, doing the very best to preserve relationships between the individuals.

We find this truth illustrated in the Bible. Sometimes God had a prophet use direct confrontation, but on other occasions, he had him use other culturally appropriate means. One example is the way Nathan confronted David about his sin with Bathsheba by telling a story about a rich man who stole a poor man's sheep. Only after David had responded in anger that the man should die, and repay four sheep, then Nathan confronted him with the withering comment: "Thou art the man." He then gave God's message to David. David repented and said: I have sinned against the Lord.

Active & Productive Versus Elderly and Retirement

The West values people who are active and productive. Many cultures place an emphasis on the elderly and have no concept of retirement. In the west, many elderly people feel abandoned and worthless. They may be "put off" in a retirement home or nursing home away from family. That would be very unusual in many cultures, where the elderly are valued for their wisdom, and also in their position as the source of life for the younger generations. They are shocked that we will put an elderly person in a nursing home and entrust the care of one of our honored senior family members to an impersonal institution! The Bible clearly indicates the importance of the elderly or experienced individual being able to instruct the young man or woman. The Bible also admonishes the young to listen, and to gain wisdom. We as missionaries should live out these truths in our lives, and in the way that we work with national leadership.

On the other hand, in Suriname among the Bush Negroes, we found that some families would put the elderly to the side if they were no longer productive and had problems with dementia or incontinence. When our director became incapacitated with Alzheimer's disease, we were determined to show respect and care for him in the best possible way. All of the mission family teamed together to give him care, not only for his sake, and to respect his contributions over the years, but to live out Christian values in front of the nationals. His wife, who was 87 at his death, was pleased to hear them say: "Joe ben sorgoe hem boen." (You took good care of him.)

The Western Approach

The West tends to emphasize seeing something, rather than hearing it, touching it or smelling it. We have a high percentage of literacy. We tend to say: "I see." Other cultures emphasize sayings and proverbs. We read in the Bible: *He that has ears, let him hear*. There is direct interaction between the storyteller and the receiver. We emphasize abstract knowledge instead of stories and situations, but we need to recognize that personal stories are important. Furthermore, we in the West often admire knowledge more than wisdom. Knowledge is knowing facts. Wisdom is knowing how to apply the facts to life.

The Biblical Approach

Coming again to the Bible, we find greater emphasis on wisdom than on knowledge. Knowledge apart from wisdom can puff us up and lead to pride. As we study Jesus' method of teaching, we find an emphasis on story-telling and oral teaching. This is not to negate the emphasis on the Word of God. Jesus quoted the Word three times to defeat Satan. Often, He said: *It is written...* As a western missionary, I think in abstract terms. I love to outline. But I have had to modify my teaching methods, using more stories and illustrations. As I have done so, the message comes across more clearly to our people. We need to use methods that are compatible with their learning methods.

CHAPTER 19: THE INCARNATIONAL MISSIONARY

One of the Missionary's Principal Tasks

One of the principal tasks of the missionary is to adapt to his new culture. We missionaries may need to become like a child again to properly learn the culture. Some are able to experience total immersion in a new culture, living with a family in that new culture. However, often this is not possible or practical. We need to become enough like those that we will reach so that we can communicate effectively with them. We must also live as Christians within a biblical framework in the new culture.

We must be willing to deny ourselves *(Mt. 16:[24] Then said Jesus unto his disciples, If any man will come after me, let him deny himself, and take up his cross, and follow me.).* Paul was willing to become all things to all men so that he might win some. *(I Cor. 9:[20] And unto the Jews I became as a Jew, that I might gain the Jews; to them that are under the law, as under the law, that I might gain them that are under the law;[21] To them that are without law, as without law, (being not without law to God, but under the law to Christ,) that I might gain them that are without law.[22] To the weak became I as weak, that I might gain the weak: I am made all things to all men, that I might by all means save some.[23] And this I do for the gospel's sake, that I might be partaker thereof with you.).* Paul was willing to pay the price to bridge the culture gap so that he could effectively witness for Christ. Another classic example is Hudson Taylor, who adopted the Chinese dress and hairstyle of a Chinese scholar to be able to reach the Chinese more effectively.[66]

Anticipation Versus Waiting

There is often a conflict between the western missionary who tries to anticipate and prepare for every problem, and the national who is much more relaxed and waits to see what develops. I have had this conflict on a number of occasions. Probably my training especially in Intensive Care has helped form my approach. There we tried to think through a variety of scenarios and then practice them until our response was virtually automatic.

The Open-ended & Non-crisis Orientation

Which of these methods is more Biblical? First of all, we must cooperate together and try to understand the working methods of each other. Remember that Jesus was often open-ended, and non-crisis oriented. What we must do is to have an unwavering commitment to the gospel and an open, questioning, non-crisis-oriented lifestyle and ministry. We must be prepared to present the gospel in a variety of different situations. *(II Tim. 4:2 Preach the Word; be instant in season, out of season; reprove, rebuke, exhort with all longsuffering and doctrine.)* We must remember that we must represent Jesus Christ. We are to be servants and consider others better than ourselves.

The Goal of Cross-cultural Missionaries

Cross-cultural missionaries are to be servants, and to minister God's love to others. We must be willing to share our lives with others. *I Thessalonians 2:[7] But we were gentle among you, even as a nurse cherisheth her children:[8] So being affectionately desirous of you, we were willing to have imparted unto you, not the gospel of God only, but also our own souls, because ye were dear unto us.* Remember that Jesus gave priority to people and their needs and not to his own tasks. We need to be humble. *Colossians 3:12. Put on therefore, as the elect of God, holy and beloved, bowels of mercy, kindness, humbleness of mind, meekness, long-suffering. Ephesians 5:1-2. [1] Be ye therefore followers of God, as dear children;[2] And walk in love, as Christ also hath loved us, and hath given himself for us an offering and a sacrifice to God for a sweet-smelling savour.*

Guilt and Shame Cultures

As mentioned above, there are two poles of reaction to confrontation with sin; guilt and shame. Guilt cultures primarily emphasize the internal conscience, and view sin as breaking the law, for which one is guilty and must be punished. Shame cultures primarily emphasize sin as letting down the group and bringing shame not only to the individual, but also to the group. I have certainly seen this difference in our church in Suriname. This culture is a group culture which emphasizes shame. When the individual fails, he brings shame to the entire group. It is very difficult for this type of individual to stand before the church and confess his faults.

Confessing one's faults is also not easy in the United States, but I believe that in our culture, we are more willing to recognize that as humans we make mistakes, often very serious ones. In the USA, personal confession does not seem as difficult, although it is never easy. Living in a shame culture, it is important to remember that God sees our guilt even though others do not. That guilt requires confession. And in a guilt culture, such as ours, we need to recognize that our sins have major ramifications in the lives of others. Our sin does not just affect ourselves. Occasionally in church discipline, it is necessary for our people to come before the church to make a public confession of a public sin. This is difficult but enables the individual to be accepted into the church fellowship in such a way that the church can minister to them.

When I wrote this chapter, our churches were struggling with this very problem. One of the prominent leaders of the church had made a significant error which he tried to cover up in order to avoid giving shame to himself, his family and perhaps his church. The problem was eventually handled appropriately, the church remained intact, and the family of those involved are still active members. As I reflect on the situation ten years after the fact, I realize that I had a better option that might have been used to allow the individual to save face and could have avoided a very difficult situation.

How to Handle Situations

There are a few principles to remember in practice in this situation.

First of all, we must be humble, which will eventually bring us honor. *James 4:[6] But he giveth more grace. Wherefore he saith, God resisteth the proud, but giveth grace unto the humble. I Peter 5:[5] Likewise, ye younger, submit yourselves unto the elder. Yea, all of you be subject one to another, and be clothed with humility: for God resisteth the proud, and giveth grace to the humble.[6] Humble yourselves therefore under the mighty hand of God, that he may exalt you in due time.*

Second, we should be willing to receive help from others as well as from the Lord. Paul demonstrates that our weakness may actually become a strength as we learn to depend on Christ's strength. *II Corinthians 12:7-10.[7] And lest I should be exalted above measure through the abundance of the revelations, there was given to me a thorn in the flesh, the messenger of Satan to buffet me, lest I should be exalted above measure.[8] For this thing I besought the Lord thrice, that it might depart from me.[9] And he said unto me, My grace is sufficient for thee: for my strength is made perfect in weakness. Most gladly therefore will I rather glory in my infirmities, that the power of Christ may rest upon me.[10] Therefore I take pleasure in infirmities, in reproaches, in necessities, in persecutions, in distresses for Christ's sake: for when I am weak, then am I strong.*

Third, we should not become self-righteous. We need to be careful about excusing our sin because we are weak. Then we can become casual about sin. But sometimes, to avoid condemnation by our own conscience, we turn around and are overly critical of others. This we must not do. We must seek ways to show respect to all believers. Remember that God has chosen the weak of this world to do his work. *I Corinthians 1:[27] But God hath chosen the foolish things of the world to confound the wise; and God hath chosen the weak things of the world to confound the things which are mighty;[28] And base things of the world, and things which are despised, hath God chosen, yea, and things which are not, to bring to nought things that are:[29] That no flesh should glory in his presence.* And remember that there will be times that we too are weak. *I Corinthians 4:10. We are fools for Christ's sake, but ye are wise in Christ; we are weak, but ye are strong; ye are noble, but we are despised.*

Fourth, we must remember to put the needs of others above our own. *Philippians 2:3. Let nothing be done through strife and vainglory; but in this lowliness of mind, let each esteem other better than themselves. 4. Look not on every man on his own things, but every man on the things of others.* As missionaries, we must become incarnate in a culture where we are working. We must work within their culture biblically in a God-honoring fashion.

CHAPTER 19: THE INCARNATIONAL MISSIONARY

Fifth, we must remember that there are problems in our own culture, and also good points in our adopted culture. We need to accept the fact that God has made us the way we are, and He will continue to shape us to use us. To become incarnate in another culture does not require that we sin. Jesus was fully incarnate as a Jew but lived without sin. We should have a heightened sense of morality as we see the blind spots in our own culture. We must have complete submission to and dependence on God. Our attitude should be like Jesus. *John 5:[19] Then answered Jesus and said unto them, Verily, verily, I say unto you, The Son can do nothing of himself, but what he seeth the Father do: for what things soever he doeth, these also doeth the Son likewise.*

Thought questions:

1. Have you been able to overcome ethnocentrism or is this still a struggle? Do you need to come to the Lord for His help in this area?
2. What are some of the areas mentioned that you anticipate might give you difficulty in a ministry to a different culture?
3. If Jesus was able to live as a Jew without sin, and He lives in you after salvation, how can this fact help you to live above sin in a different culture?
4. Is the culture where you will be ministering a guilt culture or a shame culture? How will this modify how you function within the culture?

CHAPTER 20
CULTURAL ORIENTATION AND GOSPEL PRESENTATION

Introduction

When Adam fell into sin, a new spiritual source came into play in the world, and it became possible to spoil culture with sin. Adam's sin-nature was transmitted to every person on earth. Therefore, all culture needs transformation in at least motivation, if not in content. God ordained culture, but He did not order culture. The gospel evaluates every culture in terms of its own Biblical norms. We must seek to understand the culture, not only from the perspective of the people themselves, which is looking from the inside, but also by its consistency with the Bible. In terms of changing to more Biblical norms, it is usually more successful to encourage a minimal number of critical changes than to make numerous peripheral changes. It is helpful to seek the opinions of leaders and to request their help to implement these changes.

Missionaries must be prepared to deal with other religions, not only in the area of weakness, inconsistencies, and inadequacies, but also in their strengths. It is not adequate to simply point out the weaknesses of the religion. We need to deal honestly and sympathetically with the best case that any other religion can make. Then we need to show the desperate need that still remains to be met by the true God and His redeeming Son. All false religions are based on human works. There is no certainty possible, because we humans are fallible. We as missionaries must demonstrate that Christianity is built on what Christ has already done for us. When we receive Him as savior through belief, then His victory becomes our victory too. This is the more excellent way.

When presenting the gospel to another culture, many terms may need to be redefined. The cults, in particular, redefine traditional Christian terms and change their meaning. When you have someone agreeing with you, they may simply agree in terms of their definition, and they may not really comprehend what you are saying. Furthermore, we need to give a complete message. We must use enough of the Old Testament and New Testament background to put the text into context so that it may be understood. A very effective way to work is to answer questions that other religions pose but have not answered. Another very helpful thing is to look for redemptive analogies, eye-openers, and points of contact.[67,68]

Presenting the Gospel
How Are Our Messages Understood by the People We Are Trying to Reach?
Thoughts About Worldview

It is possible to look at messages decoded into a culture through a number of different grids. (1) The first is a grid of worldview.[69] This is rarely evaluated, and we must encode messages with the other person's worldview in mind. (2) Second, there is a grid of cognitive processes, or the way of thinking. For example, does the divine truth come through subjective experience or objective revelation? (3) Further, we must remember that the language reflects what the culture sees as important, and we must use their linguistic forms properly.

(4) Another grid is behavioral patterns. Usually, we learn informally about how we ought to act. Many actions of another culture are fine for Christians, but some, of course, we must stop doing. We need to study their social structures and ways of interacting. (5) We need to be aware of the media influence which shows the way that messages are channeled to others. (6) And finally, we need to understand the motivational resources of the people, and how they make decisions.

Assessing the Individual's Response to the Gospel

After presenting the gospel, we need to be very careful in terms of assessing the individual's response. Some foreign cultures emphasize the necessity of giving approval to show respect. The individual may seem to accept the message outwardly while he rejects the message inwardly. Remember, in making decisions for Jesus Christ, there are two aspects of grace. On the side of God, there is the unmerited provision of grace. But on man's side, there is the grateful reception.

In presenting the gospel, we need to make sure that the individual personally accepts Jesus Christ, and not simply accepts the missionary or the better life that the missionary represents.[70] This is ultimately the responsibility of the Holy Spirit, but the work of the missionary is to communicate Christ so effectively that the person has the opportunity to accept or reject Christ. The missionary must rely on the Holy Spirit in making the presentation. *II Corinthians 2:15-17. [15] For we are unto God a sweet savour of Christ, in them that are saved, and in them that perish:[16] To the one we are the savour of death unto death; and to the other the savour of life unto life. And who is sufficient for these things?[17] For we are not as many, which corrupt the word of God: but as of sincerity, but as of God, in the sight of God speak we in Christ.*

Individuals Hearing the Gospel Will Reformulate it

When we present the gospel, we must realize that as the individual decodes our message, he may reformulate it as well, and may change it to something other than the gospel. Our job is to minimize this reformulation so that the individual responds to the true gospel. We need to avoid syncretism. This is a particular danger in polytheistic society. Then Jesus is simply added to the list of gods. One day, I was witnessing to a Hindu attendant who was pumping gas for my car. He asked me for a picture of Jesus Christ, but I knew that the Hindus placed such pictures upon the wall and worshipped them. I did not give him a picture. The Hindus have their multitude of gods, some 33 million of them, and it appeared that he simply wanted to add the picture of Jesus to the pictures of all the other gods he already had. "Why not cover all the bases?" is a typical attitude of some Hindus. We must be careful to communicate the uniqueness of Christ. It is not enough to accept him as a god, but as the unique God, the Creator of the universe. That young man would need to realize that the other pictures he had were false gods, and might well be demonic representations.

Protracted Decisions

When we present the gospel, there is sometimes a protracted decision. The person may tell you that he has to think about it. Sometimes this may be a rejection, but not always. Jesus Himself told others to count the cost. There is a difference between procrastination and weighing the cost. There also may be what is called symbiotic resignation. In this situation, the individual says that he chooses not to accept Christ personally, but those under him are free to decide for themselves. We saw this fairly often, where older people, who have been steeped in witchcraft, find it very difficult to leave their witchcraft. However, they see the benefits of Christian belief, and do not wish to deny their children these benefits. They will allow the children to accept Christ, although they themselves do not feel capable of doing so. My son-in-law in the interior found this particularly true, where older people told him that the spirits had known them since birth, but that perhaps a very young person could get saved. We are grateful when they allow the younger folks to get saved and baptized.

Then we continue to pray, and sometimes later the older family members may also get saved. I remember one man whose entire family was resistant except for a single middle-aged lady, his daughter. He became very sick and was expected to die. My son-in-law would visit him to pray and read scripture. One day I went in his place, and the man seemed barely conscious. However, I witnessed to him and to my surprise, he prayed to accept the Lord. A few weeks later he started improving, and eventually was able to come to church, and decided to be baptized. He lived another one or two years.

Another time, three young girls from the same family came to our Bible club. All three got saved. As time went on, the first girl married a preacher from our church. She was allowed to get baptized just a week before her marriage. The second girl, a few years later, also married one of our preachers. She was allowed to get baptized a little sooner, about a month before marriage. The third girl also married another of our preachers. She was able to get baptized considerably earlier than her sisters. A younger brother also became a preacher, and another younger brother became faithful in the church and feels called to preach. Both were baptized without any objections from the family. Finally, the mother herself accepted Jesus Christ and was baptized. She left the liberal church where she had been for years and attends very faithfully. The father made a profession and started attending church, although I understand that he is no longer attending some years later.

Worldview and Evangelism

Our worldview is important in evangelism. The Third World believers look at the Western worldview and see a number of problems. They see us as too rationalistic and preoccupied with intellectual concerns of faith and reason. They see us as molded by Western philosophies. They see us as conformed to the secularist worldview of the enlightenment, and captivated by Western individualism.

Worldview is outlined in much more detail in *Volume IV of Issues in Missiology*. In summary, a worldview is culturally structured assumptions, values, and commitments which underlie a people's perception of reality, and the way they respond to their perceptions. A worldview is composed of assumptions which are usually simply accepted without consciously requiring proof. Our worldview provides a lens through which reality is perceived and interpreted. Differences arising from different worldviews can be quite difficult to deal with. This makes conversion difficult, because true Christian conversion works at the worldview depth.[71] People follow their worldview in how they think, feel, and evaluate.

Worldview Structures

Our worldview structures are deep underlying personal characteristics which may determine the use of our wills, emotions, logic and reason. We in the West use linear reasoning, but others use more concrete situational reasoning. Our culture also determines the way we assign meaning. Our culture determines how we evaluate, with judgments about what is good and bad, aesthetics, economics, and human character. Worldview determines how people respond to what they assign meaning, and also how they relate both to those within their own people group and to the outsider. The worldview provides a pattern for how to regulate things, get psychological reinforcement, and have consistency in life.

Worldview System of Classification

In any worldview, there is a system of classification including the nature of a person and a group. The worldview determines our ideas of causality, with what forces are at work in the universe, and what their results are. Our worldview has much to do with our perception of time and space. Furthermore, when changes occur at a deep level, like at the worldview level, there is often disequilibrium in the culture and unforeseen changes may occur!

Mono-cultural Worldviews: "My Way is the Right Way"

Many people have mono-cultural worldviews; they are ethnocentric. "My way is the right way." They are often absolutist and feel that their perception of reality is true reality. Their view is superior. There is little respect for others' ways, and little desire to evaluate other customs from their perspective. The mono-cultural person evaluates everything from his own perspective. There are a couple of variations on this theme. There is the reactionary mono-cultural position, where the person rejects his own culture, and totally accepts the new culture. There is also an eclectic mono-cultural position, where the person takes the best from other cultures, but it is still one culture.

The Missionary Needs a Cross-cultural Perspective

In contrast to the ethnocentric mono-cultural viewpoint, we missionaries need a cross-cultural perspective. We need to believe that there is one God and a reality beyond our reality. We need to see that there is right and wrong in every culture, and that no culture provides all the answers to life's problems. We also need to remember that all cultures are deeply affected by our sin nature. Despite the fact that culture is contaminated with sin, it usually provides sociocultural adequacy so that the individual can adapt to his situation. Therefore, we must show respect in general to the culture, but not accept all aspects of it. Absolute relativism implies that all cultures are good in all aspects. This is not true. All cultures are somewhat unbalanced. The West is very technological. Other cultures are much better in interpersonal relationships. We need to remember that there are many equally effective approaches to solving most of life's problems. Furthermore, all languages can communicate all the human communication that is necessary in that culture.

Requirement for Evaluating a Culture

To evaluate the culture and understand it clearly, your evaluation is best from inside the culture. The prophet is an insider, not an outsider. Outsiders need to show love and patience. Furthermore, there is a crucial difference between the rights and privileges of a cultural insider or an outsider. Whatever judgments are made about the parts or aspects of the culture, we need to remember that we are not to reject the culture as a whole. When we evaluate cultural behavior, we should do this using Biblical principles that are above any single culture. We need to remember that God has allowed culture, which is important for human well-being, and provides effective strategies for dealing with the challenges of life. However, no one culture is absolute: only God is absolute. Furthermore, He does not require everybody to have the same manner of life.

Differences in Endowment and Opportunities

Missionaries should recognize that there are real differences in the endowment and opportunities of people as well as the talents that they possess. The Bible says: *"For unto whomsoever much is given, of him shall be much required . . ."* (Lk. 12:48) We know that God judges us not only on what we do, but by the revelation we have received, and our attitude toward that revelation. God is above all cultures but works through all cultures. He may allow angels and demons to work within a culture, and they are not bound by culture in the same way that humans are, but they are not absolute; only God is absolute.

Human beings are sinful and limited and interact within their cultural structures. God communicates to humans via human communication vehicles such as speech, dreams, and visions as well as the writings of the prophets. God ordinarily uses cultural structures and communication in normal ways. However, He provides supernatural trustworthy direction through inspiration of the Scriptures and revelation. We need to remember that none of the Scriptures are written from a Western cultural perspective, and as Westerners, we should probe the intent of those biblical characters and writers.

The Power of Language

What can we do to evangelize more effectively? What can we learn from anthropology to impact a culture for Jesus Christ? We need to master the heart language of the people to whom we are called to minister. The power of language is present in all humans, separating them from the animals. Adam showed his superiority by naming all the animals.

Language Word Meanings Are Assigned by the Culture

Any language can be used to communicate God's truth. Although perhaps less than 50% of people can write, all people have a fully developed spoken language. The missionary needs to have a complete set of linguistic habits for the people group with whom he ministers. Every language has a complete system which correlates with their understanding of the world, and it fits with their worldview. We need to remember that language word meanings are assigned by the culture, and are both individual, and social in character. Language is also the means by which we acquire our worldview.

Connotative Meaning: The Emotional Response to Words

Another important thing to remember is connotative meaning. This is a special term used to describe an emotional response to many words. The evaluation of the word can be good or bad, it can be active or passive, or it can be strong or weak. An example in Sranantongo is the word *winti*. This word has several meanings. It can mean the wind; it can also mean a spirit. But it most commonly refers to an evil spirit, and if you say that someone has a winti, the person usually means that the individual is oppressed by an evil spirit. When the Roman Catholic Church chose to use the term when they translated the Holy Spirit, the choice of word created major problems. This is because of the emotional (connotative) meaning attached to the word. To many, the church was describing the Holy Spirit as an evil spirit, which of course is clearly wrong.

The Use of Euphemisms

One way to avoid offense within the culture is to use euphemisms, which are polite ways to say things, while avoiding offensive connotative meanings. The Bible states that Mary was great with child instead of saying that she was pregnant. The Bible stated that Stephen fell asleep instead of saying that he died. Other terms for body functions may be considered offensive, and there may be a more polite way to refer to what happened without using an unduly graphic or offensive word.

Language Can Shape Our Thinking

Further, it important to realize that language actually can shape our thinking. Our linguistic patterns themselves help determine how a man perceives the world and thinks about it. Linguistic patterns vary widely, and this often results in very different worldviews. The language itself can shape our ideas, and not merely express them. What does this mean in presenting the gospel? The ultimate factor in receptivity to the Word is whether the Holy Spirit has been allowed to prepare the people, but we also need to prepare ourselves to speak the heart language of the people with clarity.

Behavior Also Communicates

Furthermore, our behavior also communicates. Not only what we say, but also how we say it is important. What we do is also important. All behavior is potentially communicative. Those who study communication believe that about 35% of our communication is verbal, depending on the words we say, and about 65% is non-verbal, which refers to the way that we say it and what we do. This is why a face-to-face conversation is often more successful in communication than writing or talking over the telephone. Both individuals get many visual clues that go beyond the spoken words.

Behavior is important for the missionary. We need to behave according to God's standards of Scripture. At the same time, we need to accommodate the behavioral patterns that are acceptable in the respondent culture. Sometimes we get into problems because what is acceptable behavior to us may have other connotations in another culture. Dr. Marjory Foyle described a situation when she had an innocent conversation with a colleague.[72] However it was after dark by the time they finished, and a man and woman do not have a casual conversation after dark in that culture. The man asked to come to her apartment. She immediately recognized her mistake and told him that as soon as his wife arrived back from vacation, she would be delighted to invite both of them to her apartment for tea, thus stopping the conversation.

Some of the behaviors in the other culture may not be Biblical. Then we need to distinguish between Biblical and cultural norms and do what the Bible says. Our goal must be that people see Christ in our lives. When the first believers showed the life of Christ in the way they lived in the early church, they called the people Christians. When Peter and John defended themselves with boldness and clarity before the Sanhedrin, they took notice that they had been with Jesus. (Acts 4:7-13.)

A No De Mi Gwenti (It Is Not My Custom)

We need to remember that our responses to strange behavioral patterns are often automatic, and our reflex reaction may center on our emotions and the subconscious. However, it is often possible to be prepared ahead of time to avoid certain problems. If we know that we will be asked to do something which we believe is unbiblical, sometimes we can avoid putting ourselves in that situation. Another option which is a culturally acceptable substitute may be a good solution. And sometimes we must just courteously state that we are not able to participate in that activity or behavior.[73] In Suriname, they usually do not demand too much of an explanation. Usually it is acceptable to say: "A no de mi gwenti." (it is not my custom.) Praise the Lord, we do not to have to go into a lengthy explanation of our behavior in this culture.

Be Careful to Be Not Offensive

We must be careful to try not to be offensive in our lifestyle, our physical appearance, or our clothing.[74] Our body gestures are also

CHAPTER 20: ORIENTATION AND GOSPEL PRESENTATION

important. Some are instinctive, but many are learned. Even how we position things is important, and indicates our priorities and interpersonal interactions. For example, if I come into the office of a top officer in a business, and he sits behind a big desk, and I sit in a chair across from him, it shows that he is in charge. If he wishes to be more friendly, he may pull a chair alongside the desk closer to me.

Also, we Americans cherish our privacy. We want some distance between us and others. This is quite different from those in Latin America, who sit and talk closer than we are comfortable doing. We need to be careful not to insist on too much privacy. True missionary evangelism is more than delivering the facts about Jesus. It is living out the implications of these facts in everyday life.

Time Issues

Perhaps I have put undue emphasis on time, but it has been a constant problem for someone as goal oriented as I am. Once again, remember that time is perceived in very different ways in different cultures. In the West, time is linear (it's going, going, gone.) Time is what we need to accomplish things. The symbol is the hourglass, which shows us that time is running out. In the East, time is cyclical. The symbol is the wheel. The Chinese will place great value on the past and on the present. The Africans have a long past and a very short future. And of course, the youth in the United States are focused on the present. They are the "now" generation.

Remember that the way that time is divided is cultural. You may not always agree or feel comfortable with the way the time is conceived of in other countries, but you must understand it. Remember that religious time may not be business time. A man who is always on time at his job may not be so prompt in church activities. We need to remember that people are more important than schedules, and the quality of the event is more important than the starting and closing time. Having a different perspective on time can help us to avoid making cultural blunders which inhibit our effectiveness in presenting the gospel.

Social Structure and Evangelism
Differing Emphasis in Western Society

In terms of social structure, Western society puts a great emphasis on individual freedom and the individual and emphasizes personal rights above the responsibilities that we have in society. Even in our language, we use the word "I" frequently. We often introduce ourselves by our first name. In contrast, the Japanese promote the ends of the larger group. Even the way they are introduced shows a difference. We need to remember that we are each made in the image of God, and that God said it is not good for man to be left alone. Group relationships are important, and we need to respect them to evangelize effectively.

Status

Our status shows what position we hold, and our role shows how we act them out. In Athens, Paul was a foreigner. As a foreigner, someone may come to us and say: "Sir, we would see Jesus." We need to remember that we are often considered experts in religion. We also need to be careful how we use the contacts which we make. For example, we often read in the United States about a reformed drug addict who is now saved from a life of sin and who testifies in church. But our society is unusually open. Furthermore, the church is not built on that reformed drug addict, but it is already in existence. In most cases, this type of contact would not work in other cultures. There are some exceptions. Ko Tha Byu was a converted criminal that Judson worked with among the Karen people. He ended up seeing about 1000 individuals accept Jesus Christ. However, he ministered to his own people, and not to those who despised him.[75]

Different Types of Social Contacts

Different types of contacts can help us. There are some who have prestige influence. These are usually the formal leaders. Some have personal influence. These are often the opinion leaders. If either of these people is gifted in speaking, he can be a great help to the missionary.

CHAPTER 20: ORIENTATION AND GOSPEL PRESENTATION

It is often very effective to work through the family. Different societies vary as to the importance of the family. Family is extremely important to the Chinese, but not so important in the United States. We in the United States have kindred relationships through both parents as a direct obligation, but the relationships are not extended very far. However, in many cultures, that is not true. The family kinship group is usually either paternal or maternal, but not both. For example, in the Bush Negro culture, the main lineage is through the mother's side. It is a matriarchal society, and the mother's brothers usually have the most say in what goes on. There are also non-kinship groups. Some are households where the leader had lots to say; for example, the entire family would be baptized, as in the situation of the Philippian jailer. Another example is Joshua, who stated: "...but for me and my house, we will serve the Lord." (Joshua 24:15c.) Joshua spoke not only for himself, but for his entire household.

Vertical Communication Between Classes

Communication is most difficult vertically, particularly going from the lower class to the higher class. Even from the higher class to the lower class, there may be some difficulty in communication. The higher classes have prestige but may not have much impact in terms of persuasiveness, whereas within the same class there is greater effectiveness. What is most effective is horizontal communication within a single class. In Japan, using local associations can be very effective.

Presenting the Gospel in Rural Societies

There's also a difference in evangelism between peasants in tribal societies and those in cities. The rural societies are more homogenous, traditional in values and lifestyle, resistant to change, and frequently negative to outsiders. There is not a huge range of leadership, and kinship predominates. It is not uncommon to find that decisions are group decisions. Usually, the family will take a significant amount of time before a decision is made. Effective communication is usually based on personal relationships. The initial approach may often be to those who can pass the information on within the family grouping. Then it is good to allow time to have the new ideas diffuse internally within the group. We must remember that the challenge to change must be ultimately addressed to those who are actually capable of initiating change.

Totalitarianism

The nature of totalitarianism is to control the direction and content of communication. We know that communism is totalitarian by design, and this is also true of the Roman Catholic Church. When dealing with totalitarianism, we need to remember that God wants all people to have the opportunity to hear the gospel and to be saved. We need to remember that government authority is ordained by God and must be obeyed, even if it does not recognize God. The one exception is that we are to obey God rather than man if they are in conflict. When the Sanhedrin commanded Peter and John to stop preaching Jesus and the resurrection, they answered that they must obey God rather than man.

The primary responsibility to communicate Christ really rests on the Christians in the society itself. Mission agencies have a responsibility to encourage and strengthen the witness of Christians and to avoid activities which would make it more difficult for them to function. Sometimes the mere presence of foreign Christians may put the entire Christian group at risk. We need to pray also that totalitarian societies will one day be more open to the Word.

Effective Communication

Some concluding thoughts about communication include the following. The more closely the communication follows the prevailing social structure, the more effective it will be. People communicate more effectively within the people of their own social class. The most effective way to get voluntary changes in attitude and behavior is through interpersonal horizontal communication within one social class. Prestigious communication is from the upper class to the lower class. However, prestigious vertical communication is best suited to affecting social control. The farther apart the social distance is, the more difficult communication becomes.

The more the communication is face-to-face, the more difficult it is for an outsider to communicate effectively. We need to try to communicate to the responsible members of the society to spread the word. The more heterogeneous the society, the more variety we must use for communication. In face-to-face societies, try to work with someone in a leadership position to make decisions for the group. In face-to-face societies, it is more likely that communications will go by family lines and with group decisions. Thus, in face-to-face societies you must be willing to spend more time to communicate personally.

Media in Evangelism

Media also communicates. All media are extensions of the person, either physically or psychologically. Each media has its own impact, vibrancy, and social consequences. We need to be careful of the media's impact on our lives and values. Often, simple media are very effective. This is particularly true where people think concretely. Remember that our authority is from God, Jesus Christ, and His Spirit-inspired Word.

We need to be careful of the effects, associations, and effectiveness of both the message and the media on our lives. Books have a permanent effect in many cases. However, television may be more persuasive. We need to look carefully at how the television is used in the culture. Is it primarily for entertainment, or propaganda? Mass media has relatively little effect on long-held opinions. More effective is face-to-face communication or family influence.

In recent years, the media has become far more effective in communication than when the first edition of this book was written. Most individuals are adept at using a cell phone, especially in the younger generation, and communicate through the social media. We are learning more and more to use this method effectively. As a faculty member, my learning platform is through email, but I often must reach students through texting, as some rarely look at their email.

Books, Especially the Bible, Are Very Important

Thus books, especially the Bible, are very important. They should be attractive and well-indexed, and if possible, illustrated. Tracts need to be attractive and speak to the person's needs. Otherwise, they are seldom read. Radio is economic, easy to listen to, and gives good retention, but often there is little re-exposure. Television affects both the eye and ear, but is more expensive, and must be done carefully. We are using both radio and TV in Suriname. The TV programs cost about ten times the cost of a radio broadcast of the same length. However, many people listen to the radio when doing other tasks but would have to stop what they are doing to watch television.

What about platform media? If you have evangelists hold evangelistic meetings, follow-up is very important. With films, often the response is quite deceptive. Some seem to respond but may not understand clearly. Also, some illiterate people may have difficulty following the film.

Other Media Venues in Evangelism

There are a wide variety of communication methods. Group dialogue and cell groups can bring rapid growth. Audio recordings on flash drives or a podcast can be effective if properly used, especially with gospel recordings. Videocassettes, flash drives, or DVDs are different from TV, and can be effective in pre-evangelism as well as evangelism. Slides can also be effective, especially for teaching. We began using radio broadcasts in 1991 (30 years ago at the time of this writing.) It was difficult to know how many people were reached with the gospel and decided to accept Christ. I put a brief presentation of the gospel in the introduction to every broadcast. However, I also considered that others listened to the content of the messages because they may have attended churches without much Bible teaching. A number of people with a Pentecostal background listened to our broadcasts. I also believe that by repeatedly hearing the truth of the gospel on the radio, the individual may be better prepared to respond positively when personally confronted by a soulwinner or in a church service.

When looking for mixed media, base them on the objectives desired. This includes exposure, attention, comprehension, and retention. Choose the media on the basis of the audience preferences. For instruction, it is better to have media of low speed and low transmission

CHAPTER 20: ORIENTATION AND GOSPEL PRESENTATION

such as written materials and lessons. On the other hand, for having persuasion, high speed and high transmission, such as radio and television, is effective. You must look at reach, frequency and also cost. The telephone can also be used. Computers provide new opportunities, and more and more use of the cell phone and computer will open doors in all areas of the world.

At the time of the first writing in 2012, I wrote: I believe that we will see the digital revolution radically change our methods of communication in the days to come. That day has come. With the expansion of the internet throughout the world, online communication is now worldwide. Even in a small developing country such as Suriname, our church has a website. Many have broadcasts, and such conference systems as Skype and Zoom make face-to-face conferences possible throughout the world.

Mass media usually has a supportive role but not the decisive role. Personal contact is often necessary. On a personal note, we have used radio broadcasts for 30 years. In one family, one key individual was reached by the radio. She spoke with my wife one day and got saved. Over a period of a few years, about 20 of her family members became saved, representing several households. The families became quite active, including one who married one of our preachers. The radio made the initial contact, but follow-up was necessary.

We also have a number of people from a Pentecostal background who listen to our daily radio broadcasts. As mentioned above, their churches often emphasize emotions but may lack solid doctrinal teaching and preaching so they listen to our program to fulfill that need in their lives. We have had two television programs for fifteen years now. One program is chronological, and the other is primarily doctrinal. Television does reach a different group than the radio and does have a different impact as well.

We have been especially blessed since Ethan Champlin opened a 24 hour 7 day a week radio station in Moengo, Suriname called Switi Boskopoe (a joyous message). The radio station is aimed at the Marowijne and Sipalawini districts of Eastern Suriname reaching the

Bush Negroes. We had made a wide variety of radio broadcasts over the years in addition to our standard fifteen-minute daily broadcast which went straight through the Bible. It was too expensive for us to pay to broadcast a number of these programs, but because this is our own missionary outreach, we are able to increase our programming without additional cost to us. He has Christian God-honoring music programs as well as such programs as Unshackled available. The daily news is also broadcast in an agreement with a Bush-Negro station in Paramaribo. Donations have been made to expand the outreach with a number of relay stations from towers he hopes to put up in the interior. Other donations permitted him to purchase and distribute solar-powered portable radio stations set to his frequency without cost to the recipients. They are able to hear the programs at home or even carry the radio with them when they work in their gardens.

The Instruments, the Message, the Holy Spirit

The Bible calls us to bring people to faith and repentance. Ultimately the believer is the instrument that God uses through a variety of ways. The message is the true message of salvation through the death, burial, and resurrection of our Lord Jesus Christ. The Holy Spirit can use us as His instruments to bring the message of the gospel, but only the Holy Spirit convicts the sinner that hell is inevitable if he fails to trust Jesus Christ as Savior. Only the Holy Spirit convicts the person of the perfect righteousness which is found in Jesus Christ. Only the Holy Spirit can convince the person that Satan and his evil spirits are already defeated at the cross of Christ. We are engaged in a great truth encounter and must preach the true gospel through a variety of means of communication through the power of the Holy Spirit.

The Omnipotent Triune God

The triune God is involved in missions, and He can do anything. Without Him we can do nothing. Remember that mankind is hell-bent toward self-destruction. The missionary is a servant of God, and he can depend on God's help to make his pleadings, reasoning, and preaching effective. People still reflect the image of God in their reasoning, conscience, aspirations, striving, hopes and fears. The Holy Spirit can bring the sinner to true repentance and faith in Jesus Christ.

Psychology

The Goal of Secular Psychology Versus the Goal of the Bible

What about the use of psychology? Modern secular psychology is based on naturalism, determinism, and the contention that mankind is intrinsically good. Therefore, the basis of modern secular psychology conflicts with Biblical truth. Our methods must not conflict with the truth of the word of God. Our methods must be consistent with divine purposes and aims. Our purposes must be subject to Biblical principles in the direction of the spirit of God. For example, many times the goal of the secular psychologist is to build up self-image. But the goal of the Bible is to raise up Jesus Christ, not self. Although secular psychiatry can give some helpful insights, it must be used with great caution, if at all, because of its anti-biblical foundation.

Guilt versus shame

What about guilt versus shame? Guilt concerns the violation of rules or codes by separate acts. The emphasis is on decision-making. Returning to normal health means removing wrong acts and adding right ones. To surmount guilt, we need righteousness, which is provided for the believer in Jesus Christ, who is our righteousness. At times, punishment is a consequence, but the primary goal is to restore our relationship to God.

In contrast, shame is concerned with the overall self, and not specific acts. Shame is falling short and failing to reach an ideal. Shame results in a total response involving insight that we have failed God, and let down our family or group. Emphasis is on the quality of experience. Transcending shame brings identity and freedom, with restoration to our group as well as our God. We need to remember that all men are created in the image of God. We need to recognize that our true worth comes from our position in Christ, who gives us value, and not simply acceptance by our group. The cross gives victory over both guilt and shame. We receive His righteousness, and are accepted as His sons and daughters.

Repressive Versus Suppressive Societies

What about repressive versus suppressive societies? In repressive societies, such as the United States and Germany, internal controls are important. The focus is on the individual-centered life and the search for the individual soul. Usually, the society stresses one religion and monotheism. In contrast, a suppressive type of culture is represented by China and Japan. External controls are important. Their pattern of life is situation centered, and religion is the adjusting of all powers, often leading to polytheism. As you look at this pattern, you can see that often repressive societies are tied to guilt, while suppressive societies are often linked with shame.

Individual Decisions in a Family Oriented Society

We need to be careful about how we appeal to the individual to accept Jesus Christ. In the West, there is often the appeal to the individual, even asking him to stand up alone against persecution. Even if your family rejects Christ, make your decision despite the family. But the non-Western ideal may be to also consider the family, which is important. We need to remember that group decisions are often solid. Those within the group also benefit from the support of the others in the group.

It is true that sometimes the individual must stand up against his own family and take a stance for God. This may happen especially for the first individual in the family to accept the Lord. It is not uncommon later to see a number of other members coming to the Lord. One of our preachers became a Christian and was called to preach as a teenager. His family opposed his decision, and forcibly took him to a witch doctor. Over a period of years, many received the Lord. Another man, who is currently the senior pastor in our main church, was the first in his family. His father had seen his ability (he later became the under-secretary of state for Suriname) and wanted him to replace himself as a witch doctor. He also opposed his faith, but later, many of the family accepted the Lord. These are just two of many examples which we saw in Suriname.

In approaching evangelism, it is indeed necessary to emphasize that each individual is responsible before God, but also to avoid unnecessary antagonism of the family or undermining the family structure. Truly we must be wise as serpents and harmless as doves. Sometimes those who are most antagonistic end up being strong Christians and leaders. A primary example would be the Apostle Paul. Try to work in the already existing family structure when possible.

What About Self-propagating, Self-governing, Self-supporting churches?

We in the West speak about wanting self-propagating, self-governing, self-supporting churches. But we need to be careful not to put the self of the individual in control of the church. Jesus Christ, the head of the church, must be in control. Individualism can be good, but it must be Christ-centered and not simply a reflection of Western civilization. The Scripture has a balance between self-interest and self-abnegation, between individualism, and communalism. The problem is one of emphasis and balance.

Appeal to Both Shame and Guilt

Remember that you can appeal to both shame as well as guilt. We need to be careful in a shame culture, because the problem may not be seen as what you did, but that that you were caught. But you can be in a situation where you are not caught, but still guilty. For example, while we were in Suriname, we have had a number of young ladies get pregnant out of wedlock. But the sin was not the pregnancy; that was simply the proof that immorality occurred. Often other girls may also be immoral, but simply more careful to avoid pregnancy. And often the man escapes detection and responsibility. The girl needs to realize that she is guilty, and as a result of her sin, has brought shame to her family and to her church. In a guilt culture, the individual needs to recognize the ramifications of his misdeed on others, and that his sin does not simply affect him, but those around him. Both shame and guilt are the result of sin. The cross deals with both.

Stages of Decision Making and Discipleship

Different cultures have various methods of decision-making, such as a decision to receive Christ. Some cultures feel that it is an advantage to keep your options open as long as possible, and change them if necessary, depending on the circumstances. It is very important to understand how decisions are made within the society, and further, who has the power to make them. We can look at several stages in the conversion process. **First**, there is discovery. There is a person called Christ who is the true God. He came into the world to be the Savior and Lord of mankind. **Second**, there is deliberation. There is a possibility that I or we should forsake our old ways and follow Christ. The **third** phase is determination. I, or we, will repent and believe in Christ. If this decision is made, the next 48 hours are critical, and the individual needs the support!

The **fourth** stage is dissonance. Shall I or we resist the forces that draws us back into the old ways, and follow Christ even though there are difficulties? And **lastly**, there is discipline. I will identify with the people of Christ and the church, and I will live in submission to his Lordship and to church discipline. This is absolutely vital for Christian growth. We need to remember that Jesus encouraged us to count the cost. We must weigh the benefit and cost in the balance. When He challenged persons to become a disciple, He warned about the cost, but also promised a blessing. And remember that persons are persuaded by what they consider important, and not what we consider important.

Luke 14:[25] And there went great multitudes with him: and he turned, and said unto them,[26] If any man come to me, and hate not his father, and mother, and wife, and children, and brethren, and sisters, yea, and his own life also, he cannot be my disciple.[27] And whosoever doth not bear his cross, and come after me, cannot be my disciple.[28] For which of you, intending to build a tower, sitteth not down first, and counteth the cost, whether he have sufficient to finish it?[29] Lest haply, after he hath laid the foundation, and is not able to finish it, all that behold it begin to mock him,[30] Saying, This man began to build, and was not able to finish.[31] Or what king, going to make war against another king, sitteth not down first, and consulteth whether he be able with ten thousand to meet him that cometh against him with twenty thousand?[32] Or else, while the other is yet a great way off, he sendeth an ambassage, and desireth conditions of peace.[33] So likewise, whosoever he be of you that forsaketh not all that he hath, he cannot be my disciple.

Contextualization

Critical Contextualization

What about critical contextualization? One of the big problems is that many important life events are associated with pagan religious rites, since these are virtually all-pervasive. Some people reject the old ways, which may be associated with heathen practices, but do not replace them with anything else. This may leave a cultural vacuum. Often this vacuum may be filled with Western cultural forms, although then Christianity is seen as a foreign religion. Or the individual may have a syncretic mixture of paganism and Christianity. When we contextualize, we want the Christian practices to be understandable, and at the same time not to inadvertently violate scriptural principles. We missionaries must not deny the church leaders the right to make decisions in these areas. The national church leaders are the experts in their own culture, and they understand the ramifications better than a foreigner. Of course, we also stunt the growth of leaders if they are not permitted to lead.

Uncritical Contextualization

We need to be very careful about uncritical contextualization. This may overlook that there are resulting from common practice in the culture as well as individual sins where the individual breaks the norms of society. Such sins could include slavery and idolatry. This approach opens the door to all types of syncretism, producing neo-pagans. This is also what we see with postmodernism. Therefore, we need to examine the beliefs both in terms of their old culture, and also in the light of biblical norms. First, try to understand the old ways. Then study biblically what the Bible has to say about these practices. Evaluate the customs critically in terms of the Bible. The Christians need to continually re-educate themselves, and also pass these lessons on to their children.

Theological Support for Critical Contextualization

Is there theological support for critical contextualization? Yes. **First**, there is the priesthood of all believers. **Second**, the Bible must take first place, and is available (especially if there is a reliable translation in the heart-language of the people.) **Third**, the faithful are led by the Holy Spirit. And **finally** the church is a discerning community.

It has been accepted over the last number of years that there must be a movement towards self-propagating, self-supporting, self-governing churches. They must be self-propagating; they must be taught to reproduce themselves in new churches. Otherwise they see propagation as the responsibility of the missionary. They must have self-support. Often there is a problem when the missionary started the program with foreign funds, and national churches were unable to continue the programs without outside help. We discuss these implications elsewhere.[76] Also, the church should be self-governing. They have the right to learn from their mistakes just as we have learned from those which we have made.

Self-theologizing

There is a fourth self, self-theologizing. This needs to be considered particularly with national leaders, especially after three or four generations of Christians. The Bible is the historical document of God's revelation to the human mind. Theology is the systematic and historic explanation of the truths of the Bible. But theology may be culturally sensitive and pertinent because each culture encounters specific things that the Bible deals with. For example, when we were in Suriname, demonology was an important topic, yet it is often ignored by Western theology. However, the Bible says much about Christ's victory over Satan and the demon world. This topic needs to be incorporated into their theology. Other issues that need to be addressed in other cultures may include materialism, post-modern relativism, ancestor worship, slavery, abortion, and twin murders

We need to remember that we are all sinners, and we can reject hard sayings. Therefore, we need a clear theology addressing challenges to our culture. Since our language also may tend to shape our theology, we need to consider this effect on the theology which we develop.

The Need For Clear Exegesis

What then do we need? **First**, we need a clear exegesis. We need to study the Bible text in its historical and cultural context. **Second**, we need a clear exegesis of our own cultural and historical context. We need to understand the needs of our own culture very clearly. **Third**, we need good hermeneutics. We need to make things culturally relevant for today's situation. We start with the Bible, and not our theology. We need to be willing to change if we see that we are clearly wrong. The ongoing work of the Holy Spirit will guide us into all truth. We must be humble! The Christian community has a responsibility to preserve the truth, as the church is the foundation and pillar of the truth.

Culturally Specific Theology

It may seem risky to encourage the national churches to develop a relevant theology within their culture. This is not cultural relativity or allowing the culture to change Biblical truth to fit their culture. Allowing them to develop a relevant theology will ultimately give confidence that the Bible is truly pertinent to the issues impacting that culture. We need to find the applications to our everyday lives. We need to think long term so the church does not drift theologically over the next 50 to 100 years. We need to organize and make sense of our experiences. The theology should help map our behavior and make explicit the theological ideas which we have. It must be apologetic, so that we can make ourselves clear to non-believers. Furthermore, it should be a model of reality to counteract heresy. Some may argue that the believers lack the necessary sophisticated training from a seminary. But many of the ancient heresies developed in the various religious and philosophic schools of the time. And it is in the seminaries that most of the modern heresies were developed!

Realistic Contextualization

How then can we contextualize the theology? **First**, the missionary tries to make things relevant. But we must remember that we have the bias of our own cultural assumptions and theologies. We as Westerners developed a rational organized system of thought, which may be different from the thinking process of the culture in which we are working. **Later**, every church must face the issue of making a theology in view of its own culture. The missionary should truly understand the culture but insist that the church hear the voice of God through the Scriptures and encourage national theologians. Every generation must come to grips with this truth of the Bible themselves. If we do not allow theologians to develop within the church, the nationals will often go off and start their own denomination, often without any assistance. Without any guidance, the chance of aberrant doctrine is much greater.

Trans-cultural Theology

Trans-cultural theology must be Biblically based. Its deepest concerns must be sin, salvation, and God's rule over His people. Outsiders can see the cultural bias of your theology more clearly than those who have grown up in the culture. We need to listen to each other. We must focus on God's acts in history and especially on Christ's acts in history. This must be done through the Holy Spirit with great humility. Initially, the missionary is a spiritual parent. The initial relationship is that of dependency. But our goal must be that the person becomes independent. Then it is possible to become interdependent as equals.

Missionaries Must Refrain from Giving Answers

The missionaries can leave, but they can also stay and serve as catalysts and counselors. They must refrain from giving answers, but seek the various options, advantages and disadvantages of proposed solutions. However, the national leaders should make the decisions. We must not become policemen, but help the nationals enforce rules for purity. We must model forgiveness and redemption. We must be careful also of which sins we emphasize. We must see what the culture emphasizes. We need to model confession and forgiveness. Otherwise, we put a barrier between ourselves and the nationals. We can deceive ourselves as saved sinners. Remember that Paul said that he was the chief of sinners, and yet God used him as a great theologian of the church.

CHAPTER 20: ORIENTATION AND GOSPEL PRESENTATION

Thought questions:

1. Why is it important to understand our own worldview, the worldview of our people, and the Biblical worldview when presenting the gospel?
2. How do you distinguish between contextualization, which you do want, and syncretization, which you do not want?
3. Why is it so important to learn the heart language of your people? How do you plan to do so?
4. What adjustments do you anticipate in communicating to your people group both directly and through media?
5. What are you planning to do to develop self-supporting, self-governing and self-propagating churches?

CHAPTER 21
A SUMMARY OF WORLDVIEW AND EVANGELIZATION

A brief summary of common worldviews

Naturalism

Naturalism is the underlying worldview of atheism, secularism, scientism, humanism, ecofeminism, and communism. In these situations, the supernatural is dismissed as irrelevant. Some deny that there is a God (atheism, communism), and others view that God may exist, but that He is essentially irrelevant to modern man. The pure naturalist believes that humans are simply a random collection of atoms that assembled by chance. Nature may be viewed is either hospitable or inhospitable. Some, like the humanists, view human nature as inherently good. The true naturalist usually believes in evolution as an explanation of creation. There is little basis for morality, and some naturalists will believe in existentialism, which contends that the universe is basically meaningless, and that you must develop your own morality without reference to any external standard.

In terms of approach, the missionary may be handicapped by his lack of training in philosophy and science. He must be careful not to go beyond his own expertise. However, he can show that many naturalistic systems are in conflict with each other. It is also very important to be careful of definitions. The scientist usually does not understand theological terms. The question is: where will the naturalist go to find true truth? Science is really too circumscribed. Its borders are completely materialistic. Philosophically it is difficult to live within such a belief framework. In terms of religion, then what religion is truly true? In talking with people who are naturalistic, be sympathetic to the problems that they themselves face.

Animism

Another worldview is animism. These people are usually theistic; that is, they often believe in a high god, or perhaps more than one god. The universe is moral and personal, because nature is viewed as personal. Perhaps 40% of the world has this worldview, although they nominally may be part of another formal religious system. These people are often more concerned with gods and spirits than about people. The boundaries between spirits, animals, and man are shifting, and the distinction between self and surroundings are blurred, so that you become one with nature. In the tribal worldview, man participates in maintaining the world around him, but he does not control or dominate the world.

For example, a typical animist believes in a god as the supreme being, the originator and sustainer of man. However he is far away, and has little direct contact with man now. The spirits are often involved in the destiny of man. Not only do humans have spirits, but also animals, plants, and the inanimate world, including rocks, rivers, waterfalls and rapids, and mountains and hills. The whole environment is alive. The animist's concept of time primarily focuses on the past, with a bit of present time. There is little concept of future, but he frequently goes back to the past. Ancestor worship includes fellowship with the departed of the tribe. The animist may fear the dead ancestors because he believes that if the ancestors are not placated, they may well retaliate.

Animism thus abounds with supernatural deities and spirit-beings of all kinds. They can be good and evil. Usually they are capricious, but they can be cajoled, especially by people with special secret knowledge, like witchdoctors or shamans. The animist views all nature as animate, with its own power which the anthropologist calls "mana." The animist believes that nature has influence on man's moral and spiritual environment. Therefore, mankind is in nature, and not above it. Man is somehow dependent on those who stay behind to care for those in the spirit world.

In terms of approaching an animistic culture, the people want to know who the missionary is, what he knows, and what he does. In terms of signs of authority in the spirit world, they often prefer a power encounter to a truth encounter. We as missionaries need to be secure in our resources over Satanic power.[77] We need to define who the true living God is. He is the Creator, and He supplies what we need.

We missionaries need to work within the framework which the animist can understand. In terms of practical application, we may need to go directly against the false portions of the world view. An example of this is Paul in Athens, where he showed them that the God of the universe is not like a god made with hands. We need to show Christ, and Him crucified. We do not want to depend on human wisdom and technology, but on the Holy Spirit, and work in His power.

Hindu-Buddhist Worldview

In terms of a Hindu-Buddhist worldview, one of the basic ideas is that of *maya*, which means that the visible cosmos is an illusion. The absolute lies behind the world of experience and is termed Brahman. The atman is the "impersonal" absolute in the human soul corresponding to Brahman. The highest good is nirvana, peace, or absolute bliss. In nirvana, personality disappears, and the individual is absorbed into the absolute. The techniques for gaining liberation are called yoga. Another key concept is karma, which binds humanity to the universe. What one does in life affects his karma, and what he does in this life has effects on what he will experience in the next life. The struggle is to escape from the endless cycle of existence. The belief in karma is combined with the belief in reincarnation. Death is followed by life in a different form. The ultimate goal is to escape the wheel of life and death, and merge into the nothingness of nirvana.

The Hindu worldview has a type of trinity of three gods, Braham, Vishnu, and Shiva. These are all expressions of the impersonal Brahman. All reality comes from Brahman and returns to the atman within the person. The atman is the personal equivalent of Brahman. When the Indian greets each other by saluting, they salute the divine within each person.

The question in Hindu and Buddhist worldview is how to come out of karma and be liberated from rebirths? They call this *moksha*. For the true Hindu who understands Hinduism, only Brahman really exists, and it is an illusion of the world which results in thousands or in fact millions of gods. There are different varieties of Hinduism, and some allow a sort of personality, although classic Hinduism is impersonal. In this view, the central figure is Vishnu, who manifests himself through a number of avatars such as Krishna.

Buddhism

In Buddhism, Brahman is replaced with nirvana, and atman is replaced with *anatta*. There two main forms of Buddhism, Hinayana Buddhism, with a literal interpretation of Gautama, and Mahayana, which allows more freedom. In Buddhism, karma is still present as well as reincarnation. Nothing has permanent existence. Gautama looked at himself as the greatest divine teacher. The Buddhists believe that there are other *bodhisattvas* (savior beings) beside him. However, behind everything is impersonal monism. The world of experience is ephemeral, and thus the person's gaze must be turned internal. In fact, classic Buddhism is really atheistic. Everything comes out of Brahman, including the gods and nature. There is no real personality as such. Time is cyclical, with an endless series of existences. When one applies this religion strictly, it is almost impossible to live out this type of belief except in monasteries and retreats.

To reach the Buddhist, the missionary must be people of goodwill, integrity, and creditability. You are expected to know your faith and they will expect to see some marks of austerity in the missionary's lifestyle. We must be careful as missionaries to define our terms carefully so that we do not build on a monist foundation. We must distinguish the creation from the sheer materialism of the West, and from the sheer illusion of the East. We must show that man is created in the image of God. We are not just souls or bodies, but whole persons, and our basic problem is rebellion against God and not simply ignorance.

Warnings

A few warnings are important. Hindus will often accept Christ as another avatar of bodhisattva. They must realize that Jesus Christ is a real person in history. There may be also a problem with the law of non-

CHAPTER 21: A SUMMARY

contradiction. The individual must begin to see that true truth is non-contradictory, and truth is narrow, and not broad. We must remember not to offer religion, but offer Christ. We must keep a spiritual emphasis.

Tao

Chinese thought emphasizes *Tao*. This is a force in the universe which is broken into Yang and Yin, positive and negative. Everything is one or the other. The universe forms with spirits. There are good spirits called *shen*, and evil spirits called *kwei*. The spirits should not be disturbed, and we use a term to do this called feng-shui. It is possible to be a man full of yang, who can do much good for the entire community. The great teacher Lao-tzu emphasized the *Tao*. He mentioned three major things: the way to heaven, the way of the gods, and the way of man. The main thing is to embrace Tao and not to impose your will on anything.

Confucius

Confucius, on the other hand, emphasized family relationships. His discourses were written by disciples in the Analects. He believed that we should concentrate on the practical, and not on the supernatural. Everything should work out to develop the right sort of person. In Chinese thought, each person needs to find Tao for himself, the right action that keeps things in harmony. People are intrinsically good. Lao-tzu said that the good is in nature, and Confucius looked at good and proper family relationships.

Chinese Traditional Religion

There are multiple gods also added by Buddhism to Chinese thought. Shang Ti is a god far removed, but T'ien (heaven) and Tao are more important. Nature is Tao working through yang and yin. People are good and can be kept good by education and Tao. People must maintain their proper station in life. Remember that filial worship is important. Remember the spirit lives in the body. The best times to look to are when the ancestral spirits join us in the Golden age of China. We should still plan for today and look to the future.

There are significant differences in thought between India and China. India negates the world. China affirms world. In China, people and nature have the central stage. India venerates the saint; China venerates the sage, that wise and practical man. This spirit fit for the King is the sage within and the king without. China is basically pantheistic, but believes in Tao which is the supreme spirit and the inner law of the universe.

Communists

With the coming of the Communists, significant changes have occurred. Instead of looking at past history, the Chinese look more now to the future. They replace Tao with dialectical materialism. They replace yang and yin with thesis and antithesis. They affirm humanity and the world.

For missionaries to affect a change in China, they need to present themselves as men of integrity and goodwill. They must be credible. The Chinese feel that we in the West have much to offer in science, but not in religion. We must represent Christ and not Western culture. To be effective, one must really personally know Christ as well as the Bible. We must appear knowledgeable in religious matters. Present the Bible as a holy book of history. We had a golden age in Eden, but that stopped when man rebelled against God. Christ is the one who said I am the Tao, and He is that perfect superior man, who is also the savior of the world. The filial piety can be helpful but we need to avoid ancestor worship.

Muslims

The Muslim is monotheistic. His worldview is that there is an infinite-personal God who created the universe out of nothing. Cause and effect are open ended. The universe does not exist apart from God. Mohammed rebelled against the polytheism around him. He presents Allah as the one, eternal, mighty, and forgiving, compassionate, all-knowing God, who inexplicitly assigns people to heaven or hell. The Allah of the Qur'an is basically unknowable. The Muslim thinks that the Trinity of the Christian is God the Father, Mary the Mother, and Jesus. Of course. this is not true.

CHAPTER 21: A SUMMARY

Muslims think that Jesus was talking about Mohammed himself when He spoke about a comforter who will be coming. This, again, is a false understanding of the Bible. The comforter is the Holy Spirit, who Jesus says will live in the individual, something not possible for Mohammed. The Muslim believes in angels, and countless jinn (spirits) exist between man and angels. These may be good or evil and they must do the bidding of Allah.

The Muslims have several inconsistencies. Men must abandon idols, but they are weak and helpless. In fact, fatalism is a strong theme in Islam. God is also not the God of love of the Bible.

To reach the Muslims, we must appear as people of goodwill. One of our problems is that we are not able to meet them as strangers or friends, but as a sort of enemy. We must win them with Christ-like qualities. There are number of definitions that must be made clear when witnessing to Muslims. They must realize that sin is so radical that it takes the death of Christ to overcome it. They must understand that God is a holy God, and also a self-giving God. The nature of the true Trinity, that is, that God is in three persons but with one God, must be clarified. It is quite effective to use the history and miracles of Jesus to demonstrate who indeed He was and is. Let us remember that four of the six primary Muslim prophets were Adam, Noah, Abraham, and Moses. Of course, the Muslims look at Jesus also as a great prophet. The Muslims are often organized and make application of their beliefs similar to Christian missionaries. Sometimes we may debate with them, but it is extremely important not to lose your temper or to show arrogance.

I have found that using Biblical illustrations of sacrifice can be effective in communicating with Muslims. A missionary friend emphasized to me that Muslims love stories. Adam and Eve in Genesis 3 is something most Muslims know and accept. Building on this story, they can comprehend the necessity of sacrifice. Without the shedding of blood there is no remission; the wages of sin is death. Noah made sacrifices coming out of the ark. Abraham was willing to sacrifice his own son – but God Himself provided a sacrifice in his place. And, of course, the Lord Himself is the ultimate sacrifice.

Syncretic Religions

There are a number of syncretic religions. Hinduism is a classic syncretic religion which will incorporate other religions within itself. Roman Catholicism can also show itself in a syncretic manner. God the Father may be left far away, and they may worship the Virgin and the saints. This may resemble the worship of ancestral spirits in other religions. In Japan, many people are both Shintoist in their national life and Buddhist in their intellectual pursuits. The Chinese may have three forms of religion simultaneously: Confucianism, Taoism, and Buddhism.

Presenting Christ

In presenting Christ, there is not only a difference in worldview, but in the very thinking processes between the West and the East. In the West, we emphasize conceptual ideas, followed by relational concepts and then psychological truths. In China, they emphasize concrete relational truth, followed by psychological and then conceptual truth. The Indian will begin with the psychological, then they concrete relational, and finally the conceptual. Thus, we in the West have a tendency to intellectualize the Bible into our own Western organized thought. Northrup describes the situation as follows: the East thinks more aesthetically, but the West thinks theoretically, and then checks to see if it corresponds with reality. The main point is that we think differently because our worldviews are different, and thus we must be flexible in our approach to the Bible.

The Apostle Paul's Approach

As we look at Paul's approach to presenting the gospel, he shows that the Bible is not a book that man would have authored. The Bible shows man as he really is. Even the best of men is a flawed human in comparison with the original intent of God for mankind. The gospel is foolishness to the natural man but is the wisdom of God and the power of God. Nevertheless, the Greek text shows that the force of the arguments rest on their logical validity and on the historical facts present. We must have solid thinking and persuasion. We need to do our homework, but we also need to depend on the Holy Spirit to work in the hearts of those to whom we speak.

CHAPTER 21: A SUMMARY

Note also that Paul's approach to witnessing depended on the background of the audience. In his sermon in Antioch of Pisidia, he was preaching in the synagogue to Jews and Jewish proselytes who had a Biblical understanding of God and of Jewish history. His message began with Moses. On the other hand, he addressed pure heathen in Lystra and then later in Athens, he began with creation and the Creator God.

Indians

Brahman

Indians often think that there is a higher form of knowledge, which they called Brahman. They do not allow logic, theories, doctrine, explanations, or sensory experience to invade that area. They believe that mathematics, science, theology, and philosophy are all just relative truth. They put a high priority on intuitional thinking. They believe that mystical experiences will give a deeper understanding of their own personality. and ultimately bring them to unity with the universe. They use yoga, psychoanalysis, and drugs. They don't really believe in a personal God. They talk about becoming one with Him, but ultimately, He is impersonal. In the Bhagavad-Gita, Krishna is the ultimate reality, and Arjuna bows in devotion to him.

The Indian places stress on the universal and prefers the negative. He minimizes individuals and emphasized the unity of all things. He emphasizes the static quality of universality and has a very subjective idea of personality. He gives the supremacy of the universal self over the individual self. He is subservient to universals. He is alienated from the objective world. He has an introspective stance with metaphysical qualities and emphasizes tolerance. Eastern philosophy thinks that knowledge is transient and illusionary. We as Christians should be able to understand some of this, and sometimes we jump logical gaps when arriving at a conclusion. Sometimes revelation comes from inner illumination, especially knowledge which comes from Jesus Christ through the Holy Spirit. This type of thinking has now become acceptable in the United States. We see this particularly in the emerging church movement, and also in postmodernism. We see a sort of pseudo-

Christianity with facts about God, without making the belief personal through repentance and faith in Christ.

Avoid Over-intellectualizing

What must we do? We must avoid over-intellectualizing. Christ is the way. But we must also avoid oversimplifying, with just a few premises and conclusions. We need to communicate the ministry of knowing God, and the all of approaching Him. We must take the doctrine of illumination seriously.

Doctrine and Approach to Various Worldviews

The Father reveals truths. *Matthew 16:15 [15] He saith unto them, But whom say ye that I am? [16] And Simon Peter answered and said, Thou art the Christ, the Son of the living God.[17] And Jesus answered and said unto him, Blessed art thou, Simon Barjona: for flesh and blood hath not revealed it unto thee, but my Father which is in heaven.*

The Son reveals the Father. *Matthew 11:[27] All things are delivered unto me of my Father: and no man knoweth the Son, but the Father; neither knoweth any man the Father, save the Son, and he to whomsoever the Son will reveal him.*

The Spirit leads us into all truth and the Holy Spirit bears witness with our spirit. *John 16:13. Howbeit when he, the Spirit of truth is come, he will guide you into all truth: for he shall not speak of himself, but whatsoever he shall hear, that shall he speak: and he will show the things to come.*

As we approach the Eastern mind, we must realize that Christian truth is different from the Hindu mystic's idea of the human mind. The mind is a creation of God, and not in emanation from it. We must remember that the human mind is at enmity with God. *Colossians 1:[21] And you, that were sometime alienated and enemies in your mind by wicked works, yet now hath he reconciled[22] In the body of his flesh through death, to present you holy and unblameable and unreproveable in his sight.* We cannot depend simply on inner illumination without the Word of God and the Spirit of God. We are anchored in the truth, which corresponds to actual external reality.

CHAPTER 21: A SUMMARY

Jesus calls us to come personally to him. *Matthew 11:28. Come unto me, all ye that labor and are heavy laden, and I will give you rest. 29. Take my yoke upon you, and learn of me, for I am meek and lowly in heart: and ye shall find rest for your souls. 30. For my yoke is easy; and my burden is light.* As we approach the Eastern mind, we need to remind them that God works in real history and through history. The truth of God is understood in the Old Testament and in the New Testament in their historical and grammatical sense. God's Word is more reliable than intuition, because our hearts can deceive us. *Jeremiah 17:9 The heart is deceitful above all thing, and desperately wicked; who can know it?* When we blank out our minds and meditate on nothing, or on the name of a Hindu god, we open ourselves to demonic deception. We must approach the Bible with the aid of the Holy Spirit and our meditation should be on God's Word, which is truth. *Jesus said in John 17:17 Sanctify them through the truth; thy word is truth.*

A different approach is needed for reaching the Chinese. They may use myths, aphorisms, fables, analogies, and tribal lore. The Chinese and Japanese use concrete relational thinking, and occasional intuitional apprehension. The rational or theoretical is all but omitted. Therefore, Biblical stories can be used. Once again, we need to remember the historical context. It is accurate history, as opposed to the mythological or visionary system of most religions systems.

The Bible uses truth communicated through concrete illustrations, parables, etc. We can think of how Nathan communicated to David through the story of the rich man who stole the poor man's sheep. Let us remind them also that the Word became flesh and dwelt among us. We need to be able distinguish and use types, metaphors, similes, symbols, and emblems.

We may use rituals to communicate with them as well. Two types of communication are baptism and communion service. Both are commanded by Jesus. Baptism shows that we have received Jesus Christ as savior, and we are identified in his death, burial, and resurrection. The Lord's supper shows the intimacy we share with the Lord, again remembering his death and burial, and His indwelling Holy Spirit.

We need to be careful that we do not promote idolatry. An idol is really anything that replaces God in our affections and our trust. Places of worship should be clean and orderly, but they do not need to be ornate.

It is possible to use drama as well as illustrations and pictures in teaching the Word of God. Some promote the use of an oral Bible. Many cultures are primarily oral cultures and having a form of oral communication is useful. However, the written word does not change, and can be studied carefully. If the Bible is available in the native tongue of the individual, it is a great help.

Conclusion

In conclusion, all people use all three methods of reality. For the Indian, go back to Eden, when man had direct communication with God. For the Chinese, we can find God in nature, but must not confuse the two. The Westerners must be careful not to put total trust in the rational mind. Each group does have a priority order, and we need to look at how we can present things most appropriately to them. The Bible is without error. Paul admonishes: *2 Tim. 3:16-17 All scripture is given by inspiration of God, and is profitable for doctrine, for reproof, for correction, for instruction in righteousness: that the man of God may be perfect, thoroughly furnished unto all good works.*

ADDENDUM A
THE ROLE OF THE PASTOR AND CHURCH IN MISSIONS

Introduction

I am hoping that this material will be used in settings where not only missionaries, but also pastoral students are present. If it is true that the task (or at least a major task) of the church is missions, then every pastor has a major responsibility for missions. The responsibility is not limited to the missionary. Because of this situation, and because some topics are intertwined, there will be some overlap of information given in this chapter and elsewhere in the text.

The Responsibility of the Church

I believe that the great commission was given to the church to reach out to the lost, and not primarily to another organization, whether a para-church organization or a government agency.[78] The church has the responsibility to reach the lost.[79] The church must work under the leadership of the Holy Spirit, who is ultimately in charge of missions. And the leader of the church, the pastor has both a great responsibility and a great opportunity. I believe that any church of any size can have a significant world-wide ministry, but the key is pastoral leadership.[80] In larger churches, it is not uncommon to have one of the pastoral staff who is assigned to missions. He will be the key individual to interact with missionaries. In some circumstances, the pastor in charge of the missions program may have been a missionary himself before taking such a position and is especially capable of understanding the problems facing the missionary.

The Work of the Pastor in the Pulpit
Missions Emphasis and Prayer

The work of the pastor in the pulpit can greatly enhance the mission outreach of the church. He is the main expositor of the Word, and can bring forth the missions emphasis that is present in the Bible. He also has a great responsibility to pray. He can pray for his missionaries in public. Many pastors read some of the prayer letters from missionaries before the congregation. He needs to build structure into the prayer time of the church as well. It is possible to put the prayer needs before the people in the church bulletin. Some may schedule the church to pray for different missionaries each day. Many missionaries have experienced great answers to prayer and found later that a supporting church was praying for them at the precise time prayer was needed. When the pastor relates these answers to prayer, it is a great encouragement for the entire church to continue in pray.

Educate the People About the Missionary and His Ministry

The pastor can also educate the people about the missionary and his ministry. The church needs to realize that the missionary and his people are real people with real problems. The pastor can update and give information. He can write to missionaries. As a missionary, I can state that most pastors want the missionary to write, but usually they do not write back. I prayed for my churches individually each day, but often had no idea about what I should pray. It is a great encouragement to the missionary to know that the pastor is praying for him. And he can give updates on the ministry of the missionary to the congregation.

The Pastor as Recruiter for Missionaries

The pastor can also be the greatest recruiter for missionaries in the church. He can show that missions have many options for service, including being a career missionary. He can promote opportunities which arise. He can describe the talents needed for service and provide opportunities to develop the necessary training and talents. Furthermore, many young people make significant commitments to missionary service either in church services or camp. The pastor can help preserve these commitments and encourage the young person in fulfilling his commitment as God enables. The pastor can also inform the church members of missions' opportunities through his contacts with various mission agencies and Christian colleges.

ADDENDUM A: THE ROLE OF THE PASTOR AND CHURCH

Counseling for Missionary Service

The pastor can also give counsel to the church member considering missionary service. He may discover that the individual is really not qualified, or needs additional training. He can be available for counsel as to timing to apply to a mission board. The pastor can also counsel for those who, like me, contemplate a midlife career shift. Others may contemplate early retirement to go overseas. The pastor can give encouragement and counsel for the challenges of getting on the field. The pastor can support not only married couples or single men, but also single women. Single woman missionaries have a particularly difficult time on deputation. The home pastor can be a great help in terms of setting up meetings for them by contacting area pastors.

Facilitate the Specific Needs of a Missionary

In addition to meetings, when the time of departure approaches, the pastor can arrange for help with packing and making special needs known. The pastor can also help the missionary on furlough. Any missionary on furlough has two big needs; transportation, and a base where he can stay. The pastor can help greatly in finding housing and locating furniture, etc. He can make their needs known to the congregation. Perhaps someone in his congregation has a car that he can donate or loan, or a place for the missionary to stay.

Direct the Young People

The pastor can help further the vocational and spiritual goals of the young people of his church and give direction in life. As they contemplate a Christian college, he can help them find the right school for them. For those contemplating a missionary career, he can help direct the young person to a college associated with compatible mission boards.

A Challenge to the Pastor

In summary, the pastor is the servant of the church. He is also their leader. He can have a tremendous positive impact for missions in his role. The Moravian church had an incredible outreach. From that small congregation of believers, most of whom had fled their countries, there arose a mighty mission movement, in which over twenty years time they sent out more missionaries than the entire Protestant church had sent out in the previous two hundred years. When he studied why the Moravian church had such a tremendous outreach, Murray concluded that the passionate love of Christ was transmitted from Zinzendorf to his followers.[81] What a challenge to the pastor. Do we have that sort of love? What a challenge to us on the mission field. Is our primary motive to serve Him above personal desires and above our mission accomplishments and plans, that He might have the pre-eminence? I immediately think of the church of Ephesus in Revelation 2:1-7, where the church had left its first love.

Ultimately, the work of the pastor is largely life-transfer. He must transfer his love for Christ, his devotion to doing the will of Christ, and his prayer life to his congregation. They will not be moved by words like they will be moved by a life of dedication. Murray challenges us: Seek the deepening of the spiritual life, and missionary consecration will follow.[82]

The Role of Parents

The parents are also key in terms of long-term direction of their children. There are a number of ways that they can promote interest in missions. They can open their home to missionaries. I know that my paternal grandparents were very interested in missions, and they made a point of having missionaries in their home. My grandmother ran a boarding house to help with their income, and they had different foreign students stay for months or years at their home. The man who wrote the Korean national anthem actually stayed in their house.

I have had individuals also invite my wife and I to stay in their home to encourage their children's interest in missions. They can also pray for missionaries in their family devotions, or various prayer letters and prayer prompters available. A number of families write personal letters to missionaries in order to have more family contact with the missionary. We have a few families who have taken us on for missionary support. Some make special projects for the missionaries, or even short-term visits on the field.

The Role of the Church

The church has the central role in missions under the control of the Holy Spirit. Antioch sent its two very best men, which today we might call the senior pastor and the chief Bible teacher into worldwide evangelism. The missionary candidates are obviously initially members of a church. The individual is called by God and available to do God's will. The church must evaluate the candidate to see if he is worthy. In the New Testament, the Holy Spirit used the corporate church to select and send out the candidate. The church becomes the mediating agency, with the mission board assisting.

The Role of the Home Church

The home church a has great responsibility in terms of the missionary. The church should first evaluate the individual's interest and talents as well as his character, to see if he is someone that the church can support without reservations. It is possible to have an individual receive a solid education academically, but most missionaries do not fail because of lack of education. In evaluating missionary attrition, the causes of missionaries leaving the field, or in having an unsatisfactory ministry are much more often due to personal problems, communication difficulties, or character problems.[83] The home church is in a much better position to evaluate the candidate over a period of months or years than the mission board can do in a few hours or weeks. The church can evaluate the future missionary's character and stability in a way that even the most extensive mission agency evaluation may not be able to detect.

The church can also provide the environment for the individual to practice his skills and discover his talents. He may be given opportunities to preach and hone his ability to communicate. Although sometimes this will be to the main church, it can also involve youth meetings, Sunday school, camp, church school chapel, etc. We found that working on the bus route gave us invaluable training. Our children worked with us in the bus ministry and all four are serving the Lord, and two have been overseas in Hungary and Suriname, South America for 28 and 32 years.

Here is a suggested home church procedure.[84] First the candidate is interviewed by the pastor. He then is interviewed by the missions committee. He then gives his testimony to the church committee, and if all is positive, the pastor contacts the mission board. A similar procedure is suggested for the mission agency. The candidate submits a preliminary application, including the request of the sending church. If approved, he makes a formal application followed by an application interview. The candidate attends the candidate seminar and is then formally accepted as an appointee. When the candidate is about to begin deputation, he is commissioned by the sending church, and then begins deputation in area churches. Furthermore, upon arriving on the field, he should have a field orientation.

Which Mission Board Should the Church Recommend
What is the Stated Purpose?

How does a church decide about which mission boards it should use for its candidates? It is important to know the stated purpose of the board. For example, Baptist World Mission's stated purpose is to plant like-minded Baptist churches throughout the world. Other agencies have very specific purposes, such as aviation, medicine, education, etc. It is extremely important that the goals of the board correspond to that of both the missionary and the sending church.

What are the Doctrinal Positions: Stated and Unstated

The doctrinal position is also important. One must note not only what is stated, but what is NOT stated. It is also important to see if the board actually implements the doctrinal position or not. Some mission agencies may be fine as far as what is stated on paper but fail to enforce their standards. (The same is very true of some Christian schools.) You can expect problems if there are both charismatic and non-charismatic missionaries on the same team.

Even more striking would be the difference between liberals, often unsaved, and conservative born-again believers. This created major problems on the overseas field run by denominations which had been overrun by liberalism, and then sent liberal missionaries to the mission field. If you read old mission reports of the first part of the 20th century,

ADDENDUM A: THE ROLE OF THE PASTOR AND CHURCH

you will read of many such problems. I think of the last days of Jonathan Goforth, where 100 years ago he was facing this issue. Most of the liberal boards have had fewer and fewer missionaries on the field, and at present, the vast majority of missionaries are from Bible-believing boards However, I have personally had contact with unsaved missionaries when I was in Liberia.

What are the Financial Policies of the Board?

Other questions may include what other churches support the board, and what the financial policies of the board are. For example, we have been associated with two boards. In one mission, we were considered independent agents, and in the second, we have been employees of the board. What are the board's mechanisms of evaluation, and what are their procedures? I have appreciated boards with strict financial accounting. It is easy to become sloppy in accounting, and the strict requirements we have at Baptist World Mission at least on one occasion permitted me to detect where funds were being inappropriately used in a building project.

Ordination Services

Before the candidate leaves for the field, it is important to have an ordination service, especially if the missionary is involved in church planting. In some situations, it may be required by the Internal Revenue Service. The initiative comes from the home pastor. He must make the procedure very clear to the candidate. A commissioning service may be at the same time, or perhaps more often, just before the departure of the candidate. At the commissioning service, the church identifies itself with the missionary. The church delegates to the missionary the authority of being its representative to another land and/or culture.

Churches and Their Financial Support Of Missionaries

Churches have a variety of ways of supporting missionaries. Most churches are not able to totally support a missionary, and thus the missionary usually has support from a number of churches. Some missionaries have a small number of supporting churches; others have many. For example, we had over 50 supporting churches. However, usually the sending church will give the largest amount of support. There are three basic plans that the sending church may use. One is a percentage of the total cost, or a percentage of the total budget of the church. A second method is a separate budget for missions. The church may have two budgets and two treasurers and keep the missions budget apart. The third is the faith promise method.[85]

Faith Promise

Faith promise missions are often coupled with an annual missions conference.[86] Each person is to pray about what amount the Lord would have them give. Usually, each individual or family is given a card on which they can indicate the amount they believe that the Lord would have them give per week or month. Some will have separate cards for children with suggested appropriate amounts. There are several advantages to this method. This method exercises faith. Systematic giving increases. Everyone can participate. And in most cases, the amount usually increases each year.

What is particularly interesting to me is that in many cases, the amount given to the church also increases. If we were to think in normal human terms, we would expect that the total amount given would be relatively fixed, and thus if mission giving went up, there would be less for the work of the church. However, it appears that as believers exercise faith in giving, their giving is increased to both the church and to missions. Other advantages of faith missions include the fact that no one is forced; the giving is anonymous. It is in accord with the New Testament principle that the Lord loves a cheerful giver. And it is based on personal commitment. The author advises a new pastor to go slow in terms of implementing changes. Each system can work. But I personally prefer the faith promise commitment. Not only may it increase financial support, but also prayer support. We are more likely to pray for those we support.

Budgeting for Missions

Here is a suggested procedure for budgeting missions. The first step is to survey the current mission budget, including both home missions

ADDENDUM A: THE ROLE OF THE PASTOR AND CHURCH

and overseas missions so that the facts are clear. Then one can set a specific mission goal. It is important to check with each mission board to see who is in need of additional funds, and to contact each missionary about his financial needs. It may be helpful to make a graph if necessary to demonstrate any shortfall. Then decide how to meet the needs, whether by straight percentage or more specifically based on need. It is important to realize that the needs and costs of different fields vary. Living is extremely expensive in such areas as Japan. Although our own personal expenses were moderate, our ministry expenses were substantial because of the extent of our ministry, which encompassed radio, television, publishing, teaching (Bible Institutes), and church planting, including hiring buses for transport. The budget should be reviewed at least yearly.

When we returned to the USA, I wrote to all my churches. Because I had kept my social security intact while on the field and had a bit of savings from before we went on the field, we could manage financially without continued support. Also, the churches were independent of the mission and self-supporting. However, I did hope to keep the radio and TV broadcasts going, which would have been difficult for the churches to maintain. I wrote to my supporting churches with that in mind. I suggested that they might want to either drop our support and reallocate it elsewhere, or drop the level to 50% or so, and I would use the lower amount to covering expenses for radio and TV outreach. I had estimated that I would come out with 20-25% of our regular support. That proved accurate, and we have continued the broadcasts, which at the present is an additional nine years since leaving the field.

It helps to consolidate all missions giving into the budget, including the giving from various Sunday school or other groups, special projects, etc. for a complete picture. The church should continue to take on some new missionaries and give to mission boards, either a set sum or a percentage related to the number of missionaries serviced by that board. Keep the bus ministry or local radio broadcasts apart from the missions budget. Consider giving scholarships for students considering a career in missions. Check with the mission board to see what percentage of the funds of the missionary are used to cover administrative expenses of the board. Boards vary. As I mentioned above, in my own case, Independent Faith Mission took 10% of our monthly income to cover administrative costs. When we were getting around $5500, this represented an expense of $550. When we joined Baptist World Mission, they did not take out a set percentage, but a certain amount per month – somewhere around $300 to $400 per month. This made our percentage taken out much less – about 6-7%. When we deliberately suggested that churches give us only partial support or relocate the support, the same cost represented a substantial percentage, and they dropped our monthly charges substantially.

The sending church should decide what percentage of the total support it will give for candidates from the church itself. Our initial home church supported us for 20% of our required support. Later, when our monthly support doubled, it was closer to 10%. As I had mentioned above, it is nice to have much of your support coming from a small group of churches, but if you lose support from one of those churches, you can get into a financial bind.

Some churches will band together in a group to avoid the missionary having to do so much traveling. If one member of their group approves the candidate, then each church will also add their support. Then the candidate has most of his support consolidated in a smaller geographic area, and he can speed up his deputation process. At the same time, it is important to be very careful about selecting qualified, well-trained, and capable candidates.

The Vital Factor for Missions

Prayer is vital for missions. Paul asked for prayer for himself and others many times. Pray especially for the missionaries you support, praying and for their both their general and specific needs. All missionaries need prayer for learning the language and culture, the political situation, their own spiritual growth, dealing with and helping the nationals, and maintaining good relationships with other missionaries. Some churches use a prayer calendar. Others pray in meetings and special groups, such as Sunday school. Some families have both individual personal and family prayer time for missionaries.

ADDENDUM A: THE ROLE OF THE PASTOR AND CHURCH

The person who should lead by example is the pastor, who should spend substantial time in prayer for his church's mission outreach.

Accountability

Continued contact with the home church is important to maintain accountability. The candidate should be evaluated on his initial appointment and again on his departure for the field. He should also be evaluated both on return from the field on furlough, and just before returning to the field.[87] Further reports from the field can cover such items as current support, reaching goals, and handling problems. During furlough, the home church can help the missionary re-adapt to the United States and to be spiritually and physically refreshed. Remember that missionaries not only experience culture shock on arriving on the field, but also culture shock in many cases on returning back home. The more the missionary has successfully adapted to his new culture, the more shock he will have coming back to the USA. Furlough is also a time to report back to other supporting churches, seek additional support, and possibly further education.

A Missions Committee

In many churches, a missions committee may be an important adjunct to assist the pastor in the missionary outreach of the church. However, there are advantages with having direct contact with the pastor, who often largely influences who is taken on for support and may also support special projects. I am sure that many missionaries have had that experience. I remember that we had been praying about starting a TV broadcast about 2005. We went back to a church on furlough, and as we were eating dinner with the pastor, we mentioned our thoughts. That night the pastor stood up and said essentially the following: We are not at the place to increase our missionary month support. However, the Pattons have a need for a TV program and we have a bit of money in the bank. I recommend that we give them $6000.00 toward their TV project. With that money we were able to buy the computer we needed, the software and a high-quality camera and tripod to launch the TV broadcasts, which today are continuing fifteen years later.

A mission policy for the missions committee is very helpful. It can outline the organization and qualification of both the members and the chairman. There can be a general statement of duties and also definite duties can be specified. The missions committee relationship with the church board should be clear, as well as the procedure for submitting recommendations. The mission policy can set qualifications for both missionaries and missions boards. They can outline the acceptance procedure, as well as the support policies for both missionaries and missions agencies. They can outline the expectations from the missionaries, the mission agencies, the church corporate, and the individual members of the church.

The causes for termination of support can also be outlined. I believe that if this is spelled out ahead of time, it then is not viewed as a personal attack on the specific missionary. For example, areas might include doctrinal deviation, financial mismanagement, and immorality. Other areas could be the inability to function, or major issues with other missionaries or the mission agency. It is usually best not to terminate support on the field unless the missionary refuses to make things right or come back to the USA. It is important to work things out in a Biblical manner and spirit.

The size of the missionary committee is partially determined by the size of the church. The pastor, of course, is an ex-officio member. The chairman has a vital role. He is often recommended by the pastor and confirmed by the congregation. He is responsible to oversee the entire program, and is responsible to the committee, the board, and to the congregation. Usually, he has a 2-3 year term. The members should also be spiritually qualified, mature members with a burden for missions.

The general duties of the missions committee should include the missions conference and speakers, the budget and policies. Their specific duties include educating the congregation, selecting and evaluating candidates, and evaluation of the missionaries already supported. The committee should forward financial recommendations to the church board, who then submit them to the congregation for approval.

ADDENDUM A: THE ROLE OF THE PASTOR AND CHURCH

Qualifications for Missionaries Set by the Board

What are some of the qualifications of the missionaries? First, the qualifications will reflect the values of the church. Personal qualifications include being truly regenerate and having a clear call of God on his life. He should manifest spiritual growth and have concern for evangelism that shows itself in actual practice. Likewise, the missions committee will want to be certain that the board is compatible in its doctrine, associations, and financial policies.

Financial Policies of the Church and Mission Board

Financial policies should include the support percentage if this is indicated, as well as the support policies of the church. For example, is there a difference in the amount of support for a church member? Furthermore, questions of health and life insurance, as well as retirement should be addressed. Often these questions are best handled by the board, which has experience in the varying circumstances overseas.

A Yearly Missionary Report

Each year, it is appropriate to have a missionary report including yearly goals and progress through the year as well as an evaluation of the work at the end of the year. During furlough, the missionary can report back to the churches, and also discuss future needs with the missions chairman. Again, these debriefings are very important to both the church and the missionary. The missionary needs the opportunity to share his experiences. He can process what has happened over the years and place things in perspective. As he shares with the church, they can have a more effective ministry in the life of the missionary as well.

Although the mission agency can do its best, the home church is well placed to be able to be most effective in assisting the missionaries sent from their church. For example, my field director was responsible for over 60 missionaries and families. He also raised support for the mission and his own travel. How could he possibly have close contact with all the missionaries under him, and travel to each of the fields on a regular basis? He will understand the pressures on the missionary and be able to counsel, but it is the home pastor, who has a longstanding relationship with the missionary, who should able to help in the area of pastoral care.

Other Considerations for the Missions Committee

The missions committee can do several things to promote missions. They can put up a map with up-to-date information on the mission field. They can have a place for up-to-date prayer letters. They can insert information on missionaries in the bulletin. They can use missionaries on furlough to challenge and inform the church. Missions staff from various boards are usually available to give missionary challenges. Missions professors from colleges may do the same. And it is possible to use missionary appointees as a challenge to the entire church, and especially to the youth. Another help is a good missions library, with good readable books. Some classics are helpful, as well as missions history, which often needs to be updated. Many missions agencies are happy to supply up-to-date information from the mission fields which they represent at no cost.

The Missions Conference

The missions conference is a key time in the life of the church. This is the time to both present and carry out faith promise missions, if the church has chosen to use that method to support missions. Have a goal to reach. It is a time to seek commitments to mission service. It should be planned to optimize attendance, avoiding major holidays, vacations, or times of other activities such as sports activities. There should be a challenge to the youth, rotating missionaries through the children, teenagers and the adults. One might even consider having a youth representative on the missions committee.

Prayer is a key item to have a successful missions conference. A few minutes of prayer can begin the time at Sunday school. Home prayer meetings as well as private prayer in family devotions are other ways to pray for the missions conference. The prayers can be goal directed; both for the conference, but also for the specific needs of the missionaries. In addition to praying for the conference, it is helpful to get the congregation involved to make a successful conference. One possibility is panel discussions; another is question and answer times.

ADDENDUM A: THE ROLE OF THE PASTOR AND CHURCH

The Assistance of the Mission Agencies

Mission agencies are often eager to help the church to have a successful missions conference. They are a service agency to the church in its sending function. During a conference, they may supply information concerning short term missions, and the needs in different fields. They may have ideas about teams going overseas. They can provide promotional materials, often done professionally. They are often able to provide speakers and many mission agencies have publications materials as well.

In the overall outreach of the church, the mission agency can be a vital part of the mission program. The goal of a mission agency should be to serve the local churches in their desire to reach the lost throughout the world. The agency will have outreach resources and can also provide consultation as needed. A good mission organization will have leadership with experience on the field, and practical knowledge of the challenges of missions. The mission agency can be a tremendous help in the financial area, one area that most missionaries as well as churches are ill-equipped to handle. The agency can move funds internationally. This can be very complicated legally, and often there are problems in exchange rates. They can work through the visa requirements and legal requirements for residence in the country. They may have an idea about the amount of unrest present in various countries throughout the world. The mission agency is often able to give very helpful counsel to the sending church, both on behalf of the current missionaries as well as prospective missionaries.

In terms of responsibility, the missionary is ultimately responsible to the sending church. The mission agency has been given delegated authority to supervise both the missionaries and the funds provided. The mission agency may well partner with the national churches in terms of manpower and finances. This relationship changes over the years. First the missionary is a pioneer to begin a work. As the work develops, he has a role like a parent. Later, they become partners, and finally, the missionary is a participant in the overall outreach of the church. There must be mutual respect, trust, and cooperation.

Responsibilities of the Sending Church

The sending church has a major responsibility for their missionary. They need to maintain faithful prayer support as well as financial support, and to maintain good communications with the missionary. Now with e-mail there is little excuse on the part of either the missionary or the church to lack communication, with rare exceptions.

Neal Pirolo has written a classic text called *Serving as Senders*.[88] His emphasis is that the missionary needs a support team. He compares the missionary with the soldier on the front lines. For the soldier to be successful, there must be a strong support team sending him, especially overseas. Likewise, he states that the missionary needs a support team, and identifies six major areas of support. These are moral support, logistics support, financial support, prayer support, communication support, and re-entry support. He later expanded the last item into a separate book.

Moral support is needed throughout the time on the field. It is easy to become discouraged. Knowing that there are those who are encouraging you is very helpful. This is especially true of prayer support as well. Both tie together. Logistic support can be helpful taking care of things back home, as well as getting supplies to the field. This support can also be a tremendous help during furloughs. Financial support is vital to being able to function. And communication is helpful between the USA and the field.

It is possible to have the mission agency attempt to supply these items, but it is a challenge with the number of missionaries on the field. Pirolo believes, and I believe he has biblical support, that the sending church has primary responsibility in this area. Certainly, the church can do a great deal to support their missionaries, and probably help reduce the high percentage of missionaries who come off the field before a planned termination of service.

The church's responsibility is not over when the missionary returns off the field for good.[89] He needs to be debriefed, but then many things can be done to help him re-enter the home field. Even if the individual

ADDENDUM A: THE ROLE OF THE PASTOR AND CHURCH

has seen a successful completion of his ministry, or is returning to retire, this is very important. However, it is even more critical when the departure was not planned, perhaps forced by political upheaval, or sickness in the family. And if there were other problems on the field, they need to be addressed as well. It is important to give the missionary adequate time to tell about his mission experience, and debrief him both by the church and the mission agency.

On his return, the missionary will usually have problems with both housing and transportation. The church can help in these areas. He should be involved again in ministry as he readjusts to the USA. Often, because of his unique experiences, he can make a unique contribution to the church ministry. He may need a job. The church needs to continue to work with the missionary, providing counseling and support as needed until he reintegrates into society.

In conclusion, I believe that any size church can have a significant international missions impact. The key is the leadership, especially by the pastor. Missions is a big commitment if done properly. But Jesus Christ, the first missionary, came to earth to seek and save those who are lost. He left us with a commission to do the same. We should not be satisfied with less.

ADDENDUM B
DEPUTATION: A RUGGED BUT REWARDING ROAD
By Marc Patton
Forward

The Process

In June 1991, my wife and I were accepted by Baptist International Missions, Inc. as missionaries to Hungary. At that time, my wife had one semester of college remaining before finishing in January 1992. It was my plan to begin deputation immediately after she completed her schooling. From the beginning, it was our goal to raise our support within 1½ years. Immediately after candidate school, we began preparing our prayer cards, letterhead, resume, letters of recommendation, etc. In early September, I began calling pastors and scheduling meetings for 1992. The Lord blessed us, and by the time we went to our first meeting on January 18, 1992, I had more than 80 meetings scheduled. The Lord allowed us to keep a full schedule throughout deputation, and we had anywhere from nine to fifteen meetings per month from February 1992 through May 1993. Our support began very slowly. After six months, we had only 19% of our support. By the end of our first year, we had only about 40% of our support. However, we had sown a lot of seed, and by June 1993 our support had doubled to more than 80%. We went ahead and purchased our tickets in June for an August 19th departure. By the time we left, exactly 19 months after beginning deputation, our support was almost exactly at 100%.

Success Belongs to the Lord

In a day which many missionaries spend three or four years on deputation, many would consider our deputation a success. I do not want to take the glory for that success. We have relied from the beginning on the Lord for our support. I know that He provided it, and I **know** that He can take it away just as quickly, if He desired. It is also true that most of the philosophies and methods detailed in this booklet are not original with me. A large portion of these ideas were taught to me by my father, Dr. Robert Patton, Missionary to Suriname, South America. Other ideas were gathered from talking with other missionaries during our deputation time. I have also tried to be an observer and analyzer, as I have personally watched dozens of missionaries during our deputation time. Thus, this booklet is merely a compilation of ideas that have been tried and tested by personal experience.

There Is Not One Method of Deputation

It should also be remembered that there is really no authoritative method of deputation. Our only true authority is the Word of God, and although there are certainly applicable principles in the Bible, we cannot find the step-by-step methods for deputation there. For this reason, this is not intended to be a critique of other missionaries or deputation methods. These are simply methods that worked for us, and I believe that they will work for others as well. The purpose of this booklet is to be a help and provide you with ideas.

With all these things in mind, I commend this to your reading. I have prayed over these pages, and trust that they will be a help to you and your ministry. God bless you!

Marc Patton
April 1994
Esztergom, Hungary, East Europe

Introduction

(with comments by rdp, Robert D. Patton)

In Christian work, the success of any venture is largely dependent upon three factors: Prayer, Organization, and Effort.

1. **Prayer:** without prayer, organization and effort will be in vain. Remember the words of Christ: *Jn. 15:5 Without me ye can do nothing.* One may see some external appearances of success, but

ADDENDUM B: DEPUTATION

true success is impossible without the power of God in one's life and ministry. There is no substitute for prayer and a sincere walk with God.
2. **Organization:** Without organization, prayer and effort will be without purpose and direction. *I Cor. 14:40 Let all things be done decently and in order.* Prayers must have direction for them to be useful. Effort without organization is generally wasted or misdirected. Getting organized means recognizing your purpose, (or purposes) and planning the best means of accomplishing those purposes. Organization is that which gives detail and direction to our prayers and effort.
3. **Effort:** without effort, prayers and organization lack implementation. God's Word emphasizes the importance of hard work. *Ecc. 9:10a Whatsoever thy hand findeth to do, do it with all thy might.* God will only bless those who are willing to put forth effort and do their part; likewise, organization is useless if one does not put into practice that which has been planned.

Three Critical Areas to Avoid Deputation Problems

Prayer

While on deputation, I met dozens of missionaries who were struggling with deputation. Their problems were invariably caused by a lack in at least one of these three areas. Prayer, of course, is almost impossible to measure except by self-examination; thus, each person will have to examine his own life in this area.

Organization

Organization and effort are more measurable to the observer than another's prayer life. I have met some missionaries who work extremely hard but are disorganized. Their presentation is enthusiastic but lacks cohesiveness. Their schedule is haphazard. Their records are horrendous. They misplace addresses, forget to return phone calls, and fail to send confirmation letters and prayer letters. They have a tendency to run out of prayer cards and brochures before remembering to order more. These things may seem minor, but compiled, they may double one's time on deputation.

Effort

I have also met missionaries who are organized, but they lack effort. Their displays are beautiful; their slides are professional; their presentation is efficient, but the effort is missing. This is most often demonstrated by the number of meetings they have. I have met missionaries who consider themselves busy with five or six meetings (or less - rdp) per month! I know some who spend four years going to only 200 churches. These people are organized, but do not put forth the necessary effort.

The purpose of this writing is not to provide motivation to prayer. A missionary who has not learned to pray should seek another vocation. The purpose of this writing is not to inspire effort. Any missionary worth supporting will be willing to put for the necessary effort. My purpose here is to provide ideas which will help in the organization of deputation so that the prayers and effort will be well-directed.

SECTION I: GETTING STARTED

Start Early

One of the keys to reducing deputation time is to plan ahead and start early. I would suggest that you begin scheduling meetings four to six months before you plan to begin deputation (I began a year in advance - rdp). Advance notice is necessary to schedule meetings in most churches. Some churches will be booked a full year in advance or even longer. Therefore, to begin with a full schedule, you must begin calling ahead of time. If you plan to begin deputation in June, I would suggest you begin scheduling meetings by the previous January. In my case, I planned to begin deputation in late January 1992. Thus, I began scheduling meetings in September 1991. I had over 80 meetings scheduled before I ever went to my **first** meeting. This allowed me to **start** deputation with a full schedule. In order to begin scheduling ahead of time, it is necessary to plan ahead in several areas.

Mission Board

If you plan to use a mission board, it is best to go to candidate school **at least six months before you plan to begin deputation.** This may mean going after your junior year in college rather than waiting until after graduation. Many boards will allow this, and thus you will be able to get a head start. Before calling pastors, it is helpful to have your mission board established. Having your mission board determined is also necessary to begin printing prayer cards and other material.

Printed Materials

Immediately after being approved by your mission board is the time to begin preparing your printed materials. This includes prayer cards, letterhead, letters of recommendation, and a sharp (and short - rdp) resume. Many pastors will ask you to send a packet of information; thus you will want to have all these materials ready before you begin scheduling meetings. I will give a few suggestions in regards to these materials.

1. Prayer Cards

I would suggest that you study prayer cards of other missionaries for ideas. In my opinion, the best prayer cards are simple, clear, and first class. The most important information on the prayer card is your name, your field, a nice picture, and the address of your mission board and/or sending church. Maps are also a nice touch. To add scripture verses, information about the country, your goals, doctrinal beliefs, birthdays, anniversary, etc. often make the prayer card appear cluttered and difficult to read. I would suggest if you want to include this kind of additional information, that you print it on the backside of the prayer card. (When our students at Crown College have interviewed pastors as part of their deputation training, virtually all pastors made the same comments. Rdp)

2. Letterhead

Like prayer cards, letterheads which are simple, clear and first class are to be preferred. It is not necessary to spend a large amount of money to achieve these goals. The letterhead should let the pastor know who you are and the field to which God has called you.

3. Letters of Recommendation

These are often very important to pastors. I would use a great deal of prayer and counsel in selecting people to write letters for you. It is important to use people who know you well. It is also helpful to use individuals who are well-known to the pastors who will be receiving the letters. Letters of recommendation are proper because they allow positive things to be said about you by a voice other than your own. *Prov. 27:2a Let another man praise thee, and not thine own mouth.*

4. Resume

Include in your preacher's packet a sharp resume. Your resume should not be more than a page long and easy to read. This should include a **brief** testimony, a **brief** statement of purpose, and some background information about yourself. Pastors are interested in your college education, your Christian work experience, and any foreign experience you might have. (There is a sample resume at the end of this material)

Website

I highly recommend taking the time and effort to set up a website for your ministry. I use blogspot.com and it is free. There are other options available for minimal expense. All the information that you would send out to prospective supporters should be included on your website. That would include your testimony, ministry experience, statement of purpose, statement of faith, philosophy of ministry, and letters of recommendation. You can also upload some pictures and your deputation video. Your prayer letters should also be available. And you should include a link to your mission board with your support information. **Your website should be a one stop place where people can find all the information needed about your ministry.** (Bold emphasis is mine. I totally agree. My initial packets had a lot of information, but now much more can be provided in a very compact and neat form on a website. It should be well organized, user friendly, and provide all the information that the pastor or supporter would desire – rdp)

Survey Trip

I would recommend that **every** missionary visit the field of service to which God has called him. I do not believe that the value of such a trip can be stressed too much. A survey trip provides several benefits. First, it gives you **credibility**. Pastors and churches will feel more confident of your call if you have seen and experienced your mission field. Second, it gives you **knowledge** of your field that you will never get from a book, video, or another missionary. You are able to gather your own pictures and display materials as well. Third, a trip will help **seal your call** in your own heart and mind. The field is no longer an elusive dream or desire to you, but it is a **real place** with **real people** that you have seen and experienced. It is ideal if both husband and wife can visit the field together. If that is impossible, at least the husband should go. Although the expense discourages many missionaries from taking a survey trip, I believe that it is worth the sacrifice to do it. The trip does not have to be made before you begin scheduling meetings, but I would certainly make it before beginning deputation. (I would suggest that you are included in some of the pictures to emphasize that this is your personal experience... rdp)

SECTION 2: SCHEDULING MEETINGS

Gathering Contacts

One of the most difficult things for prospective missionaries is knowing **whom** to contact. Much time and money is wasted by contacting churches that will not have you for a meeting. Most pastors will tell you that they are **flooded** by calls from missionaries. It is impossible for them to give meetings to all, or even most of the missionaries who call. Thus, it is important for the missionary to have some point of contact or relationship with the church to improve his chances of obtaining a meeting. Calling churches "cold-turkey" (for example, from a phone book or even from a Southwide Baptist Fellowship or Sword of the Lord directory) is generally a waste of time and money. In this case, the success ratio is very low. With a point of contact or recommendation, the success rate greatly increases. I was able to schedule meetings in a bit more than 50% of the churches that I contacted. Much of that success came because I used **good** lists! Here are some suggestions as to where to obtain lists of pastors worthwhile to contact.

1. Your sending church

Your sending church and pastor should provide a great deal of support and help. If they are willing to commission you, they should be willing to help you. Every pastor has a circle of contacts within which he carries some influence. Your pastor should be willing to at least provide you with a list of these contacts and write a letter of recommendation for you. Some pastors will even call some of their close friends for you, which is a tremendous help. I would seek and utilize the help of your pastor to its maximum extent.

2. Your college

If you graduated from a Bible college or Institute, this is also a tremendous source of contacts. Most graduates hold a certain degree of loyalty toward their alma mater. They are usually more likely to give a meeting from "their college" than to a stranger. Ask your college to give you a list of graduates that are pastors. Ask them also for a list of churches that are very supportive of their college. These lists will prove very useful.

3. Other missionaries

On this I would like to sound a word of caution. My current philosophy here is to only share lists with missionaries that I know very well and in whom I have a great deal of confidence. I say this for several reasons. **First**, many pastors do not appreciate having their names passed about. They get many phone calls from missionaries. If they find out that you are giving out their name to every missionary that you meet, they will usually not appreciate it. **Second**, if a missionary uses your name or recommendation to get a meeting, and later he "washes out," your name and reputation can be damaged as well. Therefore, my recommendation is that missionaries keep their own lists to themselves, and only exchange contacts in rare cases.

ADDENDUM B: DEPUTATION

4. Scheduled meetings

One of my best sources for contacts was from pastors with whom I scheduled meetings. When I would schedule a meeting with a pastor, it was my custom to ask the following question before hanging up: "Could you recommend any other pastors in your area that I could call?" Very frequently they would give me two or three names and phone numbers. I would then call up these pastors and say: "I just scheduled a meeting with Pastor _____, and he mentioned your name to me (or recommended that I call you, etc.") I am sure that I scheduled dozens of meetings as a result of this practice. There is nothing better to a pastor than a personal recommendation from someone they know well. One word of caution: some pastors will not wish to give you any names or recommendations. If that is their feeling, respect it and don't push them.

Planning Your Schedule

Once you have obtained your lists, it is time to start scheduling the meetings. Now the questions come: "Where do I start?" or "Whom should I call first?" How many meetings will I need? How long will it take? I will attempt to answer a few of these questions.

Where Do I Start?

Use your home as a base and work outward from there. We were fortunate to live in a good central location in the Midwest. Thus, with a little effort, we were able to complete our entire deputation within 500 miles of home. Over 80% of our meetings were held within 300 miles of our home. This allowed us to spend a good deal of time at home between meetings, which saved money on gas. It also saved a great deal of physical and emotional "wear and tear" of being on the road. I turned down meetings in Florida, New York, Canada, and Texas because of this philosophy. That may sound foolish, but it makes both deputation and furlough a great deal easier. I know of missionaries who cover America from coast to coast, but unfortunately, they will have to do this repeatedly on future furloughs. This either means grueling trips for the entire family, or that dad is going to spend a lot of time separated from them. I was told several times by other missionaries that "the money is on the east coast" or "you've got to go to such-and-such place."

However, I chose to stick to my plan, and found that the Lord had our entire support right in our area.

When I began deputation, I was working a full-time job. I was able to keep my job for the first five months because I scheduled meetings close to home, and thus I was able to allay the many expenses incurred with the beginning of deputation. I scheduled Wednesday meetings in the immediate area, within a two-hour drive. I scheduled Sunday meetings close enough to return home Sunday night. Eventually, of course, I had to expand, but by that time we had several churches supporting us. Every missionary must make his own decision on this subject, but my recommendation is to stay as close to home as possible!

How Many Meetings Will I Need?

This is a difficult question because so many factors are involved. The first factor is average support per church. Currently $100 per month seems to be a good average figure with most independent Baptist churches. From talking to many missionaries, I found that at best they received support from about two-fifths of the churches in which they held meetings. Many others received support from only one-fifth. Therefore, if you need to raise $6,000 per month, you would need about 60 supporting churches or individuals. This means that you would need to hold meetings in about 150 to 200 different churches to raise that amount. At this time, I believe that most missionaries will need to plan on having meetings in approximately 200 churches.

How Long Will It Take?

A big portion of the answer to this question depends on you! How long will it take you to get into 200 different churches? When we were on deputation, most churches still had three services per week. That means that there were 156 opportunities per year in regular services. Today many churches have dropped their Sunday evening services, reducing the number of available services, but there are also missions conferences to consider. We were able to hold over 220 meetings in 200 churches (about twenty churches we went to a second time) in about a year and a half. Unfortunately, I find that it takes most missionaries three to five years to accomplish this goal. Therefore, I would like to

ADDENDUM B: DEPUTATION

make a few suggestions to help you get into as many meetings as possible in as short a time as possible (Marc has additional statistics at the end of this presentation - rdp)

1. Go to two different churches on Sunday

I have missionaries tell me that it is too difficult or too tiring. They also say that it does to allow them enough time to "get to know the pastor and people." However, it adds FIFTY-TWO possible meetings each year! It is usually possible to find two churches within a two-hour drive of each other. This allows you to arrive at the first church on Saturday. You have time to go soul-winning or at least to meet and fellowship with the pastor. After church you have time for lunch, and if you are on the road by 2:30 or 3:00, you have plenty of time to arrive at 5:00 for a 6:00 pm service. After the service, you have time to fellowship with the second pastor and may even spend the night there as well. In this manner, there is plenty of time both for travel and fellowship. I do not think as a general rule that your chances for support are increased by being there an entire day. In fact, I have had several pastors tell me that it was a greater burden because they had to provide meals and accommodations for two nights instead of one! Pastors expect you to be busy and appreciate it when you are. My recommendation is that you stay for an entire Sunday only if the pastor insists upon it and that you feel that you have a reasonably good chance of support from that church.

So, what can you do when many churches have dropped their Sunday evening services? I would take advantage of the churches that still do have a Sunday evening service, by scheduling them for Sunday evenings, and schedule the other churches for Sunday morning or Wednesday evening. In other words, I would make it my goal to take advantage of as many Sunday evenings as possible, and still strive to get into two churches as often as possible on Sundays.

2. Use mission conferences to fill in meetings between Sundays and Wednesdays.

I believe that one of the biggest mistakes missionaries make is filling their schedule largely with missions conferences and then staying for each conference in its entirety. Conferences generally run from

Sunday to Wednesday or from Wednesday to Sunday. Thus, to attend the entire conference means that you can go to only ONE meeting that week instead of THREE. My general practice was to try to attend missions conferences on my "off-days" — Mondays, Tuesdays, Thursdays, and Fridays. That way I could have two Sunday meetings, attend a conference on Monday and Tuesday, and go to a FOURTH church on Wednesday, giving me four opportunities for support in that particular week instead of one (I would also mention that we have one church with Tuesday midweek services and two churches with Thursday midweek services - another opportunity to work in another meeting that same week! rdp) I remember one week where three of the four churches took us on for support! What if I had just gone to the one conference for the entire week?

Many people say that the longer you stay, the better chance you have for support. The truth is, it is quite possible that the opposite is true. The longer you are there, the greater expenses and burden you place on the pastor and church. Of course, if the pastor insists that you stay for the entire week's conference, that is a different matter. However, even in those cases you must weigh carefully the value of the meeting and your chances for support. Only on four occasions did I stay at a church for a full week conference. In each case, I stayed for the entire conference only because the pastor insisted on it and because the pastor virtually promised me support. After being on the field for eight months, we have seen only one of those churches actually take us on for support! Pastors usually mean well and intend to support everyone who comes to their conference, but truthfully speaking, it may be impossible for them to do so. In each case, when I attended a complete conference, I was only given a brief time to speak in front of the entire church. There was always a special speaker bringing the main message. That is fine, but I would rather not spend a full week in one church just to give a 15-minute testimony and show some slides, which I could have easily and effectively done in one or two nights. For these reasons, I would avoid going to conferences for the entire week except in rare cases. Rather, use the conferences to supplement your regular Sunday and Wednesday

ADDENDUM B: DEPUTATION

meetings. I remember at least one week in which I was able to have meetings in SIX different churches!

The Initial Contact

Now you have obtained some good lists. You have the basic plan as to where you want to schedule meetings. The next question is **how** to make contact with the pastor. Is writing or calling better? What should I say? I can still remember very clearly the first phone call I made. I remember the rapid beating of my heart, the parched lips, the fervent, silent prayer. It can be intimidating at first, but if you have a plan for what to say, you can be ready.

1. Make the initial contact by phone. This is an area where some would debate me, but based on my experience, it is best. I have been told by many pastors that when they receive a missionary packet from someone who they do not know, they usually throw it away. Other times, it never even reaches the pastor, but goes to a secretary or assistant or committee. The same is true for emails as well. Many pastors do not take the time to answer routine letters and emails, let alone packets from unknown missionaries. For these reasons, I recommend that you phone first. About 10% of the churches which you call will ask you if you have already sent a packet. When they do, then send a packet and call back in a few weeks. However, the other 90% of the time you are better off calling first.
2. Try to speak directly to the pastor. In most independent Baptist churches, the pastor handles the scheduling himself. If the pastor is not there, find out when you can call back rather than leaving a message for him to call you. This is more expensive but best. Many pastors will not bother answering a phone call from someone they do not know. If they do return your call, they will often be annoyed by being required to pay for a long-distance phone call that they do not really want to make, to speak to "another missionary" to whom they do not really want to speak. In other words, asking a pastor to call you back can give them an initial bad impression. Trying to reach the pastor personally can be very frustrating for the missionary, as often four or five

attempts must be made before finally reaching the pastor, but persistence pays off! In the future, when you know a pastor, you may more freely ask him to return your calls, but not the first time. It is also usually best not to spend a lot of time explaining your ministry to the secretary or pastor's wife. This will merely be a waste of time, as they do not have the authority to make a decision. If, however, the pastor has appointed an assistant or church member to schedule the missionaries, then by all means follow the channel that the pastor has established. (In some situations, I have been able to "get the secretary on my side" to get through to the pastor by a brief conversation. rdp)

3. THE OPENING QUESTION: In speaking to the pastor or his delegate, I would begin the conversation like this:

> "Hello. My name is Marc Patton. My wife and I are missionaries on deputation for Hungary. I was wondering if I could take one or two minutes to tell you a little about our plans."

The importance of this initial question cannot be stressed enough. In at least 90% of the time I received a positive response to this question. I then had permission to spend up to two minutes presenting my reasons for allowing me to come to his church. I know many missionaries that have had problems because they began their conversation like this:

> "Hello, I am John Brown. My wife and I are missionaries on our way to Outer Slabovia, and I was just wondering if we could come to your church and present our work some time?"

Now John has told the pastor nothing about himself except his name, field, and marital status. He has then given the pastor an opportunity to say "No." Now if the pastor does not know John Brown or have a special burden for Outer Slabovia, he is probably going to reply like this.

> "Well John, we would love to hear about your work, but at this time our schedule is absolutely filled with missionaries. I'm sorry, but we just can't help you."

ADDENDUM B: DEPUTATION

Now John is left with the almost impossible task of changing the pastor's "no" to a "yes." If John had begun with my suggestion, he would have two minutes to say something to distinguish himself from all the other missionaries that have called recently for meetings.

Your Two-minute Opportunity

The pastor has given you two minutes. Two minutes is not a long time, but it is long enough if you are well prepared. Consider the fact that the pastor has probably received five to ten calls from missionaries that week. It is certainly impossible for him to have every missionary come. Therefore, you must say something within the next two minutes to set yourself apart - something that will cause him to say: "this is someone that has something important to present to my church." Yes, God is in control, and we must pray, but God also gives us a mind and a tongue which he expects us to use wisely. I will mention several things that must be included and several things that can be helpful.

1. **Your background:** This would include college training, home church, mission board, and ministry experience. You should mention your wife's background as well. If your parents are involved in full-time service, I would definitely mention that, as it will help your credibility. This information is all important in letting the pastor know that you prepared for what you are doing.

2. **Your field:** It is at this point that a survey trip proves helpful. It can add to both your knowledge and credibility. You will want to tell him why there is a need for your particular field. Stress statistics about the number of people and lack of missionaries, etc. At this time, people going to Eastern Europe have an advantage because it is a newly opened field. Take advantage of uniqueness whenever you can. If you are going to one of the more common fields like Mexico or Brazil, this may be a bit more difficult. Many pastors think that countries such as those are overflowing with missionaries because they already support three or four missionaries in those countries. You must emphasize the specific needs of the area to which you are going. For example, you could say: "I am looking to the city of _____ which has a population of

100,000 without a single independent Baptist church. Of course, be honest with your statistics.

3. **Your calling:** I would end with a stress on your call to the field. How do you know that God wants you to go there? This is very important to pastors. What are your plans to get there? Most independent Baptist churches are interested in church-planting missionaries, and if that is your calling, be sure to stress it.

4. **Other helpful things:** There are other experiences which you may have had that other missionaries have not had. These things should be mentioned and emphasized as appropriate. If you are a "missionary kid," emphasize that. This tells the pastor that you know exactly what you are getting into. If you have lived overseas, mention that. This is another factor toward credibility. If you already speak the language of the field to which you are called, say so! This tells the pastor that you are prepared and will be able to be effective almost immediately. An experience or advantage that God has given you should be mentioned.

As you can see, it will take planning to fit all this into two minutes. I recommend writing out your "speech" and practicing it. If it is longer than two minutes, evaluate and edit it. Ultimately, it is better not to read it over the phone, but at least you will be organized and know exactly what you want to say. One last caution would be this. Do not go over two minutes! The pastor has given you the courtesy of a hearing. Do not abuse it. If he wants to ask some more questions when you are finished, fine.

The Final Question

I would conclude with something like this:

> "I am currently scheduling meetings in your area for the month of _____, and I was wondering if it would be possible to schedule a meeting in your church."

You have already given the pastor some information about yourself. Hopefully, something that you said will have moved his heart. You have done your part, and now "the ball is in his court." He may give you a meeting on the spot. He may ask some more questions. He may ask you

ADDENDUM B: DEPUTATION

to send some more information and allow him some time to pray about it. At this point, you simply follow his lead and accept his decision. I do not believe that it is ever proper to beg or pressure a pastor to give a meeting. If his reply is negative, do not be disheartened. If a pastor says, "I'm sorry, but at this time we cannot have you." I would suggest the following response.

> "What I would like to do is to send you our packet of information. That way, if something changes and you want to reach me, you will be able to do so. If it would be alright with you, I would like to check back in a few months to see if anything has opened up."

Usually, the pastor will agree with this arrangement. Then you should send a letter along with the packet and make a record to call him back at the appointed time. I was able to schedule many meetings on a second call back and even some on the third call back. If the calls are made with the right spirit, the pastor will be impressed with your persistence, rather than be annoyed by it. To stay up-to-date and prompt with your callback requires good records and organization, but it will prove worthwhile. I would recommend that you use good computer software to use for your letter writing and record keeping. In my opinion, the time saved will be more than worth the investment.

One other suggestion would be to add these pastors to your prayer letter list even if they do not give you a meeting. This costs very little extra time and money, but it may be worth it in the long run. I had one pastor call me back and schedule me after receiving a prayer letter. These pastors will also be more likely to remember you when you call back in six months if they have received two or three prayer letters.

A Few More Thoughts

What if the pastor offers you a meeting but says that there is no way that the church can support you? This is a tough question. I will, however, give a few illustrations based on personal experience. At first, I took meetings every time a pastor offered one, even if he said that it would be impossible for them to support us. In a few cases, we were thrilled when the church eventually took us on for support. However, there were many times when the pastor was right, and they could not and did not support us. Toward the end of deputation, I had changed my response to something like this:

> "At this point, I still have a few other possibilities for that date. If you would not mind, let me check with them first and get back to you."

This allowed me to seek another meeting with a better chance of support. If I was unable to find another meeting in a given area for that date, I would call the first pastor back and schedule him. It is always true that a meeting with a poor chance of support is better than no meeting at all!

SECTION 3 - SO YOU HAVE A MEETING

Next Things

You have now given your two-minute introduction and asked your closing question. The Holy Spirit has spoken to the pastor's heart, and the pastor has agreed to give you a meeting. Now what do you do?

1. Agree on a date and service

The pastor is doing you a favor of giving you a meeting. Therefore, do your best to accommodate his schedule. At the same time, however, you will want to stick to your overall plan. Often, if you tell the pastor that you have a Sunday morning service nearby, he will grant you a Sunday night service or vice-versa. Regardless, you will want to settle the date and service immediately on the phone.

2. Settle details

Try to settle as many details as possible on the first call. Find out what time the service starts. **Be aware of time-zones.** Decide on your arrival plans. For a Sunday morning service, you will often want to arrive on Saturday. Politely ask the pastor if that would be possible and what time you should arrive. For Sunday and Wednesday evening services, you will generally want to arrive about one hour before the

ADDENDUM B: DEPUTATION

service to allow plenty of time to set up. You may also want to ask the pastor what kind of presentation he wants. He may want you to show slides and preach or to do only one or the other. Find out what he wants done and make a note of it.

3. Request accommodations as needed

I generally made it a rule never to request accommodations for more than one night except during missions' conferences. If I was preaching on a Sunday morning, I would request accommodations for Saturday night. I know of many cases where missionaries will speak on Wednesday, and request accommodations from Tuesday through Friday. This puts a tremendous burden on the pastor and his people. If the church has a "prophet's chamber" and their pastor offers it for a long period of time, then it is no problem to stay longer. Otherwise, I would suggest that you return home on off days, or arrange your own housing with a relative, or even a motel if necessary. Missionaries often have a reputation for being "leeches," and we need to avoid making requests that feed that stereotype. We also made it a habit of returning home after meetings that were held within two hours of home. You can usually easily arrive home by midnight, and most pastors will appreciate your consideration.

4. Send a confirmation letter immediately

Within two or three days of scheduling a meeting, you should send a confirmation letter. This way the pastor receives the letter while your conversation is still fresh in his mind. It also shows the pastor that you are organized and efficient. The confirmation letter should include all the details that you discussed. Most of the pastors will keep your confirmation letter and review it just before you come. They will appreciate all the details.

5. Send a second confirmation letter

Send a second confirmation letter four to six weeks before the meeting. You would be amazed how many pastors will forget about your meeting during the months separating the scheduling of the meeting and the actual occasion. This second letter will save some pastors the embarrassment of being forced to inform you that they forgot about your meeting and scheduled something else at the same time. The four-to-six-week time frame allows him (and you) time to rearrange the schedule if things have been double booked. Your "pre-meeting call-back" one week before the meeting does not allow him that flexibility.

6. Call the pastor back

Call the pastor back one to two weeks before the meeting. This is your final confirmation of the meeting and must not be omitted. I remember one occasion when I was unable to reach the pastor on several tries and decided not to bother. I remembered very clearly discussing with him three or four months previously the details of our arrival. We were to arrive at his house at 6 pm on a Saturday night and have supper with his family. I had sent two confirmation letters and was certain that he could not forget. However, when we arrived at his house at 6 pm Saturday night, we found a very surprised pastor. The family was already eating without us, and it was obvious that his wife was not expecting guests. Needless to say, it was an embarrassing situation for all of us. He apologized profusely, but I knew that it was my fault for not making that final call!

On another occasion, I called a pastor two weeks before our scheduled meeting. It happened to be on April 1st. I told the pastor that I was just calling to confirm our meeting the following week. The pastor said: "What meeting?" I said: "You are trying to play an April fool's prank on me, aren't you?" He said: "I certainly am not." Somehow, he had forgotten our meeting. I had spoken to him once on the phone and sent him two confirmation letters. It took me several minutes of explaining before he finally said that he vaguely remembered some sort of conversation with me. I give these illustrations to say this: DO NOT ASSUME ANYTHING! You must make this phone call.

7. If an emergency arises

If an emergency arises, telephone. Despite the best of planning, emergencies do arise. Cars break down, traffic jams occur, children become ill. If you are going to arrive late for a meeting, have the courtesy to call. By arriving late, I do not mean after the time that the service begins, but rather later than your promised arrival time. There is

ADDENDUM B: DEPUTATION

nothing more unsettling to a pastor than to be wondering where you are and if you are going to make it. If you told the pastor that you would be there by 5:15 and realize that it will be closer to 5:45 give him a call. Pastors will appreciate your conscientiousness.

SECTION 4: PREPARATION FOR THE MEETING

Projects That Must Be Completed

We have now discussed the scheduling of meetings. It is possible that you will begin scheduling meetings 4-5 months before you actually hold your first one. There are several things that do not have to be completed before you begin scheduling but should be completed before your first meeting.

DVD Presentation

Over the years I have met some missionaries that were negative about video presentations. They believed that independent Baptist missionaries should "just preach" and leave the videos to the more liberal crowd. It is true that a good video presentation is a lot of work, and that I would usually prefer just to preach. However, it is also true that most churches expect you to have a video of some sort. The people will enjoy a good presentation, and if well done, it can more effectively give them an understanding and "picture" of the field than mere words can convey. For these reasons, I would encourage you to take the time and effort to put together a good presentation. Your presentation should answer the following questions:

1. Who are you?
2. What are your qualifications for this work?
3. Where are you going, and why?
4. What do you plan to do when you get there?

General Suggestions

I will now make some general suggestions in helping you prepare your presentation:

1. It should not be too long

When I began deputation, I had a fifteen-minute taped slide presentation. Halfway through deputation, I shortened it to 12 minutes. In this day and age, I would reduce it even further to about 5 minutes. I found that I often had only a total of 30 or 35 minutes to present my work and preach. If I took 15 minutes to show slides and five minutes to give an appeal for the work, that left me only 10-15 minutes to preach! I believe that 5 minutes is enough time to effectively present yourself and your country through your video presentation.

2. It should be sharp and professional

First you need to write a good script. It is best to start with a script writing down exactly what you want to say, and then add pictures or video clips that fit the script. I have tried doing it the other way around and found it a disaster. In other words, it is better to leave out some of your favorite pictures because they don't fit your script, than try to write a script that includes all of your favorite pictures or video clips. Have others review your script and pictures before recording. Make sure that it is clear, concise, and powerful. It should speak not only to the mind, but to the heart as well.

Make sure that your audio recording is done with good equipment. A recording may sound fine on your laptop, and then sound completely different when run through a church PA system. You should probably ask for some help from your mission board or your home church to make sure that both your audio and video recordings are done at a high quality.

3. (I eliminated point number three as irrelevant in this updated revision)

4. Present your family as well as the field

The first part of our presentation was devoted to our family background. We dug into old family albums, and had the pictures turned into slides. We received more compliments on that aspect of our presentation than any other. People are interested in you, and not just your field!

5. Emphasize the people more than places

The church members enjoy seeing the beautiful landscape, the unusual wildlife, and the famous sights. However, these aspects of your field have very little to do with your calling, or the purpose of this deputation meeting. Keep these slides to a minimum. Emphasize the people, their spiritual poverty and blindness, and their need for Christ. If you want to make up a second slide presentation pertaining more to the land and the customs of the people, that would be fine. It could be used in Sunday school classes or ladies' meetings, etc., while your main presentation focuses on your purpose of stirring the peoples' hearts for lost souls.

6. Tell the people what you plan to do

There are times when this can be a challenge. You may not know precisely in which city you will work, or exactly what direction your ministry will take. However, you should have a general plan in your mind, and that plan should be expressed.

If you can cover all these factors in your five-minute presentation, you will then be free to use the rest of the time preaching and sharing your heart with the people.

Display Board

Here I will simply refer you to my wife's section: The Missionary Wife. Charin did an excellent job preparing the display for us.

Deputation Messages

This is not a homiletics lesson. I am assuming that you know how to preach. I would, however, like to make a few suggestions in this area.

1. Stick to your purpose

The pastor has basically invited you there for two reasons. First is to present your work; second, to inspire his people in the area of missions. I would suggest that you prepare your messages around the mission theme. This could include messages on soul-winning, surrender and service, as well as foreign missions.

2. Stick to the given time frame

There are few things that annoy a pastor more than a guest who takes more than his allotted time. You may think "No one should tell me how long I can preach." But this is not YOUR church! You may think that the Holy Spirit told you to keep preaching, but what He actually said was to be obedient to the higher authorities. The pastor has been put in a position of authority over that church by God, and as his guest, you are under his authority!

3. Be prepared for anything

You should have messages that you can preach for forty minutes and messages you can preach in five minutes. You should be prepared to teach the "golden age" class or the toddler department. I remember in one church that I preached to the youth on Saturday night, the adult Sunday school, preached in the morning service, taught in the 6:00 hour, and preached the evening service! All this is to say, when the pastor asks you to do something, you need to be ready. This is also important for your wife as well, as she may be called on to do a variety of things (with the exception of the forty-minute messages.)

SECTION 5: AFTER THE MEETING

Follow-up

You have now concluded the meeting. You have presented your work, your calling, and your burden with all your heart. Is this the end of the work? Do you now just leave it up to the Lord? I will make a few suggestions in this area.

1. Do not be too pushy

I personally did not make it a habit of confronting the pastor directly about support. I know other missionaries that ask the pastor directly after the meeting what the "verdict" is. I believe that some of this depends on your personality and the personality of the pastor. It also depends on your relationship with the pastor. It was my feeling that the pastor knew why I was there, and that I need not remind him of this. I

ADDENDUM B: DEPUTATION

did not like to put the pastor "on the spot." Each missionary must decide to do what he believes is appropriate in this area.

2. Leave something with the pastor

Leave something with the pastor when you depart. My wife and I made up a packet to leave with the pastor. It included a questionnaire from our mission board which the pastor was asked to fill out. We also inserted some various brochures and a magazine from BIMI. Most important, it contained a brief note from us. This was a form letter that thanked the pastor for the meeting. We then closed with a line similar to this: "If the Lord should lay it upon your heart to support us financially, you may send the support to the following address...

This statement was followed by instructions in regard to sending support to our mission. I believe that this is very important. Some pastors do not know where to send the support and will just make a guess. They may send it directly to you or your home church. Worse yet, they may send it to the wrong mission board. Including these instructions in the packet can save you a great deal of difficulty in the future.

3. Send a thank you note

These I generally wrote by hand so that the pastor would know that they were personal. If you prefer typing them, try to include some specific details to let him know it is personal. It was a privilege to present your work in his church.

4. Leave the church on your prayer letter list

I know many missionaries who remove a church from their prayer letter list if they do not see support in a few months to a year. I would suggest that you leave them on your list indefinitely unless something occurred that causes you either to be certain that they will not support you, or that you are certain that you do not want their support. We recently had a church begin supporting us almost two years after our meeting with them. I have heard other such stories from my parents and other missionaries. It is well worth the money to leave them on your prayer letter list. (I would add a note - we really need prayer, and you may have people who pray for you although they do not support you. One of the strengths of the faith promise system is a broadened prayer base. I have about 55 supporting churches at present, and send out about 600 e-mail prayer letters at least twice monthly. rdp)

5. Send an occasional personal note

During deputation, I would try to write the pastor a personal note a few months after our meeting. This was not a request for support, but rather a reminder that we were still "out there." Pastors are more likely to read a personal note than a general prayer letter.

6. A follow-up phone call

A follow-up phone call can be appropriate. I did not do this as a general practice but did try it several times when we were getting toward the end of deputation. I would call and say something like this: "We are now approaching the end of deputation time. We have raised ___% of our support and are looking forward to leaving for the field by ____ date. I just wanted to check back with you to see if there was any chance that you would be able to take us on for support before that time."

I tried this procedure about ten times with different churches. I did not get any promises immediately over the phone, but two of the churches did take us on for support later. This is just a possible suggestion, and not one that I have well proven.

7. Your pastor or mission director could write a letter for you

About two months before our departure, our field director wrote a letter for us. I had it sent to all the churches in which I had meetings that were not yet supporting us. The letter informed the churches of our planned departure date, our need for support, and the urgency of getting us to the field quickly. It asked each church to consider what they could do to help. I do not really know what effect this had on our support, but I do believe that it is better to have someone else write this letter rather than for you to make a plea on your own behalf.

What Should Be Your Focus

Thus there are some things that we can and should do after the meeting. However, ultimately our support is in the Lord's hands. I personally recommend that you talk as little as possible about money before, during, and after the meetings. It is much better to focus on praying, preaching, and being a blessing to the churches, than to always have your focus on money. It is during this time that we can really learn to depend on God. We work as hard and as wisely as we can, and then trust the Lord to see us through. He knows where we are, what we need, and He can get us to the field when He wants us there. Just learn to keep your eyes on Him.

Maintaining and Increasing Your Support After You Are on the Field

So, you have raised your support and arrived on the field. It might be nice to imagine that your fundraising days are over, but that is simply not true. As a missionary, you will spend pretty much your whole life raising and maintaining your support. As the years pass some of your churches and individuals will drop your support. That support will need to be replaced. Your living and ministry expenses will also increase as time goes by. What can we do to maintain and increase our support after we are already on the mission field? Here are a few thoughts.

1. Communicate well

This is absolutely key to maintaining your support. Prayer letters should be sent out regularly - at least bimonthly. I think it is also beneficial to communicate even more frequently with those who are highly interested in your ministry. For example, we have a Facebook group for prayer supporters who have requested to be a part of it. I try to post a weekly update there. I often add pictures or a video clip. Not everyone wants this much communication, but some do. You will find that your key supporters - especially key pastors and individuals - are happy for the more regular information. And many of these people will pray for you every time they see an update from you. So, we send out monthly or bimonthly prayer letters to everyone on our list, but we also have about 80 people who hear from us every week.

2. Invite key pastors and individuals to visit you on the field!

Nothing will do more to inspire a burden for your ministry than a personal visit. Yes, it takes time and energy on your part to take care of your guests, but this will be an investment worth making. In two specific cases I invited pastors of large churches to visit our field BEFORE they supported us. In both cases after spending a week with us on the field their churches took us on for support. And in both cases a strong relationship was developed that opened many doors for joint ministry in the future. I also have several individuals who took us on for support after coming to the field on a short-term mission's trip. These types of trips are also great opportunities to deepen relationships with pastors and churches who already support you.

3. Ask key supporters to help you gain new contacts and support

I have had key supporting pastors pick up the phone and call their pastor friends to ask them to support us. We had one individual who supports us host a cookout for us. They invited potential supporters, and we had an opportunity to present our ministry to them after the meal.

4. When you are on furlough visit pastors and supporting individuals when you are driving through their area.

We generally take brief summer furloughs. It is impossible for us to visit all our supporting churches for a church service. For that reason, I will often schedule to visit supporting pastors on a weekday when we are passing through the area. I might stop by the church office or go out for a meal with them. Pastors and supporters will appreciate that personal contact even if it is only for an hour or two while you are passing through.

5. Take advantage of modern technology.

ADDENDUM B: DEPUTATION

I am writing this paragraph in 2021 in the middle of the Covid 19 pandemic. One thing Covid has taught us is to leverage online ministry opportunities. This has spilled over from our ministry in Hungary to communication with our supporters. You can now interact with a Sunday School class or small group in the US from the comfort of your home or office on the mission field! A pastor might interview you via Zoom during their church's missions conference. Instead of a prayer letter, you might want to make a 3-minute video update, upload it to your YouTube channel and send the link to your supporters. Some of your supporting churches will be happy to play that video in their next Sunday or midweek service.

These are just a few thoughts and ideas we have tried. Much more could be said. Suffice it to say, that as long as you are a missionary, raising support will be a part of your life. Take time to work out a strategy for how you will maintain and increase your support so you don't have to take an extended furlough to do so.

THE MISSIONARY WIFE
by Charin Patton
The Unique Calling of a Missionary & Family

The position of missionary is one of the most unique callings in all of Christian service. There is no higher calling than to serve the Lord, and in no other capacity is the whole family so called upon to serve the Lord together as on a foreign field. All must be willing to sacrifice, and all must be willing to work together as a team. You, as the wife, are one of the most important members of this team!

The Helpmeet

It is said of the virtuous woman in *Proverbs 31:[11] The heart of her husband doth safely trust in her, so that he shall have no need of spoil. [12] She will do him good and not evil all the days of her life.* Our number one priority is to be a helpmeet to our husbands. As a missionary, your husband will rely more heavily on you than other husbands may rely on their wives. Are you someone he can "safely trust?" Will you bring him blessing and good during these important days of his life? You can be his biggest asset or his biggest liability. What a tremendous responsibility the Lord has given you to take care of His special, chosen servant!

The Wife and Children's Responsibility

Much of a missionary's success on deputation depends on his wife. The church will not just be supporting the husband but the entire family. So as your husband holds meetings on deputation, you must keep in mind that you and your children are under as much scrutiny as he is. Pastors are looking to see if you are a blessing or a hindrance to your husband, as this will carry over to your work on the field and will often determine how effective a missionary your husband will be for the Lord. We have often been told of missionaries who have left the field after just a short time because the wife could not adjust. This fact has made many pastors very wary about taking on a missionary for support whose wife they have not met, or whose wife has left a negative impression while on deputation.

Our job as wives is to complete our husbands, building them up and enabling them to reach their full potential. Since this writing basically deals with the deputation aspect of the missionary's work, I will attempt to offer some suggestions as to how we can help our husbands reach their potentials while doing deputation work.

Ways to Assist Your Husband

There are so many numerous details involved with the deputation ministry that anything you can do to help lighten your husband's load will not only be greatly appreciated by him but will also help to create a better spirit and attitude in the whole family.

1. Before Beginning Deputation

Help with Correspondence

There are many things which a wife can do even before deputation begins that will help lighten her husband's load. If your husband is working a full-time job while he is scheduling meetings, he may appreciate your doing his correspondence work for him.

The Display Board

ADDENDUM B: DEPUTATION

Another big project is preparing the display board. Most men would rather not have anything to do with this project and would prefer to leave it entirely up to their wives. Here are a few helpful hints:

A. Have the board made or purchase one to your specific measurements. Consider carefully the amount of trunk space you will be able to spare. Do not have a board that is so large and bulky that it takes up your entire trunk, and then all your luggage must be placed in the back seat of the car along with your two children, car seats, diaper bags, etc. You will also want to be sure that the board is light enough to be carried easily.

B. Before beginning, have a plan. The purpose of your board is to present you and your field. We have often seen lovely missionary boards with beautiful pictures, but someone forgot to put the name of their country, or even worse, their own name. When people look at your board, they ought to immediately and clearly see your name and field, even from a distance. It is also important to have a large **recent** picture of your family so that folks can readily identify you.

C. I would recommend not attaching anything directly onto the board itself that cannot be easily removed. You may wish to change a picture, or something may become faded or damaged and need to be replaced at a later time. If you have glued everything directly onto the board, it will be nearly impossible to make changes without damaging the board itself. Velcro is an ideal material to use for attaching things, provided you can keep everything looking straight and even. Another possibility is to cut a piece of cardboard to fit the board's measurements, cover it with material, and then glue everything to the cardboard. This is in turn pressed into the frame of the display board, attached with velcro, and can easily be removed if necessary, with no harm done to the board itself. In this manner, one display board can be used for many, many years.

D. Chose bright, eye-catching materials. Remember to make sure these will correspond to your display items. You may wish to choose the colors of your country's flag. Your colors should be tasteful and pleasing to the eye but also attract attention.

E. Avoid clutter! Simplicity is elegant. It is better to have a few large, effective pictures than numerous small pictures all crowded together.

F. Besides just pictures, other items can be added to give your board a unique touch. Maps are always good to include. Coins and paper money, samples of the language, such as verses or tracts, and small, light souvenirs such as dolls or items of clothing can all be attached to the board effectively. This should, of course, be done in a tasteful manner.

G. The most important thing to remember, however, is to always be first class. Having no board is better than a sloppy, quickly done mess that will reflect negatively on your family's character.

2. Preparing for meetings

Before leaving for a meeting, your husband's mind will be greatly occupied on the sermon he is preaching, making sure that the car is in order, and other such matters. He will not have time to check and see if the toothpaste has been packed or the lights have been turned off. This is where you come in, and organization is of utmost importance. There are several things that you can do to get yourself organized and prepared ahead of time.

Packing the Suitcase

One of the biggest jobs will be packing the suitcase. Because you will be traveling so much during deputation, it is very wise to think ahead. What important things does your family need every time you spend the night somewhere? Toothpaste, hair spray, your husband's after-shave, deodorants, lotion, makeup for yourself, rubber pants for the baby, etc. may be needed. Make a list of the things that are necessary. I have found it helpful to purchase duplicates of all the items and place them in the suitcase to be left there permanently. This will guarantee that the shampoo will never be left at home and relieve much of the "last minute rush" to gather up all the items you just used that morning. This will save you a great amount of time and will help you leave home in a much calmer frame of mind, knowing that you have not forgotten anything important. This same method can be used for baby's diaper bag and junior's books and toys for the car.

Establish a Routine

Make a list of the tasks that you must do before leaving, and then do these tasks in the same order each time. When your "getting-ready-to-leave" routine becomes a habit, your chances of forgetting something or leaving something undone becomes greatly diminished. You should likewise establish a routine for your children. This will help them adjust to the constant, most likely stressful matter of leaving home. Perhaps each child could have his own "travel bag" of books and toys which he packs himself. Giving children their own tasks will help them feel important and help them get excited about going to a meeting instead of dreading it.

Double-check Everything

Be sure to always double-check everything before going out the door. Once you are all in the car, have another quick double check. Make sure that you have the directions to the church, proper phone numbers, maps, and that everyone has used the restroom before pulling out. This may take a few minutes but can save hours down the road when you are halfway to Timbuktu and realize that you don't have the directions to the church or that your husband's Bible, including his sermon notes, is still on the couch at home!

3. Traveling

Either Wonderful or Frustrating

You are now on the road. Will this be a wonderful time of "family fun" or a frustrating, tiring time that will cause you all to arrive at the church "out of sorts?" The answer largely depends on you, dear wife! Often your husband will not have much of a chance to be alone with the Lord before he must preach, so it is up to you to create a peaceful, happy ride for his sake. This can determine the success or failure of the meeting.

The Car Will Be Your Second Home

You will spend the majority of deputation time in the car. It will come to be your second home. My husband and I figured that we spent approximately 1000 hours in the car during our deputation! If this time is used wisely, much can be accomplished, and your whole family can be drawn closer together. It is helpful if everyone has something to do. Bring plenty of books and games for the children. Much correspondence work can be done in the car. Listen to good music and sermons. Learn Bible verses together as a family. Any activity that will keep the children calm and allow Dad time to think and prepare his heart for the meeting is to be desired.

Using the Time Wisely

When we were on deputation, I would use my time in the car to make small, cross-stitched crafts, most of which did not take more than three hours. I enjoyed doing this, and got many Christmas presents done this way. These small crafts also made wonderful gifts for the hostesses in whose homes we stayed. You may also consider having your children make their own cards or small crafts, depending on their ages. This is a great way to say thank you, and a small hand-made gift from your family will leave a wonderful impression on the dear ladies who open their homes to you. This will also help you to make many lasting friendships as you travel.

Eliminating the Wiggles

Make sure you leave home early enough to allow extra time to stop at a rest area or McDonald's playground to let the children "get the wiggles out." To sit in the car for two or three hours and then sit quietly in church for an hour and a half without a break is impossible for even the best-behaved children. Yes, they will have to learn to be well-behaved, but we must remember that they are only children, and a little consideration beforehand will go a long way. It is best not to give your children high-calorie snacks before the meeting. Cookies, chocolate, and cola will not only contribute to their "wiggles," and make it even harder to behave. Instead, choose fruit, crackers, and juice for your en-route snacks.

ADDENDUM B: DEPUTATION

4. The Meeting Itself

After so much work getting ready to leave and traveling, it is quite easy to arrive at a church and feel as if your work is done. Often you will be so tired that you feel like stretching out on the pew and taking a nap. This is not the end, however! Your family is now stepping onto center stage!

Open the Door to Conversation

Your display will probably be placed in a prominent spot near the front entrance or somewhere in the auditorium. The church people will want to get to know you but will often feel too shy or intimidated to come and speak to you. It is up to you to reach out to them. Prayer cards are a wonderful tool. When someone comes to look at your display, smile and tell them who you are as you offer them a prayer card. When you open the door of conversation this way, many people will feel more comfortable to speak with you. If you are in a mission conference, make a point of not just getting to know the other missionaries, but reaching out to the church folks also. They are the reason you are there!

Be Prepared to Do Whatever is Asked of You

As part of the "team" you will often be called upon to do various tasks. If you are prepared ahead of time, you will be able to reply positively and with a sweet spirit. Often you will be asked to give a testimony. Pastors will often ask you if you sing or play the piano. If you have talent in these areas, use it! I found it helpful to have a variety of Sunday school lessons prepared. You may be asked to teach anything from the kindergarten to the adult ladies class. It is also good to have a complete program worked out that can last an hour, as occasionally you may be asked (often on the spur of the moment) to conduct junior church. It is also nice to have a supply of candy or perhaps coins from your field which you can use for "quiet seat" prizes. These opportunities can be a tremendous help toward impressing young minds and hearts with the vision of world-wide missions.

Your Husband's Greatest Asset

Remember, you can be your husband's greatest asset! Are you friendly and positive, leaving a good impression? Or are you his worst liability, complaining and uncooperative, making everyone wish that your family had not come? Does the heart of your husband safely trust in you, knowing that he can count on you to be his helpmeet, and not his hindrance? This is our duty and privilege, ladies. Let us not neglect such a great responsibility!

Appendix A: Statistics

Type of Meeting	Number meetings	Number support	Percentage
Sunday school only	11	5	45%
Sunday AM service	37	9	24%
Sunday PM service	53	18	34%
All day Sunday	6	3	50%
Midweek service	59	21	36%
Missions conf. Partial	25	12	48%
Missions conf. Weekend	5	3	60%
Missions conf. Full week	4	1	25%
Totals	200	72	35%

ADDENDUM B: DEPUTATION

A Few Thoughts

I realize that it is very difficult to draw conclusions from only one person's statistics. It would be ideal if statistics such as these could be drawn from a large base of missionaries. However, maybe a few patterns can be observed from these figures.

1. If a pastor says that you can have only Sunday school, do not be dismayed. We did fairly well in those cases.

2. Although Sunday and Wednesday percentages are not as high as the missions conferences, the percentage is not bad. You also have more opportunities for these services. For example, suppose that I chose to go only to Sunday and Wednesday meetings averaging three meetings per week, whereas you chose to go to missions conferences averaging only one meeting per week. If I had 30% of my churches support me, you would have to get 90% to equal my support level at the end of one year! You can see the value of filling every Sunday morning, Sunday evening, and Wednesday evening with meetings in different churches.

3. You can see that the percentage for "partial conferences" is nearly equivalent to the combined percentage of "weekend" and "full week conferences. As I mentioned before, try to use the missions conferences to fill in **between** your Sunday and Wednesday meetings!

Appendix B - Confirmation Letter Sample

October 15, 1994

Pastor Steve Help
Faith Promise Baptist Church
777 Supporter Lane,
Friendship, IL 60321

Dear Pastor Help:

It was great talking with you about our future plans and ministry. We are excited about what the Lord has in store for us in Hungary and are looking forward to the opportunity of presenting our ministry to your church. I would like to confirm the plans for our scheduled meeting:

Date: March 22, 1995

Service: Wednesday evening

Time: 7:00 p.m.

Presentation: Video presentation and preaching

Arrival: My wife and I will plan on arriving at the church 30-60 minutes before the service. If possible, we would like accommodations for Wednesday night. I will contact you again closer to the meeting to finalize the details.

We are praying that the Lord will use our meeting to increase your people's world-wide vision for the souls of lost men.

Serving for His glory,

Brother Ima Missionary
4788 Rugged Road
Hopeful, IN 46555
(219) 378-4621

Appendix C - Second Confirmation Letter

February 15, 1995

Pastor Steve Help
Faith Promise Baptist Church
777 Supporter Lane
Friendship, IL 60321

Dear Pastor Help:

The Lord has really been blessing our deputation efforts. We are now looking forward to presenting our ministry in your church on Wednesday evening, March 22, 1995.

We have made a survey trip to Hungary and were able to take many interesting slides while we were there. We have put together a 12-minute taped slide presentation which we will have available. We will bring our own projector. We will also have a small screen and tape player to use if needed. We will need a small stand on which to set the projector.

We also have a table-top display. If you would like us to use this, it would be helpful if you could provide a table in the lobby.

Could you please send us directions to your church from the nearest major highway? We will contact you within the next few weeks to work out the details of our arrival plans.

Serving for His Glory,

Brother Ima Missionary
4988 Rugged Road
Hopeful, IN 46555
(219) 376-4621

Appendix D - Call-back Letter

June 30, 1995

Pastor B. Weary
Struggling Baptist Church
3563 Difficulty Avenue
Hardship, IL 60436

Dear Pastor Weary:

I enjoyed speaking with you on the phone this week. The Lord has really been blessing us in our deputation efforts, and we are excited about what He has in store for us in Hungary.

I have enclosed letters of recommendation and some information about ourselves. I am sorry that we were not able to schedule a meeting with you at this time, but I will contact you in a few months to update you on our progress, and to see if any dates for meetings have become available.

I am looking forward to speaking with you again. If you have any questions, please do not hesitate to call. God bless you!

Serving for His Glory,

ISSUES IN MISSIOLOGY, VOL. V, 2nd Ed.: MAKING A MISSIONARY

Brother Ima Missionary
4988 Rugged Road
Hopeful, IN 46555
(219) 376-4621

INDEX

A Beka, 225, 243
Adoniram Judson, 22
Adulthood, 106
advanced education, 39, 106
affective, 61
Allah, 310, 311
Ambassador, 144
Animism, 263, 306
Anthropology, 55, 64, 263, 385
attrition, 34, 119, 321, 385
Baguio,, 12
Baptist World Mission, 62, 115, 136, 137, 138, 170, 322, 323, 326, 380
Bhagavad-Gita, 313
Bible translation, 83
Birth, 104
Brahman, 79, 307, 308, 313
Buddhist, 307, 308, 312
Budget, 185
Bush Negro, 17, 47, 60, 61, 65, 66, 72, 75, 76, 94, 102, 104, 105, 108, 109, 261, 264, 270, 289, 294
call, 13, 16, 22, 31, 32, 33, 34, 37, 40, 48, 49, 53, 60, 78, 81, 111, 113, 114, 116, 117, 119, 120, 124, 135, 145, 154, 157, 159, 161, 164, 165, 167, 170, 172, 177, 178, 180, 181, 198, 200, 206, 211, 217, 218, 231, 232, 233, 237, 261, 266, 268, 307, 321, 329,341, 342, 343, 347, 350, 351, 352, 354, 360, 362, 373, 382, 385
Charismatic, 134, 221

Childhood, 105, 113
Chinese, 11, 36, 52, 60, 66, 79, 108, 206, 208, 210, 262, 264, 271, 287, 289, 309, 310, 312, 315, 316
Christian service, 47, 363
cognitive aspects, 61
Colonialism, 22
commitment, 14, 36, 37, 50, 241, 266, 272, 318, 324, 333
Communication, 234, 289, 290
Compartmentalization, 261
Conception, 104
Confucius, 309
Creator, 57, 263, 279, 307, 313
Crisis, 98
Cultural relativity, 260
Culture, 52, 55, 57, 59, 60, 61, 63, 64, 197, 198, 199, 201, 202, 245, 253, 257, 283, 284
customs, 22, 64, 121, 168, 173, 184, 217, 238, 282, 299, 357
cyclical, 57, 65, 69, 74, 263, 287, 308
Dalit, 79
Darrell Champlin, 15, 177, 189
Denominational board, 125
denominational mission board, 35, 125
depression, 197, 202
deputation, 3, 4, 7, 11, 33, 35, 38, 44, 113, 118, 121, 123, 139, 141, 142, 145, 148, 151, 154, 155, 156, 159, 160, 163, 165, 166, 167, 168, 169, 170, 171, 172, 182, 183, 185, 186,

194, 195, 231, 233, 234, 235, 236, 247, 319, 322, 326, 335, 336, 337, 338, 339, 340, 341, 343, 344, 348, 352, 356, 357, 360, 364, 366, 368, 372, 373, 382
Disappointments, 216, 217
disciple, 92, 97, 298
Display, 176, 236, 357, 364
Dr. Marjory Foyle, 224, 286
Dutch, 16, 35, 36, 47, 52, 121, 205, 207, 208, 209, 210, 379
DVD, 41, 174, 175, 189, 225, 236, 243, 355
Elderly, 269
e-mail, 167, 174, 184, 194, 332, 360
ethnocentrism, 60, 121, 258, 259, 275, 381
Evangelism, 281, 288, 291, 292
event-oriented, 45, 69
Family, 37, 51, 76, 79, 116, 223, 241, 254, 289, 296, 363
Family problems, 51, 254
Financial policies, 329
flash drive, 175, 292
Flexibility, 98
foreign language, 35
forms, 63, 90, 175, 278, 299, 308, 309, 312
Furlough meetings, 182
Gautama, 308
Goals, 217
Goforth, 26, 210, 323
GPS, 178
guidance, 33, 47, 56, 169, 302
Guilt, 92, 93, 272, 295, 297
Hindu, 279, 307, 314, 315, 381
Holistic, 87, 88

Holy Spirit, 18, 32, 33, 34, 37, 46, 47, 49, 56, 117, 133, 137, 145, 148, 152, 153, 182, 223, 279, 284, 285, 294, 295, 300, 301, 302, 307, 311, 312, 313, 314, 315, 317, 321, 352, 358
home school, 5, 51, 225, 226, 241
honeymoon phase, 198
Household help, 239
Humor, 109, 201
Informality, 268
Kingdom, 81
Kinship, 75, 76
Krishna, 308, 313
Ladies groups, 236
Language learning, 35, 210, 238
language school, 11, 27, 36, 208
Letterhead, 339
Letters of recommendation, 340
Liberian English, 121, 207, 209, 258
marriage, 14, 37, 40, 41, 43, 75, 76, 79, 106, 137, 170, 224, 231, 238, 280
Marriage, 40, 198
matriarchal, 60, 75, 76, 240, 289
Media, 291, 292
Messages, 177, 278, 357
Mission board, 119, 125, 137
missions conference, 33, 116, 166, 171, 324, 328, 330, 331, 344, 345, 363, 371
Missions professors, 330
money,, 65, 108, 150, 261, 351, 366
Mono-cultural, 282
Moravian church, 319
Muslim, 224, 310, 311

myth, 63
Nationalism, 51
Naturalism, 305
Negativism, 214
Orientation, 82, 83, 98, 120, 272
parental opposition, 38
Pastor, 4, 17, 157, 168, 178, 180, 181, 238, 317-319, 343, 371-373
pendular, 65
Pentecostal, 292, 293
Persistence, 118
Possessions, 101, 102
Prayer, 242, 317, 326, 330, 336, 337, 339, 361, 369
Prayer cards, 369
Presbyterian Church, 11, 13, 14
presentation, 159, 168, 171, 172, 175, 176, 181, 182, 236, 279, 292, 337, 338, 345, 353, 355-357, 372
Priesthood, 151
Privacy, 71, 215
projector, 174-177, 372
Psychology, 295
racial prejudice, 45
Recreation, 109
Recruiter, 318
Repressive, 296
Resume, 340
retirement, 36, 65, 107, 113, 129, 132, 251, 269, 319, 329
Ricanau Mofo, 16
risks, 25, 26
rituals, 63, 64, 315
Roman Catholic, 284, 290, 312
Rosetta Stone, 52
Satanic, 307
Scheduling meetings, 157

Self-governing, 297
Self-propagating, 297
Self-supporting, 297
Self-theologizing, 300
sermon, 171, 177, 179, 313, 366, 367
Servant, 142
sexual immorality, 62, 253
Shame, 92, 93, 95, 272, 295, 297
Shintoist, 312
Sickness, 50
single missionaries, 41, 42, 140
Spirit, 33, 46, 47, 117, 148, 279, 285, 291, 294, 314, 321, 381
Sranantongo, 16-19, 35, 36, 52, 58, 121, 174, 176, 205-211, 254, 258, 263, 284, 379, 381, 382
support, 19, 35, 38, 39, 43, 51, 52, 85, 112, 116, 119, 122-124, 128-131, 136, 138, 139, 141, 142, 145, 148, 151-155, 157, 158, 160-162, 166, 167, 169-171, 174, 181-186, 194, 195, 219, 232, 237, 251, 262, 296, 298, 300, 319-321, 323-330, 332, 333, 335, 336, 340, 342, 344, 345, 346, 349, 351, 352, 358-364, 370, 371
Suppressive, 296
Suriname, 3, 4, 5, 7, 15-19, 22, 25, 27, 34-36, 40-44, 47, 48, 51, 52, 60, 61, 65-68, 70, 71, 72, 75, 77, 82, 89, 91, 93, 100-102, 108-111, 114, 115, 117-119, 129, 132, 134-136, 138, 155, 157-159, 162, 164, 167, 169, 173, 177, 183, 184,

187, 190-194, 197, 202, 205, 208, 210, 214, 215, 219, 221, 225-227, 231, 233, 236, 239, 240, 245, 254, 258, 260-262, 264, 267, 270, 272, 286, 292, 293, 296, 297, 300, 321, 336, 379, 380-382
Suriname time, 66
symbols, 63, 315
Tao, 309, 310
Tapanahony River, 15
Television, 292, 293
Termination, 253
Territory, 72, 73
Theology, 300-302
time-oriented, 45
Tonal languages, 52
total immersion, 207, 271
Totalitarianism, 290
tourist stage, 198
trials, 25, 26, 46, 47, 117, 147, 150, 202
Trinity, 310, 311
United Methodist, 141
values, 45, 55, 57, 61, 64, 65, 93, 260, 264, 265, 269, 270, 281, 289, 291, 329
veteran missionary, 129, 182, 385
Video, 372
vocational qualifications, 40
Vulnerability, 95, 96
warfare mentality, 27
Western civilization, 259, 265, 297
worldview, 4, 44, 55, 57-60, 63, 64, 262, 278, 281, 282, 284, 303, 305-307, 310, 312, 381
Yang, 309

Yin, 309

ABOUT THE AUTHOR

Dr. Robert Patton was born on February 1, 1938 in Cambridge, New York. At age three, he accompanied his parents as missionaries to China. They were moved to the Philippine Islands and spend over three years as Japanese prisoners of war. After returning to the USA, he completed a B.A. at Hamilton College, during which he was a junior Phi Beta Kappa. He married M. Elizabeth Stringham in 1959, and completed his medical degree and was a member of AOA honor society at the University of Rochester School of Medicine. He completed four years of internship and residency in Internal Medicine, followed by two years in the Public Health Service and two years as a cardiology fellow. During this time, he became a specialist and then a fellow in Internal Medicine (FACP). At age 33, Dr. Patton went under the US Public Health Service to Monrovia, Liberia, where he was Professor and Chairman of the Department of Internal Medicine. He was decorated by the Liberian government for his contributions developing this medical program. During these years he was co-author of over 40 scientific papers and co-author of a book on Cardiac Arrythmia Agents. He also accepted the Lord Jesus as savior at age 36 while in Liberia.

The Pattons returned to the USA where he became very active in Grace Baptist Church of South Bend, Indiana while maintaining an internal medical practice with Southwestern Medical Clinic. During these ten years, he completed correspondence studies from Moody Bible Institute and Liberty Home Bible Institute, as well as additional training in counseling. They were called to Suriname, South America, arriving in 1986. During his first five years, Dr. Patton studied Dutch and Sranantongo, opened his first church, and taught in the medical school five mornings a week. He then resigned from medical practice, and concentrated on church planting, translation, and discipleship. He translated the entire Bible with a team between 1991 and 1998, and later wrote commentaries on the entire Bible as well as a number of discipleship studies. He started a Bible Institute 20 years ago, and an advanced Bible Institute in 2008. He has radio broadcasts over the entire Bible on three stations, and also two television programs weekly. He was awarded a Doctor of Divinity from Baptist College of America in 1997.

Dr. Patton and his wife relocated to Crown College in 2012 while remaining as missionaries under Baptist World Mission, where he is teaching missions courses as well as Human Anatomy & Physiology. While teaching at Crown College, Dr. Patton earned a Master of Missiology and Master of Biblical Studies graduate degrees and was awarded a Doctor of Divinity in 2021.

The Pattons have four children, eighteen grandchildren, and 16 great-grandchildren. Their son is a missionary in Hungary with his wife and four children, and his daughter is a missionary in Suriname with her husband and nine children. The other two daughters and their families are serving the Lord in the USA.

BOOKS BY DR. PATTON

ISSUES IN MISSIOLOGY, VOLUME I:

In Volume I of Issues in Missiology, Dr. Patton addresses three challenges: (1) Persecution (2) Missions & Money and (3) Missions and Partnerships. Christians are suffering in the third wave of persecution in the history of the church. The missionary needs to understand the nature and cause of persecution, and the proper Christian response. The missionary must also understand the dynamics of giving and the Biblical principles involved, especially with the increasing discrepancy between financial resources in the west and in many parts of the developing world.

ISSUES IN MISSIOLOGY, VOLUME II:

In Volume II, Dr. Patton addresses the subjects of Spiritual Warfare and The Spiritual Life of the Missionary. Spiritual warfare is a reality, not only in the developing world, but also in the ministries in "developed" countries. The missionary must be prepared to deal with these spiritual realities. All missionaries, to be effective, must walk in the Spirit. God works through the missionary to accomplish His goals as he yields to Him and works in His power and wisdom, and not in his own strength.

ISSUES IN MISSIOLOGY, VOLUME III, THOUGHTS ABOUT TRANSLATION:

In Volume III, Dr. Patton relates his personal experiences in translating the entire Bible into the Sranantongo language. The translation has been used in radio and television broadcasts, two Bible Institutes, Bible commentaries, discipleship materials, and tracts impacting the country of Suriname. He outlines the need for the correct foundational text, the proper methods of translation, and awareness of pitfalls that await the missionary translator. He concludes his book by appealing for many workers to reach the millions without the Word of God in their mother tongue, knowing the fields "are white already to harvest" (John 4:35).

ISSUES IN MISSIOLOGY, VOLUME IV, WORLDVIEW AND WORLD RELIGIONS

In Volume IV, Dr. Patton begins with an assessment of worldviews, not only those of major world religions and folk religion, but also western modernism, post-modernism, and post-postmodernism. This is followed by an assessment of the major world religions, with a special emphasis on folk religion, which is followed by 40% of the world population, though they may be nominally Christian, Islam, Hindu, etc. There is also a section on humanism, atheism, and atheistic communism, which at one time dominated nearly a third of the world's population. Dr. Patton emphasizes that it is not only necessary to understand the worldview of the religion of the people whom we wish to reach, but also our own worldview to avoid being "blindsided" by our own ethnocentrism. When possible, there are suggestions as to how to reach various groups with the gospel.

ISSUES IN MISSIOLOGY, VOLUME V, Getting on the Field; Staying on the Field

Volume V traces the life of the missionary from his call through deputation and then his ministry on the field. In addition to covering deputation and a few observations about mission boards, there is a very important section on practical cultural anthropology, which assists the missionary in his adaptation to the field. There are discussions also of culture shock and re-entry to the United States. In summary, the goals of the book are to assist the missionary in successfully arriving on the field, and how to keep him there in an effective ministry.

SRANANTONGO BIBLE

This is a translation of the whole Bible into the Sranantongo language-group of Suriname, SA. This is the first complete translation into the language using the proper textual basis, the Received Texts and the King James Bible. The Bible has been widely used in churches, in television, and on radio programs. The translation is available online here:

www.dasranantongobijbel.com.

DVDS, MP3, ARTICLES

Dr. Patton has a large collection of various DVDS, MP3 recordings, and articles from his years of television, radio, and missionary experiences. The majority of his DVDS, MP3s, etc., are in Sranantongo.

Beginning in 2020, Dr. Patton has been making daily videos on Facebook on various books of the Bible both in English and Sranantongo.

Dr. Patton may be contacted through the following avenues:

HOME

Dr. Robert Patton
7311 Brickyard Road
Powell, TN 37849
865-859-0457

ABOUT THE AUTHOR

Email: bobpattonmd@gmail.com
bob.patton@thecrowncollege.edu
His cell phone is: 574-303-9669

CROWN COLLEGE OF THE BIBLE
2307 West Beaver Creek Drive
Powell, TN 37849
Phone: 865-938-8186

BAPTIST WORLD MISSIONS
P.O. Box 2149
Decatur, Alabama 35602-2149
Telephone Number: 256-353-2221
Fax Number: 256-353-2266
Email: bpatton@baptistworldmission.org

ENDNOTES

1. Patton, M. Harmer, *Our Concentrated Life*, unpublished monograph written approx. 1945
2. M. David Sills, *The Missionary Call*, Moody Publishers, Chicago, 2008 The main thrust of the book is on the missionary call and how to know it. This brief summary gives some of the ideas of the book, but the reader is referred to the book itself for further details.
3. http://www.strategicnetwork.org/index.php?loc'kb&view' v&id'5394&mode'v&pagenum'3&lang This was a helpful source. The author, a veteran missionary who nearly left the field, has a great burden to reduce unnecessary attrition. In one study he made, 71% of the 5-7% attrition per year was preventable. It was also informative that a similar sort of results was obtained by businesses with overseas executives, with a business cost of $150,000-350,000 for those terminating early
4. I was shocked to find out that in my medical school a few years ago, the average graduate had a debt of $140,000 by the time he completed training! It would take years, even at a doctor's salary, to erase such a debt.
5. Foyle, Marjory F., *op cit.*, Chapter 8
6. www.rosettastone.com
7. Brewster, E. Thomas and Brewster, Elizabeth S., *Language Acquisition Made Practical*, Lingua House, 1976
8. www.answers.com/topic/culture
9. Steffen, Tom & Douglas, Lois McKinley, *Encountering Missionary Life and Work*, Baker Academic, 2008, pp. 180 ff. Tom Steffen gives a fascinating story of his own cultural adaptation within the USA
10. Kraft, Charles H., *Anthropology for Christian Witness*, Orbis Books, 2006, pp. 2 ff.
11. Hiebert, Paul G., *Transforming Worldviews*, Baker Academic, 2008, pp. 31 ff
12. Hiebert, Paul G., *Anthropological Insight for Missionaries*, Baker Book House, 1985, pp. 52 ff.

13. Hiebert, *Transforming...* op. cit. The entire textbook is devoted to all aspects of worldview. It is an excellent resource to consult for more details.
14. http://en.wikipedia.org/wiki/Neoplatonism
15. The father of the child was speaking in a group of men. The mother's brothers said: "Be quiet. Who are you to talk? You just "made" the child, but he is not from your "bere" (womb), meaning the matriarchal line of the mother.
16. Lingenfelter, Sherwood G., & Mayers, Marvin K. *Ministering Cross-Culturally*, Baker Book House, Grand Rapids, 1986, pp. 36 ff
17. 1 Kings 20:23-28
18. 2 Kings 5:1-17
19. Numbers 36:6-11
20. Genesis 50:13
21. Exodus 21:15-17
22. http://en.wikipedia.org/wiki/Inbreeding
23. Genesis 25:29-34; Hebrews 12:16
24. Lingenfelter, Sherwood, *Ministering Cross-Culturally*, Baker Book House, 1986, p. 100
25. Matthew 9:12
26. Lingenfelter, *op. cit.,* p. 83
27. Matthew 23 has a number of Jesus' vivid illustrations
28. Hiebert, *op. cit.*, p. 161
29. Lingenfelter, Judith E., and Lingenfelter, Sherwood G., *Teaching Cross-Culturally*, Baker Academic, 2003. The entire text, which is easy to read, has much helpful practical information
30. Lingenfelter, Sherwood, & Mayers, Marvin K., *op. cit.*, p 107
31. Lingenfelter, Sherwood, & Mayers, Marvin K., *op. cit.*, pp 69 ff.
32. Patton, Robert D., *Issues in Missiology Volume I*, The Old Paths Publishers, Cleveland, Georgia, 2012. See sections II and III
33. http://en.wikipedia.org/wiki/Ida_S._Scudder
34. I give many further details in: Patton, Robert D., *Issues in Missiology Volume IV*, The Old Paths Publications, Cleveland, GA, 2012.
35. I deal with this topic in more detail in *Issues in Missiology Volume II*, The Old Paths Publications, Cleveland, GA, 2012.

ENDNOTES

36. Iwasko, Ronald as quoted in Jones, Marge, *Psychology of Missionary Adjustment*, Ligeon Press, Springfield, MO, 2000, p. 24
37. The notes in this section were compiled from a variety of souces. One helpful resource was a notebook for use in Ambassador Baptist College entitled *Contemporary Missions Seminar* by Pastor Wayne Kirk, revised in 1994
38. Both my parents and my wife's parents went overseas under liberal boards, although they were saved. Their experience in terms of raising support was dramatically different from the experience I had with my wife, and the experience of our two children, both of whom went under faith missions.
39. Many helpful suggestions are drawn from Gambrell, Ernest C. *An Effective Deputation Ministry.* Terry Hyatt Memorial Printing Ministry. 1983, 2003, 2007 Other information has been obtained informally as well as from personal experience.
40. The basic concepts of this section are largely drawn from Harold. C. Loucks, D.D., *Mission Deputation*, Faith Baptist Church Publications, Ft. Pierce, FL. 34982. I have expanded and added some thoughts of my own as well as giving some personal examples. The reader is referred to this volume for further information.
41. *Martyrs Mirror*, Herald Press, 1938 p. 97ff.
42. Patton, Marc, *Deputation, A Rugged But Rewarding Road*, unpublished notes from BIMI, 1994. I am enclosing this monograph as an addendum
43. Barnett, Betty, *Friend Raising*, YWAM Publishing, 1991 - The entire book is on this subject
44. Dillon, William, *People Raising*, Moody Press, 1993, The entire book is devoted to raising support through persons rather than churches
45. Patton, Marc, op cit.
46. My son Marc followed the same policy. In analyzing his statistics of his meetings, he found that it was much to his advantage not to commit for the entire meeting. See his material in Appendix B
47. *Where There is No Doctor*, Hesperian Foundation, 1992
48. *Where There is No Dentist*, Hesperian Foundation, 2009

49. Dearmore, Roy F., ThB, M.D., *Biblical Missions*, Rogers Baptist Church, 1998 p. 605 ff.
50. Dearmore, op cit. p. 618 ff.
51. Hiebert, *Anthropological...* op cit., pp. 72 ff. There is a very comprehensive and excellent section on cultural shock from p 60-89 in this text
52. Hiebert, *op cit*. p. 72
53. Hiebert, *Anthropological...* op cit. pp. 78 ff
54. Jones, Marge, *op. cit.*, p. 31
55. Foyle, Marjory F., *Honorably Wounded*, 2nd edition, Monarch, Mill Hill, London, 2001, pp. 79-82 gives another excellent summary and practical suggestions
56. Jones, Marge, op. cit., p. 40
57. Fred Renich, quote in Jones, Marge, *op. cit*, p. 69
58. Myron Loss, quoted in Jones, Marge, *op. cit.*, p 71
59. Allen, quoted in Jones, Marge, *op. cit.*, p. 119
60. Foyle, Marjory F., *op. cit.*, I would suggest that a missionary couple read this entire book; it is clear, compassionate, and thorough.
61. Allen, quoted in Jones, Marge, *op. cit.*, p. 139
62. Lingenfelter, Sherwood G., and Mayers, Marvin, *op. cit.*, pp. 117 ff.
63. Kraft, op. cit. pp 70-72
64. http://www.gameo.org/encyclopedia/contents/ C653ME.html
65. This difference has caused me much frustration. My attitude has been in the past: Time is money. I liked to focus on objective productivity. This may not be so bad in a technical field, where western values are often applied along with western technology, but it is a real problem for a church-planting missionary in the developing world. I need to remind myself that Jesus was very concerned with relationships, and not focusing on completing building projects or translation projects!
66. Taylor, Dr. & Mrs Howard, *Hudson Taylor's Spiritual Secret*, Moody Press, 1989, p 67
67. Don Richards has emphasized the point of redemptive analogies in his books, especially *Eternity in Their Hearts*, but also in *Peace Child* and *Lords of the Earth*.

ENDNOTES

68 In *Volume IV of Issues in Missiology*, I gave an example of a redemptive analogy. In the Bush Negro culture of Suriname, in the interior they *"bai pasi"* (also called in other locations *"pai pasi"*) for someone who is deceased. By this term, they mean that a payment is made to open the way for the deceased to find a good life after death. What they do is fascinating. The body is already in the casket. They take a chicken, and cut off its head. Grasping the dead chicken, they knock the neck of the dead chicken along with the casket, spattering blood on the casket. Often, the chicken is then cooked and eaten by the family of the deceased. This is a wonderful illustration of two biblical principles. Without the shedding of blood there is no remission, and the wages of sin is death. **Hebrews 9:[22] And almost all things are by the law purged with blood; and without shedding of blood is no remission. Romans 6:[23] For the wages of sin is death; but the gift of God is eternal life through Jesus Christ our Lord.** The chicken dies as a substitute for the sins of the individual. His blood is placed on the casket showing identification. And of course if it is eaten, this would show participation of the family in the whole situation.

I often use this illustration as part of a soul winning effort with people from that part of the interior of Suriname. I tell them of their ancestors knew some biblical principles, but they got changed along the way, and certain things were forgotten. I then tell them the good news of Jesus Christ. I mentioned that Jesus Christ died on the cross for our sins. Then I ask them if the blood of a chicken can forgive sins. Invariably, they say that the blood of a chicken is not adequate to wash away sins. Then I say: "You are correct; it takes blood that is more worthy than that. My own blood is insufficient to cleanse your sins. I am a sinner too. Sinful blood cannot wash away sins. But Jesus Christ never sinned, and His death **is** adequate to pay for sins. When He rose, He proved that God accepted His payment for our sins."

69. Hiebert, Paul G., *Transforming Worldviews*, Baker Academic, 2008
70. When I first came to Suriname, I was not really aware of this. People would promise to come to church, or they might pray a

prayer, and I noted that the nationals were not as enthusiastic as I was. But they were able to distinguish those polite excuses which were not to be taken seriously. Later I became more perceptive.

71. Ham, Ken, What Really Happened to the Dinosaurs? Booklet from Answers in Genesis, 2007.
72. Foyle, Marjory F. *Honorably Wounded*, Monarch Books, 2001, p. 149
73. I believe that it is absolutely key to remember these points. It seems that invariably the missionary will be confronted with situations which will suggest that he compromise what he believes is right. Three possible solutions: 1. Avoid getting into the situation 2. Offer a culturally acceptable alternative 3. Politely state that you cannot comply.
74. Again, this is vital. We know a family that is heading to Saudi Arabia where the father will be working. The family has teenage daughters. They should dress, as should his wife, in a very conservative fashion. I am not necessarily suggesting a burka covering the entire body, but I would avoid either tight clothes or short or skimpy skirts and dresses, which may be offensive to the Muslim men, or worse, they may be interpreted as a come-on. We had a family for a short time living in a mission station in the bush while learning language. The wife was quite attractive and stylish. She insisted on wearing stockings and high heels going to church, and received many whistles from the men in the village - a very inappropriate response for a Christian missionary wife because of her insensitivity. In their culture, only prostitutes would dress in that manner.
75. http://en.wikipedia.org/wiki/Ko_Tha_Byu
76. Patton, Robert D., *Issues in Missiology, Volume I*, The Old Paths Publishers, Cleveland, Ga., 2012. The second and third sections deal in detail with these issues.
77. A power encounter usually involves some sort of contest. A classic example is the contest on Mt. Carmel between Elijah and the prophets of Baal, with a test to see which god would answer with fire. A truth encounter is usually confronting the powers of evil with

the truth of God's Word and insisting that the spirit yield and obey the truth, such as Jesus' confrontation with Satan in the wilderness. I give further information and examples in the section on Spiritual Warfare in *Issues in Missiology, Volume II.*

78. Murray, Andrew, *The Key to the Missionary Problem*, Christian Literature Crusade, 1979, p. 46 In speaking of the Moravian church, he states the following (italics his) She alone of all the churches has sought to carry out the great truth, that *to gather in to Christ the souls He died to save is the one object for which the Church exists.*

79. Beals, Paul A., A People for His Name, Revised Edition, William Carey Library, 1995, This excellent text gives a great challenge to our pastors to take leadership in the area of missions.

80. Murray, Andrew, *The Key to the Missionary Problem*, Christian Literature Crusade, 1979, pp. 11-16

81. Murray, *op. cit.,* p. 46

82. Murray, *op. cit.,* p. 64

83. Taylor, William D. Ed., *Too Valuable to Lose,* William Carey Library, 1997, pp. 347-349 in particular, but many references throughout the text.

84. Beals, *op. cit.,* pp. 112 ff.

85. Loucks, Harold C., *Mission Deputation: A Biblical Ministry and Classroom of Learning*, Faith Baptist Church Publications, 2006, pp. 157 ff.

86. Smith, Oswald J., *The Challenge of Missions*, Gabriel Publishing, 1999, Chapter VII p. 59 ff.

87. Pirolo, Neal, *The Reentry Team*, Emmaus Road International, 2000, pp. 21-31. Pirolo emphasizes the importance of debriefing, both by the mission agency and the sending church. He demonstrates that it is important both for the missionary and the agency and church.

88. Pirolo, Neal, *Serving as Senders*, Emmaus Road International, 1991

89. Pirolo, *op. cit.* - the entire book is devoted to the subject of returning missionaries, and focuses on the responsibility of the church.

www.ingramcontent.com/pod-product-compliance
Lightning Source LLC
Chambersburg PA
CBHW071946220426
43662CB00009B/1018